Paul Simon FAQ

Paul Simon
FAQ

All That's Left to Know About the
Legendary Singer and Iconic Songs

Dave Thompson

Backbeat
Books

Guilford, Connecticut

Backbeat Books
An imprint of The Rowman & Littlefield Publishing Group, Inc.
4501 Forbes Blvd., Ste. 200
Lanham, MD 20706
www.rowman.com

Distributed by NATIONAL BOOK NETWORK

The FAQ series was conceived by Robert Rodriguez and developed with Stuart Shea.

All images are from the author's collection unless otherwise noted.

Book design and composition by Snow Creative

British Library Cataloguing in Publication Information available

Library of Congress Cataloging-in-Publication Data available
ISBN 978-1-4935-7991-7 (paperback)

♾™ The paper used in this publication meets the minimum requirements of American National Standard for Information Sciences—Permanence of Paper for Printed Library Materials, ANSI/NISO Z39.48-1992

To Elda Gentile, with love

Contents

Acknowledgments

First and foremost, thanks to everyone who threw their thoughts and enthusiasms into this book, but most of all to Amy, for her memories of a long-ago installment of *Sesame Street*; Jen, for reminding me what a special album Art Garfunkel's *Breakaway* is; and Mo Daviau, for permission to quote from her novel *Every Anxious Wave*, and for sharing her enthusiasms, too.

And Molly, for keeping her head when others lost theirs. Usually because she had eaten them.

Introduction

Paul Simon was never *just* a singer-songwriter. It's the bag that a lot of people put him in and one from which he never particularly struggled to escape. But he's never especially fit the mold, and it has never suited him, either.

The term itself is not baggage free. It conjures—at least for listeners of a certain vintage—the image of a particular breed of early seventies troubadour, unloading his angst and his outlook on life upon a world that revolved around macramé owls and fondue parties. And, because Simon's emergence as a solo artist coincided so neatly with the peak of that parade, it was very easy to add him to the list.

But he was always an awkward match. Maybe his heart was not emblazoned loudly enough on his sleeve; maybe his humor was too sly and too sharp. Maybe his confessions weren't querulous enough. Or maybe he was just too fidgety to sit in one place for any length of time.

Whatever. The singer-songwriter boom came and went, just like all the other booms to which Simon has had his name attached, and Simon passed through its decline unscathed. A singer who writes his own songs. A songwriter who sings his own output. And one of the most remarkable of either ilk ever to pass through a recording studio.

Not through technique (although he has that in abundance); nor through musical ability (ditto). He is remarkable because he seems to sing and write for the sheer joy of doing so, and even his much-discussed retirement from active music-making is unlikely to alter that scenario.

At his best, and below that, too, Simon performs with the gusto, enthusiasm, and sheer careless beauty that we all wish we could embrace in the shower, in the kitchen, or just caterwauling along to the radio.

It's effortless, the Simon method. No matter how slick and shiny the backing track might be, no matter how syrupy the strings or how cloying the production (and there are moments when his work has fallen prey to both of those conditions), the moment Simon opens his mouth to reveal his words, all other considerations just fall away, and all criticisms fall apart.

He doesn't have a great voice *per se*. But he sings, and he makes you start singing him. And, no matter how *ordinary* a lyric might seem, there will always be one moment (*at least* one moment) when you understand why it was written.

There is more. Alongside no more than a small handful of others—Bob Dylan for sure, Bruce Springsteen and Neil Young maybe—Paul Simon is one of his era's most natural songwriters, instinctive, sharp, and literate.

Yes, occasionally he has come out with a line of such groaning pomposity that all but the most devoted listener will declare that there are times when he is so portentous that it's hard to take comfort from any place.

But even in those moments, he rescues the situation with another line of cunning simplicity, startling awareness. Paul Simon writes and he shelves our expectations in the pantry with the cupcakes.

It's not an easy vocation. A songwriter stands and falls by his pen. At his best, effortlessly spooling out classics, he is a genius. But if the classics start to falter, or are outweighed by workaday filler, then he's finished.

A great songwriter *needs* to write a great song. A great singer needs simply to hear one and then remind his listeners of the reasons why it's so great. And that, to step back to the years when Simon wasn't solo, is why Simon and Garfunkel made such a terrific double act. Why, in the decades since their partnership sundered, they remain at the top of their respective games—Simon for his songs, Garfunkel for his voice.

Few people, for example, could have been unfamiliar with Stevie Wonder's "I Believe (When I Fall in Love)," with Cliff Richard's "Miss You Nights," with Jimmy Webb's "Crying in My Sleep." Nor would anyone have denied that, in their original incarnations, all three had already been granted their definitive rendering.

Yet the solo Garfunkel redefined them, just as he defined the Paul Simon songs that he was the first to sing in the sixties.

The difference is that Simon's songs helped define him in return, and that is another of Simon's most unique talents—to write words that can't simply be sung by another person because they help shape that person, too. In the entire sphere of modern music, only Pete Townshend, writing for Roger Daltrey since 1964, can be said to have so fluidly mastered that trick, and with anything approaching the same success.

Forty years ago, British author Chris Charlesworth mused on the double act's success: "The less admiring might well conclude that [Garfunkel] is a very fortunate man whose association with a composer of Paul Simon's talents was directly responsible for earning him a vast fortune. Others rightly consider that his pure, tenor voice was an essential element *to* the formula that turned Simon and Garfunkel into the most successful duo . . . in the history of recorded music."

Those others are correct, but they only tell half the story. Just as the duo's statistics are impressive but only add up to one chapter among many.

Throughout their lifetime as a duo—indeed, across the span of just three years at the end of that lifetime—Simon and Garfunkel won no less than nine Grammy Awards, for Record of the Year ("Mrs. Robinson" in 1969, "Bridge Over Troubled Water" in 1971); Best Pop Performance by Group or Duo ("Mrs. Robinson"); Album of the Year (*Bridge Over Troubled Water*); Best Original Score (*The Graduate*, 1969), and Song of the Year, Best Contemporary Song, Best Instrumental Arrangement, and Best Engineered Performance ("Bridge Over Troubled Water"). They received two other nominations at that time and a third, for "My Little Town," in 1976. Since then, they have swept up four Grammy Hall of Fame Awards and one Lifetime Achievement Award.

In 1977, *Bridge Over Troubled Water*, both the LP and the song, received the gong for the Best International Album and Single of the past twenty-five years at the UK's BRIT Awards. In 1990, the duo was inducted into the Rock and Roll Hall of Fame. *Bridge Over Troubled Water* alone has sold over 13 million copies in the United States; the duo's total worldwide sales comfortably exceed 100 million.

And so on.

Simon's solo career has continued in that same tradition: two further Grammy-sweeping Albums of the Year (*Still Crazy After All These Years* and *Graceland*), a solo berth in the Rock and Roll Hall of Fame, and, in 2006, inclusion among *Time* magazine's "100 People Who Shaped the World."

Rolling Stone has ranked him among the one hundred best song-writers, inevitably, and the one hundred greatest guitarists (more surprisingly). In 2007, he became the first ever recipient of the Library of Congress's Gershwin Prize for Popular Song.

And toward the very end of his farewell tour, with Simon performing in Newark, New Jersey, the *Asbury Park Press* remarked upon how the first song that many people remember him ever playing, and the last song he would play tonight, remained as potent in 2018 as it did in 1964, almost five and a half decades later.

"Simon changed the arrangement of '[The Sound of] Silence.' Lines were shortened and the phrasing was altered. This was not going to be a feel-good sing along moment. Simon presented it as pointed as it was more than fifty years ago, when the world, not unlike today, seemed to be rushing into an indeterminate future."

But one gets the impression that statistics, and comparisons, mean little to Simon—which is why, for great swaths of his career, he has not even attempted to increase them.

Since 1970, when it became clear that Simon and Garfunkel were no longer a functioning unit, the Simon half of the equation has released just thirteen studio albums, three live recordings, and one remix LP. Dylan and Young enjoyed almost as many new releases in the 1970s and early 1980s alone. And while Simon's every new release is more or less guaranteed success—his name and reputation alone being worth a significant slice of sales—Simon has never chased the easy hit record.

The seventies were already two years old by the time Simon released his first solo album, and it would be disingenuous to claim that the world had *not* been anticipating it for just as long. *Paul Simon* may not have been deathless from start to finish, but it more than made up for that with the songs that *did* play to his strengths.

Similarly, while longtime listeners missed hearing Garfunkel's voice alongside him, still there was no avoiding the hits "Mother and Child Reunion" and "Me and Julio Down by the Schoolyard"; no dismissing the ribald confessional "Duncan"; and no way whatsoever of decrying "Run That Body Down"—a song so finely wrought that Eric Stewart and Lol Creme of 10cc, no mean songwriters themselves, had no hesitation in electing it one of their Top 10 songs of all time on a BBC radio broadcast a couple of years later.

Simon has marched on with similar forcefulness ever since, ratcheting up the hit singles but taking his listeners on other journeys too, and those are (some of) the corners that this FAQ intends to shed light upon.

There is his pioneering investigation of what we now refer to as "world music," although that was a term that nobody had heard of when Simon traveled to Jamaica to record with a reggae band, the first step in a restless search for new sounds and sensations from around the world.

There is his live and TV work, his (admittedly brief) career as a film-maker, and his career as a collaborative artist, not only with Garfunkel but also, more fleetingly, with Brian Wilson, Wyclef Jean, Annie Lennox, Mumford and Sons, Brian Eno, and yMusic. There are his careers as a London folkie and a Broadway songsmith, a jobbing session man and a college tutor, a questing pioneer and a tireless philanthropist.

And, of course, there are the songs.

It always comes back to the songs.

Paul Simon FAQ

Childhood Friends

I n the end, it was the Everly Brothers that did it.

Lots of kids like to sing, lots of kids *can* sing, and nobody denied that little Arthur Ira Garfunkel fell firmly into the latter category. Throughout his childhood and into his teens, the sound of music resounded within the Garfunkel family home—Art singing alone as he went about his daily activities or, more formally, joining his brothers, the older Jules and the younger Jerome (quickly shortened, of course, to Jerry), and their salesman father, Jacob ("Jack"), and harmonizing together.

All four of them enjoyed singing, but Art adored it, particularly on those occasions when they'd gather around their father's wire recorder and capture their voices for posterity. Later in life, Art would admit that it was the sound of his voice coming out of the machine that convinced him to get into what he called "the business." But it was the merciless fidelity of a recording that taught him to never be content with the sound of his voice and to instead scour it for flaws and imperfections that he could work to eliminate.

So when, at school, he met with a boy who seemed as fascinated by his singing abilities as he was, friendship was inevitable.

Paul Frederic Simon was just a shade over three weeks Garfunkel's senior. He was born on October 13, 1941 (Art was born on November 5), in Newark, New Jersey, where his parents—radio band member Louis Simon and elementary school teacher Belle—remained until the birth of their second child, Eddie, in 1945.

They then moved to a brick-built two-story home in Forest Hills, in the New York borough of Queens, just three blocks away from the Garfunkels, and that was always the place that Simon thought of as home. More than sixty years later, onstage at what he thought of as his final concert, he insisted it was "more fate than coincidence" that determined his final show would be at Flushing Meadows Corona Park.

"I could have ridden my bike from home to the park in about twenty minutes when I was a kid." He tossed a ball into the audience. "This is like two miles from where I played high school baseball. It's a little dark out, but you know what? I'm going to play a quick game of catch."

The two boys, Paul and Artie, entered first grade together in the fall of 1947 at Public School 164 in the Queens Valley—the same establishment where Belle Simon was a third-grade teacher.

It took them time to get to know one another, though. In fact, the pair were in third grade before Simon absorbed what he called "a significant memory" of his future partner, a school concert at which a tall, distinctively fair-haired boy stood up to perform Nat "King" Cole's "Too Young." He brought the house down, and Simon, though his own musical interests were far from honed at this point, was instantly intrigued.

Still, it would be another year or so before Simon, now aged ten, even thought about music as anything more than something he enjoyed listening to. He'd been selected to appear as the White Rabbit in a school production of *Alice in Wonderland*—newly released as a smash hit Disney movie with a soundtrack overflowing with future classics. Simon was up in his bedroom practicing some of the songs, singing along with the record. Suddenly he noticed his father standing in the doorway, listening.

"That's nice, Paul. You have a nice voice." Simon, retelling the anecdote many years later, exclaimed: "That was it. From that moment on, I thought of myself as someone who could sing."

Although not as beautifully as that kid at school.

His lack of interest in music as a child is scarcely shocking. With a father whose own musical career had taken him both into the recording studio and onto the television screen, Simon grew up viewing making music as simply something you did like teaching or running a store.

He admired his father and was usually allowed to stay up late to watch Louis appear on TV. But still it was a job; music was what helped pay for food, clothes, the television itself. Any glamour that may have been attached to the profession was always countered by the matter-of-fact awareness of—"well, it's just what dad and his workmates do."

Or what he did. Louis had never intended to remain a musician his entire life, and he continued his academic studies throughout his performing career. Now, in his forties and armed with a doctorate in education, he packed his bass away and joined his wife in teaching at City College.

In the meantime, *Alice in Wonderland* was getting closer, and the casting threw Simon and Garfunkel together—Art was to play the Cheshire Cat, and every day after school for close to two months, the pair were onstage together, rehearsing. Inevitably they soon discovered they were walking the same way home; they fell into conversation easily and naturally, and friendship blossomed.

Part of the attraction was that both boys considered themselves what Garfunkel would later describe as "outsiders." Although neither was at all unpopular, still they did not mix easily or willingly with their classmates. Though both were certainly interested in those topics that were considered hottest among their peers—namely, various sports—neither threw himself with all-consuming gusto into the lifestyle that accompanied them.

Artie (left) and Paul (right), two young hopefuls hoping.   *Photofest*

Their sense of unity only strengthened once the 1953–54 school year got underway. Both had graduated from PS 164 and were now enrolled at Parsons Junior High—a tough school in a rough neighborhood. To make matters worse, and to set them further apart from their peers, both had been fast-tracked into a special program aimed at gifted students.

It marked them out for bullying, both at school and, even more terrifyingly, as they walked home, trying desperately to avoid the attentions of the local gang that hung around the streets, waiting to pounce upon them.

The pair would race the short distance home in the hope of avoiding their tormentors, knowing that should they be caught, stones would be thrown, schoolbooks dropped into puddles, cash stolen, and bruises collected. Only once they'd made it back to their respective houses could they consider themselves at all safe, and that added to the sense of security they garnered from one another's presence.

Two Stars Are Born

Sunday afternoons were the highlight of the boys' week, when the pair would meet at Garfunkel's home and, as often as not, spend their time goofing around with Jack Garfunkel's wire recorder. They would sing together, concoct comedy routines, and occasionally create their own radio show, playing favorite records and doing their best to ape the mellifluous tones of the double-act disc jockeys of the day. They even concocted aliases for their "show"—Art Michaels (Garfunkel) and Ted Howard (Simon). For some reason, they didn't feel their given names had any showbiz resonance whatsoever.

The two boys were bar mitzvahed, three weeks apart of course, in late 1954, when they turned thirteen. For Paul, it was something he did largely to please his mother; theirs was not an especially religious household, but Belle would show up at synagogue occasionally, and her eldest son's bar mitzvah was one such occasion.

Garfunkel, too, was not overly keen on the ritual, but there was one aspect that he throughly enjoyed. Because nobody else had a voice anything like as good as his, he was decreed cantor—the lead singer—at his own bar mitzvah.

Singing suddenly felt even more important.

Up until this point, American radio had largely been dominated by big bands, swing, balladeers, and novelty songs. Only a handful of listeners, comparatively, were aware of what was happening in what we might now call the "underground"—the more specialized worlds of R&B and country, wherein all manner of new musical forms were germinating, if only one knew where to hear them.

Certainly they would scarcely have permeated Simon and Garfunkel's adolescent world—for them, "pop" music was the big hits of the day, and when Simon picked up his first guitar, that was the kind of music he dreamed of emulating: the sounds of Jo Stafford, Doris Day, Kitty Kalen, Perry Como, the Crew Cuts, Rosemary Clooney, and so forth.

The fabulous Crew Cuts—an early influence on the young Paul and Artie.   *Author's collection*

The boys acquired a second tape recorder and experimented with overdubbing; they were perfectionists in their zeal to sound, as Garfunkel later put it, like "real people." Face to face, they sat in the Garfunkel family basement, working on their technique and their timing, watching one another's mouths as they sang, until their harmonizing was as instinctive as it was extraordinary. And once they had achieved that, they could make it look ordinary.

The duo made their first "public" appearance during assembly at Parsons Junior High, one morning in the summer of 1955. They chose to perform an *a cappella* "Sh-boom," one of several Crew Cuts songs in their repertoire at the time. It was a wise decision. More than any of the myriad vocal groups that were floating around at the time, the Canadian quartet possessed both the sound and the material that Simon and Garfunkel saw as their own natural direction.

"Crazy 'Bout You Baby" was their first major hit in 1954; "Sh-boom" and "Earth Angel" were their biggest American chart-toppers during 1954–1955 and the blueprint for a succession of further hits. At least for now, they were also the foundation of Simon and Garfunkel's Sunday sessions.

You Can Call Me Benjamin

He was a serious child, Paul Simon. So serious that his parents, resigned never to see him smile, started calling him after the Supreme Court Associate Justice Benjamin Nathan Cardozo.

He never seemed to smile, either, but it was not the worst role model to give the boy.

Born in 1870, Cardozo was appointed to the Supreme Court by President Hoover in 1932. A lifelong Democrat, his appointment was declared (and remains) one of the few times in the history of the Court when partisan politics did not play a role in a nomination—Hoover was Republican. It was a popular decision, however; Cardozo was confirmed less than a week later.

He would serve barely six years on the Court. Following a massive heart attack in 1937 and a stroke in the following year, Cardozo, aged sixty-eight, passed away in July 1938. His impact on the Supreme Court, however, and thence on American law, has seldom been replicated—indeed, it is a tribute (albeit a most peculiar one) that, close to twenty years after his death, Cardozo's demeanor could still be recalled as readily as his decisions.

Even today, in fact, visitors to the legal website Oyez.org will find Cardoza remembered for his "felicity of expression"—in other words, he didn't smile very often.

But like so many of the formal faces that are presented to the world, it disguised a keen sense of humor, and no reluctance whatsoever to deploy it.

Such as the time he was asked to describe himself. "In truth, I am nothing but a plodding mediocrity—please observe, a plodding mediocrity—for a mere mediocrity does not go very far, but a plodding one gets quite a distance."

Rock 'n' Roll Is Coming

It was a gradual process, but as 1955 began to trickle through the egg timer, and with increasing pace as the year wore on, a different kind of music began leeching into Top 40 radio. Bill Haley and the Comets, Little Richard, Fats Domino, and Elvis Presley were coming and, with them, a new terminology. "Rock 'n' roll" was on its way, and it coincided with the next major landmark in the two friends' lives, as they moved on to a new school, tenth graders at Forest Hills High.

The shift in the musical firmament was, in some ways, a mixed blessing for the boys, particularly for Art, whose voice and tastes continued to lean toward the harmony-strong likes of the Crew Cuts and the Hilltoppers. But he was also a big fan of Alan Freed, the firebrand Cleveland disc jockey who had made the New York station WIN's airwaves his own; and the fact was, you couldn't have one—Freed—without the other—rock 'n' roll.

And besides, who was to say that you couldn't like both sides of the musical coin, Nat "King" Cole *and* Jerry Lee Lewis, "Earth Angel" *and* "Heartbreak Hotel"?

It was Simon—seated in the family car, waiting while his parents picked up some groceries from Waldbaum's Supermarket—who heard Elvis first. Heard him, and fell for him. As much as his father complimenting his voice, as much as the applause his White Rabbit received in *Alice*, Elvis Presley set Paul Simon on his musical way, but for wholly different reasons.

Elvis did *not* receive the plaudits of parents and teachers; Elvis did not sing in a voice that the older generation might consider "nice." He was down and dirty, suggestive and sly. He sang in English, but it was coded in a way that only a teenager could understand, how *this* phrase meant *that* observation, and *this* intonation meant *that* inflection. And when you saw him on TV, or even in pictures, his guitar slung as low as his quiff soared high, you *knew*. This was what music was really all about.

Louis Simon bought his son a cheap Stadium guitar, and the boy practiced till his fingers were as raw as his and Garfunkel's throats sometimes felt. His parents encouraged him, too; Louis had already tried to persuade Paul to learn piano, while his mother, Simon later remembered, "was extremely supportive." He went on, claiming: "[She was] the first nourishing person in my life. She made me feel as if I could take my needs very seriously because she did. By the time I was twelve or thirteen, I felt that I was special because I could play the guitar and write songs."

Actually, he was a couple of years older than that, but the point remains unaltered.

Those Sundays gathered around the wire recorder, aping the popular DJs of the day, were now devoted to making music. Simon was not so much playing his guitar at this point as pounding on it, creating rhythms that were more akin to the sound of a speeding locomotive than they were a handful of chords. Garfunkel, too, was experimenting, gathering the licks and tricks he'd learned from his favorite balladeers and merging them with the moments he loved best in rock 'n' roll.

"I loved Elvis Presley," Simon admitted later. He taught himself to sing a little like him, and to play and move like him as well. But he was also realistic enough to know, even then, that he could "never *be* Elvis Presley," determining that he would "go and find something else to do."

Garfunkel, years later, could still marvel at the knowledge that Simon "does have an Elvis Presley style which he can always pull out of his back pocket."

But Elvis was not alone in there.

Sam Cooke impacted heavily on Simon. "I think Sam Cooke was the best voice," he told *Spin* in 1987. "I don't think anybody was in Sam Cooke's league. And he also tended to be more of a soft singer and phraser, so there was more for me to learn because that's what my voice is naturally. Although he could belt too, essentially for me it was the smoothness of his voice. I was a big Sam Cooke fan, still am, even more for his work with the Soul Stirrers than for his pop stuff."

There was Dion and the Belmonts, New York street kids with a direct line to doo-wop heaven. Hits like "Teenager in Love" and, later, when Dion DiMucci went solo, "Runaround Sue" and "The Wanderer," would become eternal touchstones in Simon's life. In fact, he would perform with Dion on several occasions, first at the singer's 1989 induction into the Rock and Roll Hall of Fame and then in 2015, when the pair duetted on the title track from Dion's latest album, *New York Is My Home.*

"It's my 'street rock 'n' roll song,' my love song to the city and my girl," Dion explained.To my eyes the city is pure; it lifts me to a higher reality. I experience the fullness of life in New York. It's all here."

And, almost as soon as the song was written: "I knew I had to sing it with Paul Simon. I knew Paul would 'get' this song. And he did. Soon after I sent it to him, [he] called and said he'd become obsessed with it and added his own distinct touches to the production. This was a labor of love for us."

Even so, these other names scarcely mattered. Early in 1957, the boys found another force to emulate. It was called the Everly Brothers.

At a time when rock 'n' roll was considered a nasty, greasy, evil noise, the Everly Brothers almost single-handedly turned it into a national obsession and, in an age when rock 'n' rollers were widely regarded as untalented yobs making an unnatural racket, the Everlys' close harmonies proved that even devils could sound like angels.

In the midst of the most tumultuous upheaval that popular entertainment had ever witnessed, Don and Phil Everly established themselves as the bridge between the pop harmonies of the old wave and the earthy rhythms of the new. And there was nobody else like them.

Siblings born two years apart in Brownie, Kentucky (the elder Don), and Chicago (younger Phil), and raised in Shenandoah, Iowa, they were born into showbusiness. Their father, Ike, a coal miner by trade, had a show on local Shenandoah radio, presenting his own family group, the Everly Family, and quickly singling out the boys with their own moment in the spotlight, as Little Donnie and Baby Boy Phil.

Their fame followed them to Knoxville, where the family moved in 1953; teenagers now, the pair were "discovered" by Chet Atkins, and in 1956—by which time the boys were living in Nashville—they cut their first single for Columbia, Don's own country-fied "Keep a-Lovin' Me."

Fame was still some years away, but the boys already knew how to cut a shape.
Photofest

It didn't sell and Columbia lost interest. Atkins, however, kept the faith, introducing the duo to Wesley Rose, one-half of the Acuff-Rose publishing house. In return for the Everlys pledging their songwriting to the company, Rose arranged an introduction to Archie Bleyer, head of the Cadence label, and in early 1957, their very first single for the company, "Bye Bye Love," soared to number two—held back only by the omnipresent Presley. The first time Simon heard it on the radio, he phoned Garfunkel immediately. "There's a record we have to go and buy."

Indeed, no matter what else the rock 'n' rollers of America could fling at the charts, that was how it would remain for the rest of the decade—Elvis was King, none could dispute that. But the Everlys were the princes-in-waiting, and the string of hits with which they confirmed that status still reads like one of the greatest hits collections that could ever be compiled: "Wake Up Little Susie," "All I Have to Do Is Dream," "Bird Dog," "(Till) I Kissed You," "Ebony Eyes," and more.

For five years, between 1956 and 1962, the Everly Brothers enjoyed an almost unbroken run of success on the *Billboard* Top 20. Even more pronounced than their hits, however, was the sheer weight of influence that the Everlys brought to bear, not only on great swaths of the music scene, but upon impressionable young listeners as well.

Across the United States, and over the ocean in Europe, too, the notion that rock 'n' roll had not, after all, chased harmony into the hills was one that more than one aspiring pop singer rejoiced in. The Beatles' trademark harmonies—along with those of other British Invaders—were straight out of the Everlys' songbook. Buddy Holly was a fan, and he wrote "Wishing" for the Everlys. And for Paul Simon and Art Garfunkel, there could have been no greater influence or idol.

In his 2017 autobiography, *What Is It All but Luminous*, Garfunkel confesses their hero worship: "The Everlys were our models, Paul and I wrote our songs together [their first was called "The Girl for Me"] and practiced getting a tooled, very detailed accuracy in our harmony."

They were serious in their endeavors; "The Girl for Me" was even legally copyrighted. They completed the necessary forms, paid the required fee (four dollars), and lodged their composition with the Library of Congress.

Tom and Jerry

They also took to riding the subway into Manhattan after school, Simon's guitar in tow, to tour around the record company offices. They did their homework, too—they would only visit labels who released records they liked.

Still unconvinced by the marketability of their own names, they introduced themselves as Tom Graph (Garfunkel) and Jerry Landis (Simon); although, of course, it was not their names that saw so many doors slam in their faces before they'd even had a chance to play their songs. They were not, after all, the first fifteen-year-old kids to think that all they needed do was knock on a door to get a record deal, and they wouldn't be the last.

They were offered one deal, by one Morty Kraft, who "signed us and locked us away from all competition for six months," as Garfunkel put it. Nothing happened, but the pair didn't give up. Not immediately. But High School was coming to an end; college and adulthood were just around the corner. It was time, both boys knew, to place their childhood dreams on hold and step out into the real world. They would give music one last try.

2

Harmony and High School

One evening during the summer break of 1957, the Everly Brothers performed a new song, "Hey, Doll Baby," on television. Watching the show from their respective homes, both Simon and Garfunkel were blown away by it, and the next time they got together, they were intent upon recapturing what they'd heard. (The Everlys would not include the song on a record for a few months more.)

It took them a while, so long, in fact, that they didn't even notice as their attempts to recapture one song began gradually morphing into the creation of another one entirely—a wholly different song that may have been firmly rooted in the Everlys' trademark sound but was utterly Simon and Garfunkel's own creation.

And when they did realize this and had titled the song "Hey Schoolgirl," they knew exactly what they needed to do with it.

Stars for a Day

Down on Seventh Avenue in Manhattan, the Sanders Recording Studio offered would-be pop stars the opportunity to cut what was called a demonstration disc for just two dollars. There were a lot of places like that around in those days, and many people took advantage of their largesse—Elvis Presley himself got his "big break" when he dropped by Sam Phillips's Sun Studio in Memphis to record a demo disc for his mother; Cliff Richard made his recorded debut in a similar setup in a London record store.

It was a rudimentary process. The performances would be recorded live and cut direct to acetate. There were no retakes, no overdubs, nothing. If you made a mistake, you either lived with it or you forked over another two dollars and tried again.

Tom and Jerry made no mistakes. They completed "Hey Schoolgirl" and were taking a break before moving on to a second song when a stranger approached them. Sid Prosen was awaiting his turn in the studio and listening to the teenagers while he did so. Immediately after they finished, he came over and, as Art put it to *Rolling Stone*, told them, "When you're finished, I want to talk to you guys."

Tom and Jerry recorded their other song, and Prosen made his move. "[You're the] greatest thing since the Everly Brothers. I'm going to make stars out of you."

The pair shrugged. They may not have heard those exact words before, but they knew the pitch and, particularly in the wake of the Morty Kraft experience, they weren't impressed. They agreed to sign with Prosen only if he could guarantee to record them and release the disc within sixty days.

Prosen had no problem with that. They signed, they recorded, and, sure enough, "Hey Schoolgirl" was released that fall, as both a 78 and a 45, on the Big Records label. Even more impressively, Prosen was already hard at work promoting it, beginning by pointing the pair toward a suitably clean-cut image—red blazers and white loafers.

There was even a performance on Dick Clark's nationally syndicated *American Bandstand*, filmed at the show's studio on Market Street in Philadelphia, on a bill that they shared with, among others, Jerry lee Lewis.

In fact, Tom and Jerry were broadcast immediately after the Killer's riotous rendition of "Great Balls of Fire" when the show aired that Thanksgiving—a sobering scenario for a couple of teenaged schoolboys, but a thrill regardless. After all, they'd been avid viewers of *American Bandstand* since it was launched that summer. And now they were on it.

Tom and Jerry Discography

1955: "The Girl for Me" (Simon/Garfunkel)—unreleased; song copyrighted at the Library of Congress
1957: "Hey Schoolgirl"/"Dancin' Wild" (Big 613, reissued King 5167)
1958: (by True Taylor a.k.a. Paul Simon) "True or False"/"Teenage Fool" (Big 614)
1958: "Our Song"/"Two Teenagers" (Big 616)

1958: "That's My Story"/"Don't Say Goodbye" (Big 618, reissued Hunt 319)

1958: "Baby Talk"/"Two Teenagers" (Big 621)

1959: "I'm Lonesome"/"Looking at You" (Ember 1094)

1961: "I'll Drown in My Tears"/"The French Twist" (Mercury 71930)

1962: "Surrender, Please Surrender"/"Fighting Mad" (ABC Paramount 10363)

The duo hit the road—a string of record shops in Cincinnati and a lowly spot on the bill at the Hartford State Theater, where they were the only white guys on a nine-act roster, playing to an almost exclusively

The fifties kids.   *Photofest*

black audience, too. But even on a stage overflowing with R&B, they carried it off, and back home in Queens, they were regarded as royalty—local superstars no matter how well the record did.

In fact, it didn't perform too badly. Coupled with local New York airplay, the *American Bandstand* performance pushed "Hey Schoolgirl" as high as number fifty-nine on the *Billboard* chart. It sold around 100,000 copies and kept the duo busy with additional live appearances. Simon was even able to purchase his first car with his share of the proceeds.

Unfortunately, that was as good as it ever got for Tom and Jerry . . . and for Big Records, too. Further Tom and Jerry singles sank; Big itself went out of business, and that, as Simon later said, "was the end of it, so we went back to school."

He didn't even have the car to show off, either. Out one night, the carburetor caught fire. He got out of the burning vehicle in one piece, but his share of the duo's moment of fame was left a blackened, charred wreck.

Anybody else might have taken that as an omen.

There Goes Sideman Simon

Over the next five years, Simon, more than Garfunkel, would continue to release occasional singles. None were especially successful, but they scratched an itch, and besides, every new session, every fresh live performance, every sour recording deal, every new musician encountered and befriended, all these experiences added up.

They also made it increasingly obvious that, like his father, Simon was destined to try and make his way in the music industry. Unlike his father, however, he believed he was in it for the long haul.

He just had to find his voice. And it was while he was finding it that he took the step that, years later, Garfunkel would throw at him as the single most damaging thing that ever occurred in their career together.

The revelation came as the duo's early 1980s reunion wound down into rancor and bitterness. Anxious to clear the air, Simon asked point blank why their friendship had always had an edge to it, as though Garfunkel either didn't like or didn't trust Simon.

The response shocked him.

"We are indescribable. You'll never capture it. It's an ingrown, deep friendship," Garfunkel explained in one interview. "Yes, there is deep love in there. But there's also shit." "Shit," apparently, that was born the day in December 1957, with "Hey Schoolgirl" still a fresh, happy memory, when Jerry recorded his first ever solo single, "True or False," without telling Tom that he'd even made a deal to do such things.

Why should he have? Simon considered the record irrelevant—he'd been asked if he wanted to do it, and he said yes. Garfunkel had no interest in singing rockers, whereas Simon ached to let rip on one. But Garfunkel didn't see it that way. To him, it was a betrayal, and he carried that betrayal with him for the next thirty-five years. Simon, like a lot of other people too, was astonished when he discovered that.

The two friends graduated in the summer of 1958 and moved on to college—Garfunkel at Columbia College, on Manhattan's West Side, and Simon majoring in English literature at the local Queens College. He had always been an avid reader, and he was growing increasingly fascinated by poetry, attending readings by both the great (E. E. Cummings) and the average (the local hopefuls) while accumulating an impressive library of the classics.

Suddenly T. S. Eliot, Robert Frost, and Emily Dickinson were as much a part of Simon's creative landscape as Elvis and the Everlys, and their influence would soon be communicating itself to his songwriting. Indeed, of all the criticisms that can be leveled at Simon the writer, the most frequently made is that he rarely takes the easy way through a lyric, preferring well-spoken profundity to quick and easy rhymes and maintaining a particular pride in his ability to do so.

Indeed, even when, in 1966, he did "loosen up" his language for "We've Got a Groovy Thing Goin'," with its fresh-as-daisies incorporation of the latest buzzword *du jour*, it remained a ferociously defended point of pride, as fellow songwriter Carole Bayer Sager recalled in her autobiography, *They're Playing Our Song*.

She had recently penned (with Toni Wine) her first major hit single, "Groovy Kind of Love," and a family friend, who happened to be Simon's aunt, arranged for the two songwriters to go on a date.

The evening started badly. Simon was due to pick her up at eight, and bang on time, the doorbell rang. But when Carole's mother looked through the peephole in the front door, there was nobody there. Nor when the bell rang a second time. But this time, she looked down as well as out and saw the diminutive young man, all five foot two of him, looking up. "Forget it," Carole's mom stage-whispered. "Midgets."

"I think the highlight of the evening was behind me," Bayer Sager wrote. "Because all I remember of our 'short' date was an argument about which of us first used the word 'groovy' in a song."

Simon was not deterred. "Groovy" reappeared in his vocabulary later in the year, in his "The 59th Street Bridge Song," and that, too, was guarded fiercely. When Simon's name was added to the songwriting credits of Sid and Marty Kroft's theme to *HR Puffenstuff*, it was because he had pointed out that song's similarity to "The 59th Street Bridge Song."

He could reach for pretension with the best of them. The lyric "I have my books and poetry to protect me" is no less a toe-curler today than it was when it was first heard in "I Am a Rock." But he could also puncture such loftiness, as in "A Dangling Conversation," with its razor-honed denunciation of the supercilious intellectuals who read their Emily Dickinson and Robert Frost but have nothing meaningful to say about either—or anything else.

At the same time, however, such quirks (if quirks they be) are wholly unconscious. At least through the first years if his career, he has insisted, he would never have dreamed of writing for posterity, or even fame. As he reminded *Rolling Stone* in 1972, between the ages of fifteen and twenty-two, he had scored one minor hit at the dawn of that period and nothing but flops ever since.

"So I expected everything to be a flop," he said, and that took the pressure off. He viewed himself as a complete unknown, so who cared whether or not he wrote the occasional bad song? He wasn't important enough to criticize.

Or, as he put it on another occasion, that was when he started to travel on a considerably less traveled path compared to most people.

With college the biggest thing on their horizons, Garfunkel had stepped away now—not from their friendship, but from the musical partnership. Instead, Simon began casting around for whatever musical employment he could get, including a period working with a clutch of song publishers, recording whatever songs were thrown to him.

The system was quite simple. A writer would send in a song; the publisher would listen to it and then determine which hit artist it should be offered to. Simon's task, together with a handful of other salaried musicians, was to record a demo that sounded like that hit artist. He explained: "A publisher would get a song and they'd say, 'This song would be great for Dion.' So I would be Dion, and then I'd sing all the background ooh-ooh-wah-ooh."

He was earning fifteen dollars a pop for these sessions, a neat little earner even if it was not exactly the greatest use of his talents, not even when he was paired with another aspiring songwriter, Carole Klein. Going under the name of the Cousins, they too recorded demos—Simon playing bass and guitar, Klein the piano and drums. They would sing them together and then split the thirty-dollar fee between them.

Neither was called upon to lend their own pen to the proceedings, but when one of the demos they made, for a Mary Kalfin composition called "Just to Be with You," became a hit for the vocal group the Passions in 1959, Klein announced that she was going to go full bore toward a career in music.

Simon advised her against it, just as his father was now counseling him, but Klein didn't listen. She simply changed her surname to King and, with her husband Gerry Goffin, set about establishing herself as the most successful female songwriter in pop history.

While Simon got on with not being much of one at all.

Jerry Landis, Session Man Superstar

1959: "Anna Belle"/"Loneliness" (MGM 12822)
1960: "Just a Boy"/"Shy" (Warwick 552)
1960: "Just a Boy"/"I'd Like to Be" (Warwick 558)
1960: (The Mystics; a-side written/arranged by Jerry Landis) "All Through the Night"/"To Think Again of You" (Laurie 3047)
1961: "Play Me a Sad Song"/"It Means a Lot to Them" (Warwick 616)
1961: "I'm Lonely"/"I Wish I Weren't in Love" (Canadian American 130)
1961: (By Tico and the Triumphs) "Motorcycle"/"I Don't Believe Them" (Madison 169, Amy 835)
1962: "Lone Teen-Ranger"/"Lisa" (Amy 875)
1962: (By Tico and the Triumphs) "Express Train"/"Wildflower" (Amy 845)

1962: (By Tico and the Triumphs) "Get Up and Do the Wobble"/"Cry, Little
        Boy, Cry" (Amy 86)

1963: (By Tico and the Triumphs) "Cards of Love"/"Noise" (Amy 876)

The High School Love Explosion

His poetic predilections notwithstanding, the songs Paul Simon was writing during this period were very much the children of their time—that late 1950s/early 1960s era, when the initial flamboyant flourish of rock 'n' roll had first been tamed and then been neutered.

Not one of the stars who emerged from the initial big bang of feral ferocity remained a reliable hit maker, at least in any shape or form that their original fans considered similar. The nature of the music business at that time, after all, was either to hype a newcomer to the stars and then drop them the moment the next one came along, or, if somebody did show some staying power, to begin tailoring them toward a wider—mom-and-pop-friendly—audience.

Elvis was the classic example of that, readily identifiable by the seismic shift he underwent in the comparatively short period that elapsed between "Heartbreak Hotel" in 1955 and "Love Me Tender" the following year. (By the time he got around to "Jailhouse Rock" in 1957, it was already an anomaly.) But he was by no means the only one.

From a financial point of view, which of course is the only consideration that the music industry really cares about, it was a smart move. The business had long since grown accustomed to sudden crazes emerging out of nowhere to hypnotize the record-buying public, and there was no reason whatsoever to believe that rock 'n' roll was any different to those musical upheavals that preceded it.

Indeed, even among its own practitioners—Buddy Holly, for example, and the Everlys, of course—there were signs that the music's more raucous attributes were losing their appeal. With but a handful of generally one-off exceptions, by 1959, rock 'n' roll was dead.

It was replaced with what was effectively its corollary. Rockin' and rollin' (most people knew the term was a euphemism for sexual intercourse) was replaced by kissin' and cuddlin'. The frantic jitterbug was now a mild-mannered smooch. Adult themes were supplanted by teenaged ballads, leather jackets by letterman cardigans, seething hormones by cheerleader chastity. All of which, in turn, served up a pretext that Tin Pan Alley—the traditional soul of the American music industry and the source of much of Paul Simon's current employment—understood.

It was nothing less than pop music, of course, but it was more than that, as well. It was a way of life. And the market was milked for all it was worth. In 1959 Tommy Facienda recorded a song called, quite simply, "High School USA," and then rerecorded it almost thirty times—"High School USA (Boston)," "High School USA (Buffalo)," "High School USA (Chicago)," and on and on to Washington DC, each version targeted at a specific geographical marketplace. One presumes that, had the records' sales justified it, the list could have gone on forever.

Ten Great High School Anthems

The Shangri-Las—"Leader of the Pack"
Carole King—"It Might as Well Rain until September"
The Dixie Cups—"Chapel of Love"
The Shirelles—"Will You Still Love Me Tomorrow"
The Everly Brothers—"Devoted to You"
Johnny Tillotson—"Poetry in Motion"
Brian Hyland—"Sealed with a Kiss"
The Paris Sisters—"Love How You Love Me"
The Poni-Tails—"Born Too Late"
Tico and the Triumphs—"Motorcycle"

The new sound was everything rock 'n' roll wasn't, and that included the chain of command that created the songs in the first place. No more sweaty musicians writing chords in the back of the van on their way to or from a show.

Hit songs now were written in Hit Factories, places like the Brill Building, where the office equipment was two chairs and a piano, and a good day's work meant a song that would rule the Top 10.

Goffin and King, Bobby Darin, Barry Mann and Cynthia Weill, Neil Diamond, Ellie Greenwich and Jeff Barry, Gary Sherman, and Howie

Greenfield all filed into work at ten every morning and clocked out at five, and in between those times, they wrote songs.

Such an environment was a principle that both Tamla Motown and Kasenetz-Katz were later to employ, and according to English songwriter Graham Gouldman, who was to work at the latter during the late 1960s, the system ran along the simplest lines imaginable: "We were employed to write songs. Every morning we would clock in, go up to our offices, sit down at the piano, and write. It was like any factory, only instead of little bits of cars, you'd make little bits of music."

The criteria which bound their efforts were equally simple. Was a song easy to learn? Was it easy to sing along with? And, most crucial of all, was it a hit? That was all that mattered. You're writing for teenagers, so write *about* teenagers.

This was the world that Paul Simon was so keen to enter, and all the more so after Carole Klein set herself up within it. Whether under his own steam, as Jerry Landis, or as producer and session man for others, he was involved in a succession of singles throughout this period, most of which he subsequently dismissed as "dumb teenage lyrics."

"I'd Like to be the Lipstick on Your Lips" is an especially gratuitous example, and with a title like that, there's no surprise. But Tico and the Triumphs' "Motorcycle," which Simon produced and sang on in 1961, is sensational, a rocking doo-wop stomp, shot through with the roar of a speeding hog, while its breakneck lyrics do nothing more than sing the praises of the titular vehicle through the besotted eyes of its teenaged owner.

"Every day after school, I'm a motorcycle fool." This wasn't dumb, this was life!

What his elder self ignored, or perhaps had forgotten, was that "dumb teenage lyrics" were what the market demanded; "dumb teenage lyrics" were where the hits were. Even his beloved Everly Brothers ("Wake Up Little Susie," about oversleeping at the movies; "Ebony Eyes," about mourning a sweetheart who perished in an air disaster) were not above jamming the juvenile jukebox with their gems, and today music history can look back on that scene as one of the last truly innocent eras in the history of American pop.

And, though so much of it sounds like cotton candy, one of the most influential.

An early promo photograph.   *Author's collection*

3

Blowing in the Wind

It was, Simon later mused, "age" that prompted him to change the kind of music he wanted to make. He was twenty-one, twenty-two years old—too old to continue delighting in the frivolities of his youth and, from an intellectual standpoint, too serious to ignore what was going on in the world around him. And not just from a musical angle.

It's true what he later said: "[Rock 'n' roll became] very bad in the early sixties. Very mushy." But perhaps that was only to counter the increasingly abrasive world into which its audience had been cast.

By 1963, the past two or three years might have been marked by a certain stagnation within the mainstream pop music industry, but potent undercurrents were swirling elsewhere—a movement that the industry, once it got its own hands on the sound, would dub "the folk revival," but which was a far purer beast than that in its infancy.

It was spawned both by an intellectual curiosity for the music that pre-dated pop in the American lexicon (Alan Lomax's mammoth *Folk Songs of North America* was newly published) and by growing unease over the plight of America itself.

The Cold War was in full swing, the threat of nuclear obliteration real enough that even elementary schools interrupted lessons so the kids could practice hiding under their desks in readiness for the Bomb. ("Duck and cover" was *not* a joke.)

The tensions that would culminate in the Cuban Missile Crisis were already being felt, and President Kennedy was moving the first pieces into place as America lurched toward the Vietnam War. The anti-Communism panic of the fifties was still in play. Culturally, the split between "old" and "young" had never felt wider, as one side pushed toward the bright utopian future they dreamed was around the corner while the other clung doggedly to the values, laws, and prejudices that made America great in the first place.

The civil rights movement was struggling to assert itself; the sexual revolution was a political volleyball. Division was everywhere, and for the generation that was born within the grip, or the aftermath, of the Second World War, the optimism of youth was fast decaying into cynicism, fear, and rage.

Folk music, that aforementioned intellectual pursuit, became the vehicle with which that rage would be conveyed.

Folk itself is not, and never has been, simply a gathering of antiquated phrases and rhymes, most of which seem to involve nut-brown maids dil-lydallying in the hedgerow. It is the voice of the people from a time when their voices were the only weapons they had—a time before newspapers, or even literacy, were truly embraced within society.

Songs were sung about life in all its shades, from the sweetest love to the blackest murder, and from the darkest disaster to the brightest smile. Politics, and its effect on the average person, was as much a part of the lyrical lexicon as any other.

Woody Guthrie is, quite rightly, regarded as the grandfather of what was now being called protest music. The songs he wrote to chronicle the American struggle through depression and the dustbowl hung a bitter alternative to the histories that the textbooks liked to retell, and, though

Simon and Garfunkel strike a moody pose. What else?   *Photofest*

his personal powers were waning as illness wracked his frame, his disciples—led by Pete Seeger—were adamant that his lessons would not be forgotten.

That Seeger was himself drawn into Senator McCarthy's Communist witch hunt in the early 1950s and was effectively blackballed by the browbeaten world of popular entertainment only piled intrigue upon interest. The idea that folk music, the purest and most authentic of all American musical pursuits, could be regarded as somehow *un*-American was itself as instrumental in the music's rise through the very early 1960s as any of the songs or personalities that were now espousing it.

Queen of the folk world at this time was Joan Baez; the king, though he was still celebrating the release of his first album in 1962, would soon be Bob Dylan. And all around them, folk clubs were springing up across the nation, and folk singers were lining up to fill them.

Some remain legends today: Phil Ochs, Richard Fariña (whose wife and musical partner, Mimi, was Baez's kid sister), Eric Von Schmidt, Dave Van Ronk, Caroline Hester. Others are forgotten, perhaps even by the people who witnessed them performing in the coffee houses of Greenwich Village and Cambridge, Massachusetts, or out in the open at Manhattan's Washington Square Park.

Some followed Dylan's lead and wrote their own music—usually styled after Guthrie or adapted from an earlier source but with a sharp topical lyric that could disguise any number of borrowings. Others followed Baez and adhered to the traditional song sheet yet confirmed their own topicality by selecting songs whose resonance remained electrifying.

Simon approached this new musical currency cautiously, seeing it not so much as a possible new direction but as simply a respite from pop. But attending events in Washington Square Park, ground zero for aspiring folkies and fans alike, he found himself becoming increasingly drawn toward its deceptive simplicity—the power that a simple lyric could convey, the weight that the right words could adopt.

In the past, his love of poetry and his interest in pop had been very different sides of two similar (but not quite the same) coins. In this new music, however, he heard the two disciplines collide—not only in the lyrics of Bob Dylan, who was already being spoken of in terms that had never hitherto been applied to a simple songwriter, but elsewhere, too. Of course Simon was intrigued. It would have been strange if he hadn't been.

At the same time, he was adamant. "I didn't think 'my gosh, music is changing and I have to shift now'." In his heart, he knew that this was what he should have been playing all along—and would have, had he known it existed.

He wouldn't completely abandon his pop ambitions. In 1963, "Jerry Landis" even scraped the Top 100 with "Lone Teen Ranger." He was still working in Tin Pan Alley, too—having graduated from Queens College with a BA in English, Simon landed a job at Edward B. Marks Music, touring around the record companies in much the same manner as he and Garfunkel once did, only now he was trying to interest them in his employer's catalog of newly acquired songs.

Among all the composers he was peddling, incidentally, there was one who especially excited him—a young man by the name of Paul Kane. It was Simon himself.

But he was losing interest in such frivolities, all the more so once Garfunkel began joining him on his excursions into the folk world.

Garfunkel, too, was smitten by what they heard. He had done little to maintain his own share of Tom and Jerry's musical legacy over the last few years, cutting just a couple of singles under the name Artie Garr in 1960. But he had continued singing, and several songs in the folk repertoire were already familiar to him. Indeed, even today, Garfunkel still cites Joan Baez's first album, darkly colored by traditional mayhem as it is, among the albums that most profoundly influenced his young self.

Slowly, the revitalized Tom and Jerry started to venture out as a duo once again, two voices and one acoustic guitar, performing both folk standards and the first of the songs Paul was writing in this new format. Gigs around the Greenwich Village coffee houses and folk clubs followed, together with occasional Sunday morning appearances in Washington Square Park.

It never felt like anything more than a passing fancy; Garfunkel was attending architecture school in Berkeley, California, and would be leaving New York City in June. Simon, for his part, was simply feeling restless, and around the same time as Garfunkel headed west, Simon flew east to Paris for an extended vacation.

Paul in Paris

He had made no arrangements. For the most part, he would be living and sleeping rough; busking for change with the guitar that was more or less his sole possession; hanging out at Shakespeare and Company, the renowned Parisian bookstore; and simply reveling in the same Bohemian lifestyle that had attracted hundreds of other kids, from America and elsewhere, to *La Ville Lumière*.

"We'd sit on the banks of the Seine, and when tourist boats would go by, I would yell out 'Capitalist Pig,'" he recalled years later.

It was not necessarily an uplifting experience. Busking can be a rocky profession at the best of times, but when you are just one of dozens of likeminded kids, all of them competing for the prime spots outside the metro stations and bus stops, it becomes even harder.

He sang whatever he thought would make the most noise—particularly, he later remarked, if it had "a loud, high ending." He explained: "I was particularly good at loud, high endings. If you sang a note for a long time, you tended to get money for it."

Of course he concentrated on the big hits of the era—there was little room, or patience, for self-composed material in the world of street musicians, but it was good experience regardless.

The best (as in, the most successful) buskers tend to be those who can not only attract a crowd but can hold it as well, and it's ironic that, though the language barrier might ordinarily have been an additional obstacle for him to overcome, it only forced him to put even more feeling into his performance. So as far as he was concerned, he was simply finding new ways of earning a few extra centimes. But he was learning stagecraft, too, and expanding his musical tastes.

He fell under the spell of Jacques Brel, the Flemish songwriter who had gripped the French music scene for much of the previous decade. In years to come, songsmiths as far removed as Rod McKuen, Scott Walker, David Bowie, and Marc Almond would sing Brel's praises loudly, recording his songs as their lyrics were translated into English. At the end of the sixties, Brel would even become the subject of a major Broadway stageshow, *Jacques Brel Is Alive and Well and Living in Paris*.

Simon, however, was entranced much earlier, before anybody had thought to give English words to Brel's vision—indeed, as Simon remarked in the mid-1960s: "He doesn't bother about having his stuff done in English. He's my favorite writer. He comes from the French school of Chansons singers. He writes about French life in the provinces. Some of his stuff is like mine, except it's set in France. They idolize him in France. He works with a piano, bass and drums, and sometimes just his own guitar accompaniment."

A few years later, *Hit Parader* magazine asked Simon whether he could recommend one Brel album in particular. No. "Any number of Jacques Brel albums will suffice."

He Was My Brother

Simon returned to New York City that fall, and with Garfunkel passing through town at the same time, the pair immediately resumed their partnership around the clubs.

Simon had written a handful of songs while he was away, two of which were immediately incorporated into their live set. "Sparrow" and "He Was My Brother" were both very different to any he had played to Garfunkel in the past—the former a plaintive and gentle paean to loneliness, the latter an impassioned tribute to the civil rights struggle as the violence and murders mounted.

Indeed, the song's message would become especially personal for Simon the following year, after one of his former classmates at Queens, Andrew Goodman, was murdered in Mississippi in June 1964. When Simon and Garfunkel's debut album was released that October, "He Was My Brother" was dedicated to Goodman.

A volunteer for the Congress of Racial Equality's "Freedom Summer," an initiative designed to encourage disenfranchised blacks to register to vote, Goodman and two other activists, Mickey Schwerner and James Chaney, were in Philadelphia, Neshoba County, investigating the recent burning of the Mount Zion Methodist Church.

There they were arrested, allegedly for speeding, and fined and released, only for the arresting deputy to then pursue them and order them out of the car again, just as they were about to cross the county line. The cop took them to a deserted patch of land, with two carloads of

Simon and Garfunkel onstage in the mid-1960s.   *Photofest*

Ku Klux Klansmen bringing up the rear. The three were then beaten, shot, and buried.

Nobody was ever convicted of their murder; in fact, it would be forty-one years before anyone—just one man—was even found guilty of manslaughter, and the investigation into the so-called Mississippi Murders was closed in 2016, on the eve of the killings' fifty-second anniversary.

Simon and Garfunkel—The Protest Years

October 1964: *Wednesday Morning, 3 A.M.* (Columbia CS 9049)

All songs composed by Paul Simon unless otherwise noted

"You Can Tell the World" (B. Gibson/ B. Camp)

"Last Night I Had the Strangest Dream" (Ed McCurdy)

"Bleecker Street"

"Sparrow"

"Benedictus" (Trad., arranged and adapted by Simon and Garfunkel)

"The Sound of Silence"

"He Was My Brother" (Paul Kane)

"Peggy-O" (Trad.)

"Go Tell It on the Mountain" (Trad.)

"The Sun Is Burning" (Ian Campbell)

"The Times They Are A-Changin'"
    (Bob Dylan)

"Wednesday Morning, 3 A.M."

Produced by: Tom Wilson; Engineered by: Roy Halee

Musicians: Barry Kornfeld—second guitar; Bill Lee—acoustic bass

1964: (by Paul Kane) "Carlos Dominguez"/"He Was My Brother" (Tribute 128)

September 1965: "The Sound of Silence" (overdubbed electric version)/"We've Got a Groovy Thing Goin'" (Columbia 43396)

Produced by: Bob Johnston

Musicians

(a-side) Al Gorgoni—guitar

Bob Bushnell—bass

Bobby Gregg—drums

March 1966: *Sounds of Silence* (Columbia LP CS 9269)

"The Sound of Silence"

"Leaves That Are Green"

"Blessed"

"Kathy's Song"

"Somewhere They Can't Find Me"
    (rewrite of "Wednesday Morning,
    3 A.M.")

"Anji" (Bert Jansch credited on record
    label, Davy Graham on record
    sleeve)

"Homeward Bound" (not included on
    US album)

"Richard Cory"

"A Most Peculiar Man"

"April Come She Will"

"We've Got a Groovy Thing Goin'"

"I Am a Rock"

"Recorded in December 1965 at CBS studios in LA and Nashville

Produced by: Bob Johnson

March 1966: "Homeward Bound"/"Leaves That Are Green" (Columbia 43511)

June 1966: "I Am a Rock"/"Flowers Never Bend with the Rainfall"

Debuted at Gerde's Folk City on March 30, 1964 (three months before the murders), "He Was My Brother" was the first indication that Simon and Garfunkel were ready to add their voices to the protest movement, although in truth, it would be some months more before Simon was confident enough in his own songwriting to truly embrace the topic.

As late as that aforementioned first album, the duo was still looking elsewhere for suitable material, to the songbooks of Ed McCurdy, Ian Campbell, Bob Gibson and Bob Camp, and, of course, the master, Bob Dylan. Even "He Was My Brother" was initially credited to Simon's Paul Kane alias.

Meanwhile, the bulk of the remainder of their live repertoire (which again carried over to the sessions for that first album) was drawn from the traditional milieu—and beyond. In fact, "Benedictus" was a Latin prayer, sensitively arranged for two voices.

The Bonnie Lass o'Fyvie and Other Tales

The best known of Simon and Garfunkel's traditional excursions, "Peggy-O" was an adaptation of the Scottish folk song "The Bonnie Lass o' Fyvie." It told the saga of the love of the captain of an Irish Dragoons regiment for a Scottish girl, presumably during one of the English military's periodic incursions into the then-rebellious Scottish highlands—Fyvie itself was a well-fortified town in the Scottish Northeast.

Taking the same route as many other Scottish folk songs, "The Bonnie Lass o' Fyvie" arrived in the United States aboard the boats that delivered the first great wave of Scottish emigrants during the mid-eighteenth century. When the great song collector Cecil Sharp set about compiling his monumental (if somewhat misleadingly titled) *English Folk Songs from the Southern Appalachians* from 1916 to 18 (the book was published in 1932), "The Bonnie Lass o' Fyvie" was among the songs that awaited him.

Manifold variations of the song (and its title) exist, but it is likely that Simon and Garfunkel first encountered the song when it was recorded by Bob Dylan in 1962. They may then have renewed their acquaintance via Hoyt Axton and his 1963 album *Greenback Dollar*, coincidentally closing the circle of influence that was opened by Simon's love for Elvis Presley, as Axton was a cowriter of "Heartbreak Hotel."

Both men base their renditions on the song's Americanization, with Fyvie renamed as "Fennario," Aberdeen as "Louisiana," and the captain's insistence that, if the bonnie lass does not accede to his romantic demands, "all your cities I will burn." Most researchers agree that this particular version is probably descended from the Civil War and, specifically, the destruction of Atlanta.

As for the location of Fennario itself, however, even Dylan's spoken introduction to the song admits he is at a loss. "I've been around this whole country, but I never yet found Fennario."

Since that time, "The Bonnie Lass o' Fyvie" has been recorded by acts as far afield as the Grateful Dead, Martin Carthy, and Jefferson Starship, the former and latter, at least, lifting it far from the mellifluous, folky air within which Simon and Garfunkel enfolded it.

The pair were also prone to a joyous recounting of "Go Tell It on the Mountain," an Afro-American spiritual that again has been dated back to the Civil War. (It was first noted in 1865.)

Interestingly, the song probably started life as a Christmas number; however, it would also become a standard bearer for first, the emancipation movement, and a century later, the civil rights struggle. Indeed, Peter, Paul and Mary's 1963 recording confirmed that linkage by incorporating the impassioned demand "Let my people go" (from another spiritual, "Go Down Moses"). Simon and Garfunkel returned to the earlier lyric, but the association was made regardless.

The duo's support of the protest movement was in every way sincere. Nevertheless, Simon's own songwriting was naturally stepping out of that specific (and somewhat oversubscribed) milieu and into the more urban observations that would soon see a new subsidiary movement arise from within the folk scene, the so-called "city folksingers."

The term itself was coined by writer Paul Nelson while penning the liner notes to Tom Rush's eponymous Elektra Records debut, and it was then popularized further by Robert Shelton in the pages of the *New York Times*. The New Hampshire-born, Harvard-educated Rush, he wrote, was one of the most important of that ilk through the "unusual synthesis of sensitivity in statement and guts in feeling, in his music."

Paul Simon would have read those words with especial interest.

What distinguished the "city folksinger" from his presumably rural cousin was Rush's insistence that, whatever he was singing, whether one of his own compositions or a cover, he was "working for the song."

"I always tried to find a little bit of a different take on things," he said. "I remember being really impressed with a guy named Bobby Jones, he specialized in Woody Guthrie songs, hearing him one night doing 'Pastures of Plenty.' It was like a religious experience. I'd heard the song a thousand times, but I'd never heard it. Bobby did it in such a way that it was a brand new song and I was so impressed that ever since then, I've tried not to just sing a song, but to find a way of doing it that would make the song fresh again. I'm working for the song."

Of course, subject matter also played a part in the genre—an awareness of the writer's surroundings, a sensitivity to the lives of his audience, a keen eye for familiar scenes and situations.

There is nothing whatsoever wrong with singing a sixteenth-century ballad about a shoemaker and conveying your audience back to his humble abode. But how much more intriguing to take whatever observations that song may have made and transpose them into modern-day surroundings—and more intriguing still to replace the everyday events of an idealized past with those of a very real today.

The Sounds of Bleecker Street

That was what singled out "Bleecker Street," and established it as Paul Simon's first truly great composition.

Bleecker Street runs east to west across Greenwich Village. Laid out in 1808 and named for the wealthy Bleecker family whose former farmland the street would cross, it originally reached from the Bowery to Broadway. Two decades later, however, it was extended to Abingdon Square, and that is the route it still follows today.

The street had long been a magnet for live entertainment. In the Village of the very early 1960s, however, it was best known as the home of two of the most significant clubs of the age—the Bitter End and the Village Gate. They would be joined, in 1964, by Cafe Au Go Go; but, of course, it was not only the established venues that were open to performers. The streets outside, too, were littered with hopeful talent, all dreaming of becoming the next Bob Dylan, and the teenaged runaways who were likewise being lured to the Village by the promise of the folk boom.

The "voices leaking from a sad cafe" that Simon conjured in his lyric, the shadow that touches another shadow's hand, the poet reading his "crooked rhyme"—these are images that everybody who passed down that street, and its neighbors, would have recognized, and the images, too, that singled out what would quickly become Simon's most potent weapon.

He not only recorded reality. He touched it, too.

Only one other song he wrote during this initial period comes close, and of course, it is the song that would eventually establish Simon and Garfunkel's name and fame, both in the Village and across the world beyond it.

Simon started writing "The Sound of Silence" in the aftermath of the assassination of President John Kennedy in Dallas, Texas, on November 22, 1963. Utterly blindsided, like so many people, by the senseless loss of America's youngest president since Teddy Roosevelt, Simon turned to his songbook as a means of escaping and making sense of the shroud of grief that now enveloped the nation.

The song's melody and its basic theme—the ease with which the rush of everyday life can crush people's ability to communicate with one another; the all-pervasive power of capitalism ("the neon god"); the horrors of apathy and ignorance and how, in so many tiny ways, society encourages them to flourish as a means of keeping organized dissent and argument at bay—were all in place very early on.

The lyric, however, could not and would not be rushed. Every line, Simon knew, needed to count. Every word. There could be no wandering off into a "la la la" chorus or a few random insertions of "baby" to bridge the gap between one thought and another.

Six months it took for him to complete the lyric, for he was deleting and inserting and redeleting words and lines as he honed it into its final shape.

As he explained to NPR, the "key" to "The Sound of Silence" was the sheer simplicity of the music and lyric. It was a song of "youthful alienation," and it was, he conceded "not bad for a twenty-one-year-old." At the same time, however, he admitted that, no matter how sophisticated the thoughts behind the song might have seemed, they were simply something he had discovered in his reading. "It wasn't something that I was experiencing at some deep, profound level—nobody's listening to me, nobody's listening to anyone—it was a post-adolescent angst, but it had some level of truth to it."

Finally, he was able to show the final composition to Garfunkel. Neither knew what the song would ultimately help them to achieve, nor were they yet ready to attempt it onstage. But both were vividly aware that it was Simon's most important creation yet.

4

Paul Simon's London

Most people contemplating what folk music aficionados called *The Child Ballads*—the vast collection of English and Scottish traditional songs collected by a Harvard professor in the mid- to late nineteenth century—know that you need only browse through a few random pages and then the murders begin.

Of course the songs are popular!

The young Paul Simon certainly understood their appeal. Three times did he delve into the pages of Professor F. J. Child's monumental work—in 1964, when he took to opening his live performances with "Scarborough Fair" and "The House Carpenter" ballad, and a couple of years later, during the sessions for Simon and Garfunkel's second album, when "Barbara Allen" was one of three folky favorites recorded during the sessions.

And all three are as darkly supernatural as any other in the books.

Suitcase and Guitar in Hand

Paul Simon returned to Europe in early spring 1964.

The New York folk scene was not dying, but it was certainly ailing. Earlier in the year, the Beatles arrived in the United States in a cloudburst of wild hysteria and even wilder haircuts, and what had once been a thriving scene of earnest young singers filling coffee bars with music, and equally devoted listeners nodding thoughtfully to their revelations, was already shifting on its axis.

Last month's folkie was this month's beat musician, and for those performers who had not taken the next step up the live circuit—which, by early 1964, was almost every one of the worthwhile ones—it was a case of adapt or die.

Simon, however, did not want to adapt. Not yet.

During his time in Paris, Simon fell in with a young Englishman named Dave McCausland, who ran a folk club at the Railway Hotel in Brentwood, a small town in Essex, about an hour outside central London.

Folk music was just as popular in the United Kingdom as it was in the United States at that time, and Dylan and Baez just as admired. More than that, however, the United Kingdom was where the music was born—so many of the folk songs Simon had sung, or had heard, started their centuries-long life in the British Isles; Professor F. J. Child himself was a Bostonian whose interest in folk music was initially aroused by hearing old British songs performed by American singers.

The English and Scottish Popular Ballads: Vol. 3
F. J. Child Ballads sung by Ewan MacColl   Folkways Records FG 3511

Although the first Child Ballad recordings were made in the days of cylinders, it was the 1950s before any serious attempt was made to record them as folk staples. This album is one such effort.   *Author's collection*

Just as he would in the early 1970s, when he travelled to Jamaica to capture an authentic Jamaican sound, and in the 1980s, when he visited South Africa and returned home with *Graceland* (see chapter 11), Simon knew that if he was ever to understand the music he played, he needed to investigate it at its source.

But that knowledge was not his sole reason for going to England; it might not, in fact, even have occurred to him. He simply needed to get out of New York, and the possibility, first raised by McCausland, that he could continue his career in Britain was all he needed to hear.

Simon traveled first to Paris but did not remain there for long. In the meantime, he had reconnected with McCausland and was offered not only a place to stay but also a gig at the Railway Hotel. Arriving in London on the boat train on April 20, 1964, Simon was onstage at the folk club just twenty-four hours later.

That was also the night he met Kathleen Chitty, the woman who become his muse throughout his time in London and the subject of some of his best-loved period compositions. The first time he saw her, she was collecting the admission fee at the door of the folk club.

Kathy herself has never talked publicly of her relationship with Simon—how she not only inspired so many of his early compositions but also titled one ("Kathy's Song") and was named in "America." Even when the British *Daily Mail* newspaper tracked her down, in 2014, to the small village in Wales where she now lives, she remained silent.

But the paper nevertheless struck a chord with its readers as it recalled "Her elfin qualities, huge eyes and aura of gentleness through her shy personality [which] caught [Simon's] attention" while explaining that "she still has requests for interviews from music biographers across the world about her time with Simon, but all they have received is the sound of silence."

The songs will have to suffice.

Over the next few months, Simon enjoyed several changes of address, circulating though the more affordable hinterlands of the metropolis, while he also enrolled at King's College, close by Waterloo Bridge. And, inevitably, he infiltrated the folk scene, gigging not only around London's most legendary venues—Bunjies Coffee Bar, Les Cousins in Soho, the Troubadour in Earl's Court, and so forth—but also around the country.

One show took him into the West Country, to the town of Bridgewater, where, according to one legend, a dispute over payment subsequently gave rise to the punning slogan "Trouble over Bridgewater." One tour, a lonely scouring of England's northernmost climes, induced him to write "Homeward Bound."

These venues were crucial to the music. Clubs the length and breadth of the country formed an informal but nevertheless tightly linked network, each reliant upon the experiences of the other when it came to

Written towards the end of his time in England, Paul's "Homeward Bound" remains one of his most beloved composition.   *Author's collection*

booking unknown talent, each dependent upon the discernment of its own loyal audience, and the fairness of its organizers, to maintain its ability to attract the right names.

Even the late Sandy Denny, the doyen of British folk singers, once described her early career as time spent flitting round the country by herself, trying to find her way to one obscure pub after another, while the characters that members of one club recall with such affection were to be found in every other one.

History recalls Simon performing alongside the likes of Denny, Roy Harper, Bert Jansch, Ralph McTell, Al Stewart, and so many more, and so he did. All were stars of the future, for sure, but now they were united by nothing more tangible than the sheer obscurity in which they dwelt, utterly unknown beyond the confines of their own smoke-filled world of guitar and vocal.

Mention Ralph McTell to the average passerby, and you might as well have been singing the praises of Meg, the toothless old lady in plimsolls and a headscarf who used to make regular appearances at Bunjies to sing "Danny Boy," or the Armenian-born Hrath Garabedian, who could set grown men sobbing with his rendition of Woody Guthrie's "Deportees." Or even the character whom singer Steve Ashley recalls performing with his young son seated, and singing along, on his lap.

Yet without these people, and these venues, the face of folk on both sides of the Atlantic would now be unrecognizable.

In this world, Simon may not have been a "star," but he was a minor celebrity. He had a recording deal with CBS in New York and an album (Simon and Garfunkel's debut *Wednesday Morning, 3 A.M.*), which would soon be available on American import.

He also had a single out under his Jerry Landis alias on the Oriole label, a raw interpretation of "He Was My Brother" backed by "Carlos Dominguez," a yearning but darkly hard-hitting ballad about "an unhappy man" who is "searching for something that I cannot find"—truth, eternity, answers, love—but only finds lies, death, fate, and hate.

So yes, he was a celebrity. Even if his fee for live performances was no more likely to buy much beyond a drink and a sandwich than that collected by anybody else.

So much of the music Simon wrote at this time was influenced by the sights and sounds of the British Isles, from the lonely musician waiting for a late-night train who laments his way through "Homeward Bound" to the idiosyncratically joyful "'The Big Bright Green Pleasure Machine," which he composed in the all-night laundromat around the corner from an apartment he shared on Dellow Street in London's East End.

A recording exists of a live show he played at his old alma mater, Queen's College, later in 1964, a twelve-song tape that includes both "The Sound of Silence" and "He Was My Brother" alongside a clutch of new songs—"Leaves That Are Green," "A Church Is Burning, " and "Going to the Zoo"—and covers of American folkie Tom Paxton's "Can't Help But Wonder Where I'm Bound" and Englishman Ian Campbell's "The Sun Is Burning."

Opening the show, however, were four songs best guaranteed to put his audience at ease: Woody Guthrie's "Pretty Boy Floyd" and the spiritual "The Good Old Gospel Ship," as if to spotlight his homeland credentials, and "Scarborough Fair" and "The House Carpenter," two songs that he adopted on his travels.

Professor Child's Balladry

Since its initial publication in the late nineteenth century, the multi-volume collection of English and Scottish Ballads compiled by the Harvard professor Francis J. Child—"the Child Ballads," as they are most commonly known—have become *the* essential songbook for successive generations of folk artists.

From Oscar Brand to Bob Dylan, Sandy Denny to Joni Mitchell, Ewan MacColl to Jefferson Hamer, the 305 ballads that Child brought together have influenced, inspired, and informed every aspect of folk's continued history, a relationship that is without peer in the annals of either traditional or popular song.

The songs were never confined to the pages of Child's writings, after all. For centuries past (Child's earliest inclusion, "Judas," dates to the thirteenth century and is, in fact, the oldest extant English ballad), the ballads had been passed from singer to singer, from troubadour to minstrel, without any recourse to the printed page, and this tradition would only continue after Child completed his task.

Ever-evolving, the ballads moved through time as though time itself had stood still, with fresh versions (that themselves were often ancient) being rediscovered deep into the twentieth century as such researchers as Alan Lomax, Cecil Sharp, and Pete Seeger delved into their homelands' surviving folk traditions, seeking out the skeins that Child and others of his era had overlooked.

The difference was that Child wrote his discoveries out on paper. Lomax and company recorded theirs on tapes (that then became records), which in turn would be studied as avidly by modern scholars as Child's work was by the antiquarians of his time. And, as the popularity of folk music spread throughout the post-war West, the Child Ballads were at the forefront of the movement.

The appeal of the Child Ballads was, and remains, instantaneous. Alive with some of the most sensationalist plots in musical history—a succession of murders, betrayals, and supernatural occurrences—the Child Ballads are living history refracted through populist prisms that are as alive today as they were in centuries past.

Haunted castles, vengeful ghosts, violent death, perfidious spouses, merciless rulers, deathbed curses, evil stepmothers, lovelorn suicides, Satanic pacts, wicked witches, victorious heroes, vainglorious cheats—they all tumble from the ballads, a true kaleidoscope of calumny.

Even the legends of Robin Hood, so familiar today from television and film, exist primarily through the medium of the ballad, and Child devoted almost one-eighth of his collection to the deeds of Robin of Sherwood.

Recordings of these tabloid epics are legion. In 1949, Burl Ives recorded two Child ballads on his album *The Return of the Wayfaring Stranger*. Less than a decade later, Ewan MacColl and AL Lloyd recorded more than seventy of them across a series of albums that would in turn become many young folkies' introduction to the canon.

Across the LPs that preserve highlights of the first Newport Folk Festivals in 1959 and 1960, the likes of Oscar Brand and Will Holt are already paving the way for the generation that would burst forth amid the folk boom of the early 1960s, a well-thumbed copy of the Child Ballads at their side: Bob Dylan ("The House Carpenter"), Joan Baez ("Geordie"), Judy Collins "The Great Silkie of Sule Skerry"), Buffy Sainte Marie ("Sheath and Knife"), Tom Rush ("Barbara Allen"), and so many more.

The Child Ballads underpinned the successes enjoyed by Martin Carthy, Pentangle, Fairport Convention, Steeleye Span, and the Albion Band—British concerns whose arrangements of the ballads would themselves become regarded as definitive standards.

And today, the Ballads live on across recent albums by English legends Shirley Collins and Current 93 as well as American performers like Stonebreath and, most notably of all, Jefferson Hamer and Anaïs Mitchell, a Northeastern Seaboard duo whose award-winning 2013 album was titled, and comprised of, *Child Ballads*.

Neither is it the folk tradition alone that has kept the music alive. Led Zeppelin's "Gallows Pole" was a fresh interpretation of one Child Ballad; classical composer Gustav Holst's "King Estmere" was another.

Whenever Bob Dylan performs a rocking rendition of "A Hard Rain's A-Gonna Fall," he is revisiting the sixteenth-century Child Ballad "Lord Randall." When former Deep Purple and Rainbow guitarist Ritchie Blackmore leads Blackmore's Night into "Barbara Allen," they are performing a song first noted by Samuel Pepys in 1660.

Child Ballads have been adapted for novels (Lindsey Barraclough's *Long Lankin*, Pamela Dean's *Tam Lin*) and incorporated into television (*Penny Dreadful* and *The Living and the Dead* both made eerie use of them). They have been transformed to heavy metal, goth, and industrial; they have become woven into the fabric of modern storytelling.

Indeed, throughout the story of traditional music in the twentieth century, the Child Ballads have stood on the cusp of every major step forward, every great advance.

Professor Child would be proud of them.

Simon's Child Ballads

"Scarborough Fair" is a deceptive song, misleading in as much as melody and the most recurrent lyric ("a true love of mine") paint it with a romantic sheen that its true origins utterly belie.

Ewan MacColl outlined the story in the liners to his album *Classic Scots Ballads*:

A universal theme of both folk tale and ballad is that of impossible tasks. In this ballad, the form it takes is that of the courtship, with one flirtatious lover setting a series of tasks and his companion meeting the challenge by setting an equally difficult series.

In early forms of the ballad, an elfin knight posed the tasks, to be answered by a maiden who remains free by devising tasks of no less difficulty which must be answered first. Modern folk have made both characters mortal enough. Child had nineteen versions of this ballad, which he traced in his affinities through many languages of Europe and Asia. It is well known in England and America.

"Scarborough Fair" is, in fact, just one of several titles by which the song is known; the earliest appears to have been "The Elfin Knight," to which a somewhat longer title was abridged when it appeared in a volume of *Ancient Scottish Poems* in 1673: "The Wind Hath Blown my Plaid Away, or, a Discourse betwixt a Young [Wo]man and the Elphin Knight."

Passing time and the ministrations of other singers and performers saw the ballad undergo considerable alteration; the "wind has blown" chorus was lost, and with it a great deal of exposition.

Soon, all that remained were the tasks—"tell her to sew me a holland sark, and sew it all without needle-wark" and "tell her to wash it at yon spring-well, where ne'er wind blew nor yet rain fell"—with each command beautified by the pledge "and syne we'll be true lovers again."

The version that is most common today trims even more away. In 1810, the unimprovably named *Gammer Gurton's Garland* offered up a version that replaced the earlier refrain of "sober and grave grows merry in time" with the now-familiar "parsley, sage, rosemary and thyme"; and, by the time Lucy Broadwood and J. A. Fuller Maitland published their *English Country Songs* in 1893, even the Scots setting had been displaced.

"Is any of you going to Scarborough Fair?"

"Remember me to a lad as lives there."

Versions of the ballad, in different forms, were already commonplace on the British folk scene of the early 1960s, and on record, too. MacColl, A. L. Lloyd, the Copper Family, and Shirley Collins, the very cream of the era's British folk vanguard, had all recorded versions by the time Paul Simon reached London.

Parsley, Sage, Rosemary & Thyme took its title from the Child Ballad "Scarborough Fair."
Author's collection

He learned the song from Martin Carthy, who would soon add his own name to that canon of legends. At the time, however, he was better known as a member of the somewhat less than folky Three City Four. He was also, for a time, Simon's neighbor in a bedsit in Belsize Park, North London.

Carthy was, however, a familiar face around the club scene, frequently performing his own vivid arrangements of favorite ballads in a voice that was as distinctive as his guitar style. And, though he would not record the song for another year or more, "Scarborough Fair" was already one of the high points of his repertoire.

In the liner notes to his debut album, Carthy wrote of the song: "Folklorists and students of plant mythology are well aware that certain herbs were held to have magical significance—that they were used by sorcerers in their spells and conversely as counter-spells by those that wished to outwit them. The herbs mentioned in the refrain of 'Scarborough Fair' (parsley, sage, rosemary and thyme) are all known to have been closely associated with death and also as charms against the evil eye."

In other words, the maiden might be tormented by the Elfin Knight, but clearly she has defenses of her own. In fact, Carthy continued, "Sir Walter Scott in his notes to *Minstrelsy of the Scottish Border* recalled hearing a ballad of 'a fiend paying his addresses to a maid but being disconcerted by the holy herbs she wore in her bosom.'"

The version of the song with which Simon opened his Queens College concert—and that which appears on (and, via its refrain, titles) Simon and Garfunkel's third album—is clearly modeled upon, but does not credit, Carthy's own. It was an oversight that, for many years, left a furious Carthy barely even acknowledging Simon's existence. It would be three and a half decades before the dispute was finally salved, when Simon invited Carthy onstage to perform the song with him at London's Hammersmith Apollo in 2000.

"The House Carpenter," the second song in Simon's set, had likewise undergone a considerable metamorphosis over the centuries. The great seventeenth-century diarist Samuel Pepys was the first to set it down in writing (at least that we know of), under the grand title of "A Warning for Married Women, being an Example of Mrs Jane Reynolds (a West Country woman), burn [born] near Plymouth, who, having plighted her troth to a Seaman, was afterwards married to a Carpenter and at last carried away by a Spirit, the manner how shall presently be recited."

Small wonder that it was soon retitled "The Distressed Ship Carpenter" and, soon thereafter, "The Daemon Lover." It is under that latter title that it became best known in England; in the United States, however, it became "The House Carpenter" and had already been recorded by Joan Baez, the Doc Watson Family, and Bob Dylan, among others, by the time Simon began performing it.

The third Child Ballad in Simon's repertoire was "Barbara Allen," and during the sessions for Simon and Garfunkel's second album, the duo recorded it alongside versions of the Irish drinking song "Wild Rover" and "The Rambling Gambler," a song introduced to the popular imagination via the 1938 edition of John Lomax's *Cowboy Songs and Other Frontier Ballads*. (Simon and Garfunkel retitled their version "Rose of Aberdeen.")

All three songs were eventually shelved, partly because they had been hammered into the ground by every aspiring folkie for the past five years, and for decades before that, too, but also because Simon's own appetite for writing left little room for further covers.

It would be forty years before the performances were finally released, by which time the duo's straight-faced, straitlaced rendering of "Barbara Allen," one of the loveliest death songs ever sung, had been absolutely superseded by Garfunkel alone, a strings-and-things-driven reenvisioning that became one of the highlights of his solo debut album.

The song itself is one of the most enduring of all the Child Ballads. Samuel Pepys records hearing actress Mrs Knipp "sing her little Scotch song of Barbary Allen" in 1666; poet Oliver Goldsmith, a century later,

Two fine young folkies.   *Photofest*

insists that "the music of the finest singer is dissonance to what I felt when our own dairymaid sung me into tears with 'The Cruelty of Barbara Allen.'"

Cruel, indeed. Garfunkel abridges the ballad somewhat—there are versions that stretch to forty-one separate stanzas; he disposes of it in nine. But the gist of the song remains the same—William lies on his deathbed and begs his servant to send a message to his lady friend, Barbara Allen, apparently forgetting that just a few nights earlier, he had snubbed her at the tavern.

She, however, has not forgotten and will not forgive him either. But later, as she hears the death bell tolling, the full force of her hard-heartedness hits her, at which point she, too, drops dead.

The pair are buried side by side, and in death they are finally joined together.

> From William's grave, there grew a rose, from Barbara's, a green
>   briar.
> They grew and grew in the old church yard,
> Till they could grow no higher,
> And there they tied in a true lover's knot,
> The red rose and the briar.

And, in that single, sad performance, Garfunkel answered every criticism that could have—and did—attend the release of *Angel Clare* in 1973.

Yes, his old partner might have been singing the harder-hitting songs, might have been comfortably (and perhaps even calculatedly) taking his place within the then-prevalent pantheon of contemporary singer-songwriters whose musings on love and life and the futility of human existence were the soundtrack of so many student common rooms.

Yes, Paul Simon might have been the voice of the people.

But Art Garfunkel had the voice of an angel.

"When I listen to ['Barbara Allen'], I think, 'Oh man, were you blushingly crimson,'" Garfunkel confessed to *Mojo* in 2015. "Songs are different colors and that one is red, red. I'm doing so much breath control and the heart is way out on my sleeve."

He ranked it, for the magazine, among the top five vocal performances of his entire career.

Songs and Singers

Simon made several trips between Europe and the United States during 1964–1965, continuing to do so even in the aftermath of the release of the first Simon and Garfunkel album, *Wednesday Morning, 3 A.M.*, in late 1964.

Back home, the record was neither well received nor kindly reviewed, and Simon's presence was largely ignored. The London folk scene, on the other hand, regarded him as one of its own.

He befriended folk guitarist Davy Graham and would subsequently include Graham's instrumental "Anji" on Simon and Garfunkel's *The Sounds of Silence* album. He also spent time with Sandy Denny's boyfriend, the fellow American expat Jackson Frank, even producing Frank's recording of the future classic "Blues Run the Game." That's Al Stewart on guitar, by the way.

He saw his songs recorded by Harvey Andrews ("A Most Peculiar Man"), Val Doonican (Paul Kane's "Carlos Dominguez"), the Bachelors, and the Hollies. And while he did not necessarily enjoy them all, he didn't dislike them as much as he was alleged to. He told the *New Musical Express*: "Let's take the Bachelors. I've never said that I think their version of my song is 'disgusting,' as one paper reported. I don't sit in judgment over them. They've pleased an awful lot of people with that disc." Their interpretation, he conceded, was "a good clean version," and it racked up a lot of airplay—unlike Simon and Garfunkel's, which he sighed, "did not sell here."

He found it "strange," however, that the Bachelors should even have considered recording the song. They were a smartly suited vocal group whose music could scarcely have been further from the rough and tumble of pop and rock, and Simon was mystified why "the Bachelors should choose to record a very hip song when their style is so conflicting" and said, "I feel that some artists never get as much out of a song as I have put into it."

He also enjoyed Them's version of "Richard Cory," and when a *Hit Parader* journalist remarked on the beauty of the performance, Simon swiftly agreed, albeit with one caveat: "You and me are the only ones who think it was beautiful. I thought it was great. In fact, the melody changes they made in the song, I adopted. I do it their way in concerts."

The Hollies' upcoming version of "I Am a Rock," on the other hand, did bother him: British radio at the time could be almost painfully prudish—so much so that many bands deliberately set out to find ways of foiling the authorities demand for cleanliness. The Beatles famously constructed a backing vocal (in the song "Girl") that simply repeated the word "tit" over and over, just to see if they could get away with it. (They did.) The Rolling Stones were reportedly delighted when they dropped a reference to menstruation into "Satisfaction" ("I'm on a losing streak come back next week").

Simon did not play such games. But still the Hollies felt that the word "womb" was sailing too close to the censorial wind. They removed it and Simon was not happy. "Changes in my lyrics upset me some. Anyone would think there was something dirty about the word—I never wrote a dirty lyric in my life."

Simon also cowrote a clutch of further of numbers—"I Wish You Could Be Here," "Someday One Day," and "Red Rubber Ball"—with Bruce Woodley of the Seekers, an Australian folk band that was topping the UK charts at the time.

There was an onstage reunion with Garfunkel when the latter visited London, and the pair were asked to fill in at the Flamingo Club in Soho one evening when the scheduled headliners, the Ian Campbell Group, failed to arrive—Garfunkel came onstage for at least one song, "Sparrow." But he would also recall, from the stage in 2003, some of their other adventures: "We were twenty-two years old, we were out of college, and we'd go to England and sing in these clubs all around the country; we'd sing on the sidewalks for money, we were poor, and we'd bring our friend Kathy, she'd collect the money."

The London Sessions

January 1965: *Five to Ten* (solo BBC Radio performance, introduced and linked by Judith Piepe)

"I Am a Rock"	"A Most Peculiar Man"
"Leaves That Are Green"	"He Was My Brother"
"A Church Is Burning"	"Kathy's Song"
"April Come She Will"	"The Side of a Hill"
"The Sound of Silence"	"A Simple Desultory Philippic"

"Flowers Never Bend with the Rainfall"   "Bad News Feeling"
"Patterns"

May 1965: "I Am a Rock"/"Leaves That Are Green" (CBS 201797)

June 1965: LP *The Paul Simon Songbook* (CBS 62579)

"I Am a Rock"	"He Was My Brother"
"Leaves That Are Green"	"Kathy's Song"
"A Church Is Burning"	"The Side of a Hill"
"April Come She Will"	"A Simple Desultory Philippic"
"The Sound of Silence"	"Flowers Never Bend with the Rainfall"
"A Most Peculiar Man"	"Patterns"

Recorded: May 1965 at Levy's Studio, Bond Street, London

Produced by: Stanley West and Reginald Warburton

July 1965: *Ready Steady Go* (UK television performance)

"I Am a Rock"

5

Paul Simon's *Songbook*

I n London in May 1965, Simon recorded his first solo album—one man
with a single microphone, a guitar, and a £60 recording budget.

Slip-sliding out of print since the end of the 1960s, *The Paul Simon
Songbook* was destined, equally slipperily, to fade in and out of favor too.
Its maker himself has seldom been overly kind about it—in fact, it was
apparently at his request that it was deleted in 1969. It would not reap-
pear until an early-eighties box set of his LPs-so-far. The vast majority
of listeners, too, usually write it off as little more than a set of demos for
songs that Simon and Garfunkel would soon be rerecording to far greater
effect (and acclaim).

Of its twelve songs, just two—"The Side of a Hill" and "A Church Is
Burning"—would not be officially released by the duo. (An in-concert
version of "Church" would ultimately surface on the *Live in New York City
1967* album, many years on.)

"The Sound of Silence" and "He Was My Brother" were both reprised
from the *Wednesday Morning, 3 A.M.* album (which had yet to be released
in the United Kingdom at that point); the remainder—"I Am a Rock,"
"Leaves That Are Green," "April Come She Will," "A Most Peculiar Man,"
and "Kathy's Song"—were destined for the *Sounds of Silence* album; "A
Simple Desultory Philippic (or How I Was Robert McNamara'd into
Submission)," "Flowers Never Bend with the Rainfall," and "Patterns"
would be revisited on *Parsley, Sage, Rosemary and Thyme*.

Nevertheless, there are those who may argue *The Paul Simon Songbook*
represents one of his strongest-ever albums. The sheer strength of the
songwriting, and its (comparatively) unaccompanied rendering, ensures
that the vision that is so implicit in the songs remains unscathed by the
individual songs' own subsequent popularity and arrangements.

A stark "I Am a Rock" packs a desolate urgency that Simon and
Garfunkel's later revision could never recreate, while "The Sound of

Silence" conveys an empty-street loneliness that is worth a new verse or two on its own.

Indeed, it is remarkable just what a difference it makes, stripping away Garfunkel's so pristine vocals and hearing only Simon's own, still occasionally tentative, tones.

Written about a suicide that Simon read of in the paper one day, "A Most Peculiar Man" radiates a damp dinginess that is absolutely redolent of London's once notorious "bedsit-land"—street upon street of former family homes that were sliced into spartan one room apartments—bedroom, kitchen, wash basin and all—decorated decades back in styles that would have been cheap even then, and every one radiating the scent of past residents, at least some of whom would certainly have taken the same way out as the subject of Simon's song.

Unerringly English, too, was "Kathy's Song (Written by Paul in New York for Kathy in London)"—a reminder, also, of why love songs always sound better when sung by one of the lovers. In fact, if any criticism can be leveled at the *Paul Simon Songbook* it is, simply, that it was recorded so quickly. But Simon was busy, and about to get busier.

Recorded in London, this was Paul's first-ever solo album.
Author's collection

The Singer-Songwriter

The UK newspaper the *Guardian* put it best. Reviewing Paul Simon's 2016 show at the Royal Albert Hall in London, writer David Bennum declared: "Being seventy-five must feel like second nature to Paul Simon, who has been looking back reflectively for fifty years now." Unlike so many of his peers, Simon had never felt the urge to do his growing up in public; the characteristics he bore when he first emerged on the songwriting scene—"pensive, heartsore, and complex"—were those that he had maintained ever since. "The chief difference now is that he seems a tad more cheerful," Bennum said. A line drawn beween the oldest songs on display that night ("Homeward Bound" and "America") and the most recent would be a very short one indeed.

Simon writes, and has almost always written, about what Bennum called the "unravelling of lives over time, and his signature style is the combination of musical jollity with lyrical melancholy."

Yet it was not a formula, if that is what it can be called, that he arrived at immediately. As a teen he could not; as a young adult, he would not. But firsthand experience—first of the American protest boom and then of the British folk revival—pointed out a new direction, and thenceforth, he needed only refine it.

The sudden rush of songs that Simon wrote in and around his time in the United Kingdom came as a complete surprise to many of the people who knew him back in New York. There had been little evidence of them in Simon and Garfunkel's live performances, still bound as they were to more regular folk material; it was in London, where audiences expected more from a performer than a flood of familiar material, that he truly let fly.

Nowhere is this better illustrated than when the cool and so-assured *The Paul Simon Songbook* is lined up against the hodgepodge of material that packed out *Wednesday Morning, 3 A.M.*, Simon and Garfunkel's debut album.

Producer Tom Wilson first encountered Simon in his job hustling songs for the music publishers. Simon visited him at his Columbia records office one day, shortly before the singer left for London. Wilson showed interest in "He Was My Brother," at which point Simon mentioned that he had some other songs of his own that weren't a part of the publisher's portfolio.

Wilson asked to hear them and arranged for Simon and Garfunkel to audition for him. They performed four songs that were already a part of their live show—"Wednesday Morning, 3 A.M.," "Sparrow," "Bleecker Street," and "The Sound of Silence"—and Wilson had heard enough. Already regarded as "Mr. Folk" in some circles, on account of his work with Dylan, Wilson signed the duo to Columbia and set them to recording an album.

That night, home after performing for Wilson, Simon called Garfunkel on the phone. "How come you're not the greatest singer, Artie?" Meaning, translated out of typical Queens slang, "How come you are?"

Simon and Garfunkel's debut album—a little ragged, but it showed a lot of promise.

Author's collection

The ornate picture sleeve accompanying the
European "April Come She Will" 45.
Author's collection

"He was so pleased that we sang so well and that [my] voice was so
useful for his desires," Garfunkel told *Mojo* almost fifty years later. And
then the barb. "It's one of the only times I can recall Paul giving tribute to
me. This is a big part of Simon and Garfunkel. I was a brilliant audience
for Paul, and the fact that I could sing so well was almost invisible. The
world gets it. I got it. But the vibe between us treated that as nothing."

The recording sessions themselves were quick—three weeks in March,
1964; it took longer, apparently, to decide what name the album should be
released under. Simon and Garfunkel themselves were unsure whether or
not they should use their real names or continue their earlier vinyl aliases
of Tom Graph and Jerry Landis, or even Artie Garr and Paul Kane.

There was still a great deal of anti-Semitic prejudice abroad in the
early 1960s, and there were fears that such distinctly Jewish names as
theirs would count against them or see them written off as a musical
comedy act.

At the same time, however, it was already common knowledge that
Bob Dylan had been born Robert Zimmerman, and there had been no
appreciable backlash against him. Besides, both Wilson and his Columbia
records associates agreed—it was the music that mattered.

Yet the record with which they emerged is barely an out-of-focus
snapshot of what was to come, the five Paul Simon/Paul Kane originals
notwithstanding. Indeed, the album can be valued more for introducing

the duo to engineer Roy Halee Jr., who remains alongside Simon still, than for its musical content, a ragbag of cover versions that reached a nadir of sorts with an astonishingly unenthusiastic cover of Dylan's "The Times They Are A-Changing."

Long Islander Roy Halee Jr. was born in 1940, the son of voice actor Roy Halee—the cartoon duo *Heckle and Jeckle* was among his manifold guises. Originally working as a cameraman and, later, a sound engineer at CBS TV, the young Roy then moved to the audio division first as an editor and then as a studio engineer.

His first session was for Bob Dylan's "Like a Rolling Stone." He told *Mix* magazine: "I didn't know what the hell I was doing. But I ended up doing that album [*Highway 61 Revisited*], and that evolved into my doing Simon & Garfunkel and the Lovin' Spoonful and a couple of dates with the Yardbirds. And then interspersed with that was all the pop stuff that Columbia had at the time. They sent me down to the Bon Soir nightclub and I did Barbra Streisand's first session."

He recalled his initial exposure to Simon and Garfunkel for *Analog Planet*.

"Tom Wilson's bringing in these guys to do an audition. And in walks these two kids, Simon and Garfunkel. They're going to come in and do an audition. Two guys and a guitar—this is going to be great, I can't miss. This was at the 799 7th Avenue studio, which later turned into A&R Studios. A great studio, and they sold it! And they later moved to 49 E. 52nd Street. Terrible studios. So anyway, I do this audition for Simon and Garfunkel. [And] it was the whole album, man! The whole *Wednesday Morning* album was the audition." Halee would engineer the entire LP.

His Simon and Garfunkel work, as engineer and producer, remains his best known, not only in terms of accolades (he would receive Grammy Awards for his work on "Mrs. Robinson" and the albums *Bookends* and *Bridge Over Troubled Water*) but also longevity—his most recent project with Paul Simon was 2018's *In the Blue Light*. He is even mentioned in song, in 1965's "A Simple Desultory Philippic (or How I Was Robert McNamara'd into Submission)."

Halee's technique and innovation was swift to win recognition. In 1971, the magazine *Recording Engineer/Producer* asked him about the special effects that he brought to *Bridge Over Troubled Water*.

"We wanted to get an explosion effect, so I put the guy out in the hall next to an elevator at 49 East 52nd street in New York. The hallway itself was extremely live, so I put mikes in the shaft and in the hall, and limited the hell out of them. And we got an explosion sound. It's in 'The Boxer.' In 'Bridge Over Troubled Water,' there is a snapping sound, like a whip in the distance. It was created by physically placing the drummer inside an echo chamber."

The relationship continued following the duo's breakup; Halee would produce both Simon and Garfunkel's debut albums, while the 1970s saw him producing the likes of Journey; Blood, Sweat & Tears; Laura Nyro; and Rufus and Chaka Khan. He would then return to Simon and Garfunkel for the *Concert in Central Park* album and Garfunkel's solo *Scissors Cut* (both 1982) and *The Art Garfunkel Album* (1984).

By the time of the latter, however, he had also reunited with the solo Simon, and he has remained an integral part of the singer's career since then. As Simon has said on more than one occasion: "Roy's brilliant. He's a brilliant sound guy. He was great with echoes, he always had a great sense of echo. I really think that Roy was the best."

It is no surprise that, almost as soon as it was recorded, Simon should head off for his British adventure, nor that the album barely made a splash when it was released in October.

It is no surprise, either, that his London sojourn should prove such a productive period for Simon as a songwriter. Despite a measure of popularity in New York, Simon and Garfunkel were very much outsiders on a local scene that might once have been closely knit but was now as cutthroat as any other popular musical movement.

A hierarchy had formed, a pecking order of performers that naturally favored its elder statesmen far ahead of any Johnny-come-latelies, who were, in any case, usually regarded as little more than hapless bandwagon-jumpers, seizing upon the folk movement as a commercial vehicle as opposed to a way of life.

Simon, with the handful of originals in his pocket, had demonstrated that he could write good songs, and the smattering of people who heard them appreciated that.

It was just a smattering, though.

In London, on the other hand, the mood was somewhat more inclusive. The wave of singer-songwriters in which he found himself were not yet jockeying for position, were largely operating beneath the radar of any but the most devout folk fans, and, more importantly, were bound by a camaraderie that was unknown in Greenwich Village. They slept on one another's floors, they attended one another's shows, they helped each other whenever they could. In New York, if Simon was struggling with a song, he had only Garfunkel to turn to. In London, he had a club full of fellow writers.

"In New York," he said, "I was a kid from Queens. That was bad. In England, I was an American. That was good."

So many of the songs included on *The Paul Simon Songbook* are now regarded among Simon's finest-ever compositions, even beyond the reprises of "He Was My Brother" (updated now to directly confront Andrew Goodman's death) and "The Sound of Silence." The alacrity with which Simon rerecorded so many of them with Garfunkel speaks to that, while the flood of inspiration that he focused on the record was still a long way from drying up.

Late in 1965, Simon set out on a solo tour of northern England. Many of the dates were ones that he organized himself, browsing through the *Folk Directory* magazine, calling the promoters to introduce himself, and forever keeping an eye on a map of the country to ensure the schedule retained some kind of orderly geographical shape.

He reminisced on the outing from a Manchester, England, stage in 2018, during his farewell tour, admitting, "This is probably my last chance to do it." The clubs that he played on that outing, he reminded his audience, were not purely dedicated to music. They often served other functions too, and he delivered a note-perfect impersonation of the kind of MC that would welcome him onto the stage, by telling the audience: "Shut *up*! You've 'ad your fun, you've played bingo, now shut up and give the ah-tist a go."

The tour would also prove to be his final solo excursion for six years, but it also inspired another of Simon's most memorable songs.

"Homeward Bound," legend insists, was written at Widnes railroad station as Simon waited on a train to Manchester. There is even a plaque at the station to commemorate the fact, and while some researchers are convinced that the tale isn't true, the precise location really doesn't matter.

What is important is the pinpoint accuracy with which Simon conjured a mood—an accuracy from something so mundane as "sitting on a railway station." You can feel the cold, taste the fog, and see the night refracted in the glare of the sodium lamps. But, most of all, you can sense his loneliness.

For the most part, he loved England. "I was consciously aware that I was ecstatically happy," he told *Rolling Stone*. "I'm sure that those will be the purest, happiest days of my life."

But this tour was grueling. "I missed my girl and my friends," he told *Hit Parader* magazine. "It was kind of depressing. I was living out of suitcases, getting on trains every day and going to the next place. It wasn't a pleasant ten days."

And in another interview, with the *New Musical Express*, he simply quipped, "If you know Widnes, then you'll understand how I was desperately trying to get back to London as quickly as possible."

That said, any nostalgia he may now feel for London itself is tempered by remembrances of its less romantic practicalities. A 2016 interview with *Drowned in Sound,* taking place during Simon's latest visit to the city, asked him whether he missed the metropolis, or the lifestyle, of his youth. He didn't.

"No, not really," he said. "You can't be young when you're not young, you know? I don't particularly want to ride the tube and miss the last bus and hitch-hike out in the rain. I'm fine to be spoiled a little bit now."

And besides, it quickly became obvious, back in 1965, that his career was no longer so firmly rooted there. Back in New York City, Columbia Records had released "The Sound of Silence" as a single after learning that the album track was picking up airplay in Cocoa Beach, Florida.

First, however, Tom Wilson decided to give it a makeover. Less than a year after its release, after all, the performance already sounded old-fashioned; Dylan had embraced electric music that summer, and controversial though the move was, it had not dented his popularity in the slightest.

The *Sounds of Silence* album was Simon and Garfunkel's breakthrough.   *Author's collection*

Now everybody was rushing to follow suit, and although Simon and Garfunkel had been slow in climbing aboard the folk movement, there was no reason whatsoever why they should be so tardy with "electric folk."

Overdubbing twelve-string guitar, drums, and bass onto the original track, Wilson created a record that was utterly in tune with the times and was swiftly rewarded accordingly. Entering the *Billboard* chart at the end of November, the single of "The Sound of Silence" began slowly to rise. Simon was vacationing in Denmark when he saw it was number 111. He was back in London and it cracked the Top 100.

He told the *New Musical Express*: "I don't know how to react to it. The fact of the matter is, I don't even feel it at all. You see, here I am in London and this record is supposed to be selling well. I'm here in England and I'm going to folk clubs and I'm working like I was working always. It hasn't changed me at all. Oh, I'm happy, man. I've got to say I'm very pleased. It's a very nice gift."

His opinion slowly changed. He was never "violently against" the overdubbing, he admitted, but he certainly had feelings about it: "I didn't think it was great. I didn't say, 'Oh, they screwed up my song with electric guitars and drums.' I was pleased with that. It grew on me."

It grew on a lot of people. Shortly after that interview, "The Sound of Silence" was number one in America. And, for the next five years, Simon and Garfunkel were seldom too far away from that same peak.

Simon's writing played a major part in accomplishing that, and of course, it has maintained that preeminence today, both as a salable entity and as an influence upon others. A subject, incidentally, upon which Simon is rarely drawn, as this 2016 exchange with *Billboard* magazine reveals.

> Q: Do you ever hear a record and think: "Ah, he has been listening to some Paul Simon"?
>
> A: Yeah, sure.
>
> Q: Can you give me an example?
>
> A: Nah, I don't want to.

Singing for the Sixties

The sixties are often regarded as a halcyon era for songwriting in its purest state. Some might say that better, and more memorable, music has been composed in the five decades since then—few rundowns of the greatest songs ever written, after all, are complete without "Stairway to Heaven," "Bohemian Rhapsody," and I'm Not in Love," suggesting that the early to mid-1970s were rock 'n' roll's peak, and from Springsteen to U2 to Oasis to Harry Styles, a host of other songwriters have arisen to challenge the claims of that now distant age.

Yet there is also the argument that, in the sixties, songwriters still wrote *songs*, and that, thereafter, they made records, and there is a difference. A record, after all, can be whatever one wants it to be—an overblown operatic parody, a lumbering hard rock symphony, an exquisitely produced *tour de force.*

Whereas a song is simply that—a voice, an instrument, a tune, and some words, plus that indefinable *something* that, as Simon remarked in 2016, is the listener's own responsibility.

"Do songs ever end?" he asked *Billboard.* "I think the ending is in the listener's ear. If they like the song, they like it for reasons that have nothing to do with the songwriter's intention."

Nevertheless, a great song is a "record" that can be stripped of *all* the technique and virtuosity, production tricks, and marketing gimmicks that accompany it, relayed in its own most barebones form, and *still* capture the imagination. And that is a lot harder to do.

Simon's own songwriting method, at least in the years before computer technology rendered such practices old-fashioned and clumsy, was simply to sit down with either his guitar (or, less commonly, a piano), find a key, and start to play, singing whatever words came into his head.

Circulating tapes of his demos, on the occasions that they have leaked out, testify to this—even his first recorded attempt at "Bridge Over Troubled Water" is a morass of lost lines and as-yet-unfilled blanks, with only its chorus firmly in place.

He still improvises today; "The Werewolf," from *Stranger to Stranger,* took its title, and theme, from the sound made by the instrument he was playing with at the time, an Indian instrument called the gopichand. It sounded to him as if it was saying *"The-weeeeerewolf."* And he thought to himself, "OK, this song's 'The Werewolf.'"

It is during this "stream of consciousness" phase, as he once described it, that the first glimpses of the finished song will emerge—lines or phrases that possess "a naturalness and a meaning."

Along with the jokes. It is a seldom-remarked upon aspect of Simon's songwriting that he litters his texts with humor—not just the obvious "novelty"-style numbers like "50 Ways to Leave Your Lover" and "You Can Call Me Al," but the more intense numbers as well.

"My father was a fisherman, my mother was a fisherman's friend," he puns in "Duncan," while "The Werewolf" must surely be the only song to rhyme "decent wife" with "sushi knife" as in, "she killed him [with a]."

He teases, too. One of the key lyrics in "Me and Julio Down by the Schoolyard" is the one which insists that "what mama saw" was against the law. But ask Simon what exactly mama did see and he happily confesses that he has no idea. It's the same reason he mentioned Gatorade in "Papa Hobo." The word, he insisted, did not belong in a song. So of course it had to be in one.

"A lot of people believe 'first idea, best idea,' but I don't," he told the BBC in 2016. "I rewrite songs, not because I'm trying to make them more commercial, but because there's something about them that's unsatisfying to me." He worked, he said, according to the theory that the human ear will naturally pick up on the things it *doesn't* like in a song before it considers the things it actually lkes. His job, therefore, was to isolate those "irritants" and remove them. "Sometimes it takes me a year or two. I'll be in denial about it. But once it goes, then I'll try and fix it."

———

Amid the plethora of collections, compilations and compendiums that litter the Simon and Garfunkel discography, the greatest frustration has always been the absolute disdain for the serious collector that shines through the exhumations.

True, the CD release of Simon's *Songbook* album, after decades in the dumper, was cause for celebration, but the most recent bonus-tracked remasters of the duo's five albums could muster no more than another LP's worth of unreleased material between them, and most of them were mere alternate takes.

The internet steps in where the record racks disappoint, rightly or wrongly liberating a vast corpus of radio and TV performances, outtakes and all-round oddities that, gathered together, paint a portrait of Simon and Garfunkel that stands in sometimes stark and often hilarious opposition to the increasingly po-faced and humorless picture that stares out of their official output.

A live "Sparrow," for example, with Simon talking an audience through the song's "true" meaning before leaping into a slice of demented doggerel; a jolly ramble on the importance of producer Tom Wilson; and a rocking beat version of "Wednesday Morning, 3 A.M." designed, Simon explains, to break the duo into the mid-60s pop market.

There are those moments when you could almost believe you're listening to a comedy act, so deftly does Simon (for the most part) taunt the audience with his wryest observations.

We slip from a raucous live performance to the protracted studio session that produced "For Emily, Whenever I May Find Her," with Garfunkel attempting to perfect an angelic harmony. (And it *is* protracted—by the time you reach take fourteen, you're almost desperate for Emily to reveal where she's hiding.)

We hear Art detailing the convoluted photo shoot for the duo's debut album (a preamble to "Poem on the Underworld Wall") and a painfully polite TV rendering of "Overs" before moving on to a version of "Bye Bye Love" that makes the *Bridge Over Troubled Water* take sound positively neutered.

There's a surprisingly funky "Why Don't You Write Me" backing track, a scratchy "The Only Living Boy in New York," and a joyous reprise of "Hey Little Schoolgirl," recorded at the very tail end of the 1960s. And that's not even the best of it.

Happy hunting!

For Simon, Not Garfunkel

Of all the reasons why Simon welcomed the demise of Simon and Garfunkel in 1970, the freedom it offered his songwriting was among the most tangible.

"I had written so many more songs by then," he told SiriusXM interviewer Bill Flanagan in 2016. "A lot of songs that we weren't doing because they weren't Simon and Garfunkel songs."

It infuriated him. "There was pleasure in the blend. That was always fun, to get the blend right. But to have to stay with the songs that were from my earlier writing, and the first half of my earlier writing was more generic than individual, there was a limit to how much I wanted to do."

Discussing his songwriting in the introduction to *The Songs of Paul Simon*, the mammoth songbook that he published in 1972, he was adamant—"I think the best songs are those where words and music really come simultaneously"—and he singled out "The Boxer" and, indeed, "Bridge Over Troubled Water" as examples of that serendipity.

It is not a gift that can consistently be relied upon, however; "Mother and Child Reunion," "Duncan," and "Peace Like a River," three of the finer songs with which he inaugurated his post-Garfunkel solo career, were all completed melodies some time before he had conceived lyrics to match.

Nor does lightning strike every time, even among those songwriters who are considered the kings of their castle. Bob Dylan, the first songwriter ever to be granted the Novel Prize for Literature, has written more than his fair share of duffs over the decades was writing them even during his so-called prime.

Not every Lennon-McCartney composition was a stone-cold masterpiece. And not all Paul Simon songs are equal, either. For every sublime "The Only Living Boy in New York," there is the garish Dylan parody "A Simple Desultory Philippic"; for every "Duncan," there is a "[name your least favorite here]."

But how joyous it was to pick up 2018's *In the Blue Light* and hear "Some Folks Lives Roll Easy," a *Still Crazy*-era composition that always felt as though it demanded more stately surroundings, now hanging so spectral over Sullivan Fortner's lonely piano as a jazz trio wanders into earshot. Jazz itself is not a genre with which Simon is naturally associated. But he pulls it off.

Simon himself keeps quiet about which of his compositions he especially dislikes; again in *The Songs of Paul Simon,* he confesses that of the handful of songs that were omitted from an otherwise all-encompassing collection, two were "really bad ones [he] wouldn't want to look at." (Three more were songs for which the necessary publishing clearance could not be obtained, and one was a new number that he "[hadn't] had a chance to record.")

Yet the songs for which, over the decades, Simon is most frequently lionized are also the songs by which our entire culture can be appraised—for, of course, few songs can ever be said to have been written in a vacuum.

Under the Covers—Forty Great Paul Simon Cover Versions 1964–2017

"A Hazy Shade of Winter" (1968) by the Bangles (1987)

"A Most Peculiar Man" (1966) by Harvey Andrews (1965)

"A Simple Desultory Philippic" (1966) by Swamp Zombies (1988)

"America" (1968) by David Bowie (2001)

"American Tune" (1973) by Shawn Colvin (2015)

"Baby Driver" (1969) by Ringmasters (2012)

"Bookends" (1968) by Stacey Kent (2003)

"Bridge Over Troubled Water" (1970) by Elvis Presley (1970)

"Cecilia" (1970) by Bruce Ruffin (1970)

"Cloudy" (1966) by the Cyrkle (1966)

"Diamonds on the Soles of Her Shoes" (1986) by Mika (2016)

"El Condor Pasa" (If I Could) (1970) by Yma Sumac (1972)

"50 Ways to Leave Your Lover" (1975) by the Drifters (circa 1978)

"Flowers Never Bend with the Rainfall" (1966) by Toast (1970)

"Graceland" (1986) by the Tallest Man on Earth (2010)

"Homeward Bound" (1966) by Willie Nelson (1983)

"I Am a Rock" (1965) by the Hollies (1966)

"I Do It for Your Love" (1975) by David Sanborn (1976)

"Kathy's Song" (1966) by Eva Cassidy (2000)

"Keep the Customer Satisfied" (1970) by Marsha Hunt (1970)

"Kodachrome" (1973) by Percy Faith (1973)

"Loves Me Like a Rock" (1973) by Ramsey Lewis (1974)

"Me and Julio Down by the Schoolyard" (1972) by Me First and the Gimme Gimmes (1997)

"Mother and Child Reunion" (1972) by the Uniques (1972)

"Mrs. Robinson" (1968) by the Lemonheads (1992)

"Old Friends" (1968) by Caravelli (1971)

"Punky's Dilemma" (1968) by Barbra Streisand (1969)

"Richard Cory" (1966) by Paul McCartney and Wings (1976)

"Something So Right" (1973) by Annie Lennox (1995)

"St. Judy's Comet" (1973) by Kenny Loggins (1994)

"Still Crazy After All These Years" (1975) by Karen Carpenter (recorded 1980; released 1996)

"Take Me to the Mardi Gras" (1973) by Johnnie Taylor (2003)
"The 59th Street Bridge Song" (Feelin' Groovy) (1966) by Harpers Bizarre (1967)
"The Boxer" (1970) by Emmylou Harris (1980)
"The Boy in the Bubble" (1986) by Patti Smith (2007)
"The Dangling Conversation" (1966) by Joan Baez (1967)
"The Only Living Boy in New York" (1970) by Marc Cohn (2010)
"The Sound of Silence" (1964) by the Dickies (1978)
"Was a Sunny Day" (1973) by Rosemary Clooney (1976)
"You Can Call Me Al" (1986) (retitled "Bodyguard") by Ghost (2013)

Time and place are as essential as timing and the placement of words—the very enunciation of words, too. In 1997, upon stumbling across a particular curse within the soundtrack to *The Capeman*, the *Village Voice*'s Rob Sheffield remarked: "Paul Simon tries really hard with the word 'motherfucker.' But he has trouble with it."

Yet Simon returned to the term during "Cool Papa Bell," a song from 2016's *Stranger to Stranger*, and this time he nailed it, although he admitted that he "must have sang 'motherfucker' 500 times to get it right."

On other occasions, the words themselves can be dictated by outside circumstance, as Simon and Carole Bayer Sager revealed on that dismal date in 1966 when they argued over who was first to use "groovy" in a lyric. Just as "Mrs. Robinson" might never have been written had director Mike Nicholls not suggested Simon write a song about the lead female character in his movie *The Graduate* (see chapter 13).

It was that awareness, whether it was conscious or not, that enshrined Paul Simon's writing in the popular consciousness of the sixties and—a rarity among his contemporaries—the seventies and beyond as well, when the best of his solo work proved as striking a contrast to the domesticated slickness of his "singer-songwriter" peers as his earlier writing had when lined up alongside the sweet and easy pop of the era's other harmony bands. He understood that, in writing songs that touched upon his own fascinations and interests, he needed to touch upon those of his audience, too.

But not, as in the days of protest, by littering the landscape with current affairs and popular fads. That rarely works, as Simon discovered very early on.

"We've Got a Groovy Thing Goin'," after all, is a fun slice of rock 'n' roll, but its very title gives it an antique sheen, one that became achingly apparent the moment the word "groovy" was co-opted by the mainstream to prove that it was hip to the kids' latest lingo (a process that is still alive today, of course, every time the evening news reader drops some hot new buzzword into a report). "The 59th Street Bridge Song" "feeling groovy!" is an even crasser example.

But "Hearts and Bones"—recounting a journey, Simon explained, taken by "one and one-half wandering Jews"—is universal, no matter how personal its actual subject matter might have been; and so is "Mother and Child Reunion," a song about death whose intrinsic sadness is only amplified when paired with its almost insatiably gleeful melody and delivery

A French advertisement for the next Simon and Garfunkel 45.   *Author's collection*

and whose title, absurdly, was inspired by a meal Simon ate at a Chinese restaurant: boiled eggs and fried chicken.

"Diamonds on the Soles of Her Shoes" might be best regarded for its startling arrangement, and the involvement of Ladysmith Black Mambazo (the first time many Americans had ever heard their sound), but it is as real, and sincere, a lyric as any of Simon's other reflections upon past love.

He discussed these triumphs with the *New York Times*'s Jim Dwyer in 2016. He was surprised, he said, when he wrote "The Sound of Silence" because it felt like such a vast leap forward from the songs he was writing beforehand. Of how he made that leap, he said, "I have no idea." But he would continue to do it. "When I wrote 'Bridge Over Troubled Water'—whoa, that song is better than what I've been doing. Different chords and something special about it." "Still Crazy After All These Years" was another; "Graceland," too.

"All of a sudden you're there, and you're surprised." A lyric spills out and, just for a moment, he said, "I have to stop, because I'm crying. I didn't know I was going to say that, didn't know that I felt that, didn't know that was really true. I have to stop and catch my breath." There was just one caveat.

"It doesn't happen too often."

He is talking of the songs as he first writes them, often before anybody else has even heard them, and long before he slathers on the production and the arrangement that are the things that make a song into a record. If a song can thrive without either, then it is immortal—and even more so if it can also withstand their addition.

True Simon purists probably despise it, but prog rockers Yes's *ten-minute* version of "America" retains all the fragility and yearning of Simon and Garfunkel's original, even with the synth and guitars-led bombast going hell for leather around it—just as the contrarily, but so beautifully, stark and spartan rendering of the same song with which David Bowie dignified the Concert for New York in 2001 left the entire auditorium blinking back tears.

Of course, Simon has never been above the notion of beautifying his art with production tricks, or musical mannerisms, some of which *can* now resemble museum pieces. Yet the decision to slip a recording of an evening news bulletin over a gentle rendering of the Christmas carol "Silent Night" *still* works as a piece of performance art, more than half a century after the combination closed the *Parsley, Sage, Rosemary and Thyme* album with such stark commentary upon the horrors unfolding in the world.

And while there are certainly moments on *Graceland*, so widely regarded among the greatest triumphs of Simon's career, where the excision of mood and momentum would leave a song stranded and gasping for air, for the most part Simon has used such devices both sparingly and thoughtfully. It's a trick (or, perhaps, a talent) that many of his peers could learn from.

6

The Teacher

Bridge Over Troubled Water was still racing up the chart; Simon and Garfunkel had yet to part. They were no longer simply the most successful singing duo of the decade—they were among the biggest acts the music industry had ever seen.

So how did Simon celebrate the achievement?

By going back to school to teach the art of song craft—not, of course, to his fellow musicians but to the generation of aspiring songsmiths who dreamed they might succeed them.

In the fall of 1969, Simon contacted the respective music departments of Columbia University, the New School for Social Research, and New York University to inquire whether they would be interested in sponsoring a workshop class in songwriting.

Columbia rejected the notion. New York University, however, leaped at the prospect—the head of the arts department there, David Oppenheim, was a former public television executive with whom Simon had worked on an ultimately abortive attempt to stage, and broadcast, a Simon and Garfunkel concert in the Soviet Union.

It was agreed that the class would be held every Tuesday evening, beginning at the start of the spring semester in January and running through May, with just a short break in April when Simon and Garfunkel would be playing some European concerts.

It would be open to all comers and not only those from the NYU campus. Simon himself would select the students, basing his determination upon the submissions (music and/or lyrics) that he received once the course was announced and the occasional recommendation from elsewhere—joining Oppenheim at the meetings was Jeffrey Sweet, a member of Broadway composer Lehman Engel's theatrical music writing class, and it was he who recommended Simon give an ear to one Melissa Manchester, a former NYU acting student.

Sisters Maggie and Terri Roche, on the other hand, approached Simon as he crossed campus one day and convinced him to give their songs a listen in a nearby empty classroom. They, too, were selected.

Slowly the class took shape. Tommy Mandel, later to find fame as a keyboard player, was one student; rock/beat poet Joe Linus became another. All looked to their celebrity tutor to offer them guidance in the field that he had so effortlessly conquered. But even once lessons were underway, Simon admitted that he was very much flying by the seat of his pants, not at all certain how the class was going to pan out.

For his students, of course, that was of little concern. They were spending three hours a week with one of the biggest stars of the age. But the students wouldn't be listening to him perform his songs; instead, he'd be listening to them performing theirs.

One week, a student or two might distribute a chosen lyric around the class and then deliver the song. Simon would listen and then, along with the rest of the class, offer up his thoughts and opinions. On other occasions, Simon would introduce the class to a song that *he* was writing

Simon and Garfunkel around the time of *Bridge Over Troubled Water*.   *Photofest*

and talk about his own processes. The final class would be held at the CBS Studios, where Simon would demonstrate how a "song" could be turned into a "record."

His lessons still hold true today.

He argued against sitting down to deliberately write a hit, pointing out then—as he would again when interviewed by *Drowning in Sound* in 2016—that few people can predict where lightning strikes, and the more you try, the less you are likely to succeed.

"I was just writing songs," he said, "and a bunch of them turned into hits but, if I wrote '50 Ways to Leave Your Lover,' it wasn't as if I thought: this is going to be a hit. I just wrote the song. I didn't even think that 'Bridge Over Troubled Water' was a hit. I thought it was really good, but I didn't think that it was a hit."

Sometimes his instincts were correct; "Kodachrome" and "Cecilia" were among the songs that he was sure would do well. But more often than not, it appears, he completely misjudged. "Mother and Child Reunion"? Not a hit. "Love Me Like a Rock"? Not a hit. "Any number of odd things that I tended to like"? Not a hit in sight.

It was for that reason, perhaps, that he counseled against writing for a particular musical fashion. Interviewed by *Rolling Stone* toward the end of the course, he insisted that it was "songs, not styles," that were important. Styles, after all, are ephemeral; already, he had lived through the ascendancy of folk rock, the British Invasion, and acid rock. "Now the Band is on the cover of *Time* magazine and they call it country rock or raga rock. Anything like that is not important; the only thing that matters is the songs. If a song lives for a couple of years then that's a pretty good thing."

He railed against cliché. Years later, talking to journalist Chris Ingham about the song "Darling Lorraine" (from *You're the One*), he admitted that he'd deliberately thrown one in—"All my life I've been a wanderer"—*specifically* so he could shoot it down in the next line: "You know, I say, 'what a load of crap, he's a liar.'"

He explained: "So, 'All my life I've been a wanderer / Not really, mostly I've lived near my parents' home', that was the joke. And, as I did that, I said I don't think I've done that joke before, say, 'that line's a big lie, anyway, back to the story.'"

Whether his own writing religiously obeyed the principles he suggested is questionable. But he was certainly on safe ground when he told the class that a key element in the learning process is the ability to imitate others, and if everything else failed and a lyric felt uninteresting, open a Bible and steal a phrase. "That's what they're there for."

He talked at length about remaining true to oneself, a topic he returned to when discussing songwriting with writer Anthony DeCurtis in 2000 (and on other occasions): "In [my] early songs, there was a lot of posing. And there comes a time in every piece of work where I turn on it and say, 'Why don't you shut up?' Then I say, 'I can't shut up. I'm a songwriter. I'll try to be more truthful.' [Songwriting is] an attempt to tell the truth, to say who you are at this point."

BOOKENDS/SIMON & GARFUNKEL

Nobody could have guessed it at the time, but *Bookends* would prove the duo's penultimate LP.
Author's collection

But he also advised steering clear of one's own comfort zone, another point he reiterated in the *Rolling Stone* interview. Far better , and far more enjoyable, too, to "do all different kinds of songs." His personal comfort area, he knew, lay in slow songs, reflective songs, simple songs. That was what came the most naturally. But what fun it was, he said, "to try writing in other styles just to see what will happen when I do that."

Bridge Over Troubled Water, newly released at the time of the interview, was a particular case in point. He and Garfunkel never set out consciously to create an album of so many different moods and tempos. In fact, they were some way into the process when they realized that's what they were doing. But they didn't back down. It made things interesting, both for them and, ultimately, for the listener. "I think that's good," Simon said. "I enjoy that."

He encouraged his students to actively seek out situations that could be put into song and pursue words and couplings that fell out of the norm, whether or not they corresponded exactly with the song. According to Simon biographer Peter Ames Carlin, he once suggested Melissa Manchester change the phrase "laughing lagoons" to "laughing da goons," "because it sounded more interesting"—in much the same way as "Mama pajama rolled out of bed" became such a peerless opening line to "Me and Julio Down by the Schoolyard."

Indeed, he reinforced the importance of having a good opening line as well, a point that journalist Charlie Gillett, reviewing *There Goes Rhymin' Simon* in 1973, assures readers he was eminently capable of living up to: "'When I think of all the crap I learned in high school, it's a wonder I can think at all.' For ten years I have been struggling to describe that feeling of being cheated. [Author] Paul Goodman devoted a lifetime to writing books exploring that paradox, which were never so clear and succinct. Paul Simon's LP starts out with that line, and it is by no means a downhill slide from there."

Simon was not necessarily a kind or even encouraging tutor. Perhaps he had learned during his own education in the worlds of sessions and publishing that, no matter how good you thought you were, there was always somebody better—a mindset that would either send a young hopeful crashing into despair *or* encourage them to up their game. Again, the difference between the Paul Simon who left New York in 1964 and the one who returned from London in late 1965 comes to mind.

Building the Bridge

But even if a student wanted to question Simon's methodology, it would have been a fool's errand. Every week, it seemed, *Bridge Over Troubled Water* became a little more successful; every day on the radio, it was impossible to avoid hearing one song or another from the album. And when the title track went to number one, even the dourest cynic would have been forced to admit that Simon was in a songwriting class of his own.

Even today, in the canon of "the greatest songs ever written," "Bridge Over Troubled Water" is regarded as standing head and shoulders not only above the rest of his catalog but the bulk of the competition, too.

It has been estimated that there are over 250 recorded cover versions of "Bridge Over Troubled Water" by "mainstream" artists alone—that is, everyone from Aretha Franklin to Mary J. Blige, and from Johnny Cash to Annie Lennox.

Elvis Presley was so enamored with it that he was performing it in his Las Vegas live show as early as August 1970; in fact, he recorded it in June, less than six months after Simon and Garfunkel's own version was released. Apparently, Paul Simon was present at one of the Las Vegas shows and is said to have remarked after hearing his song, "That's it. We might as well give up now."

Yet Elvis was not even the first to record the song. Stevie Wonder, B. J. Thomas, Glen Campbell, the Jackson Five, and Skeeter Davis all got in before him, while the full list of artists who took a shot at "Bridge Over Troubled Water" within the first year of its original release is an unimpeachable testament to its impact. (See sidebar.)

"Bridge Over Troubled Water"—The First Twelve Months of Covers

Al De Lory	Byron Lee and the Dragonaires
Andy Williams	Caleb Brooks
Anita Kerr Singers	Chairmen of the Board
B. J. Thomas	Charlie Byrd
Barbara Mason	Claude Denjean and the Moog
Bill Medley	Synthesizer
Boots Randolph	Davy Graham

Elvis Presley

Ferrante and Teicher

Frank Chacksfield and His Orchestra

Frank Ifield

Gerry Monroe

Glen Campbell

Helmuth Brandenburg

Hugo Winterhalter Orchestra

The Jackson 5

Jerry Reed and Chet Atkins

Jerry Vale

Jerry Walsh

Joe Dolan

John Davidson

Johnny Mathis

King Curtis

Larry Santos

Living Guitars

Merry Clayton

Mike Batt Orchestra

Nana Mouskouri

The Now Generation

The Osmonds

Patricia Cahill

Paul Desmond

Paul Mauriat

Peggy Lee

Quincy Jones

Ray Conniff Singers

Ronnie Aldrich and His Two Pianos
    with the London Festival Orchestra

Ronnie Dyson

Skeeter Davis

Smokey Robinson and the Miracles

Stevie Wonder

The Supremes

Terry Baxter and His Orchestra

The Top of the Poppers

The Ventures

Wayne Newton

The last song to be recorded during the album's sessions (but the first to be completed), "Bridge Over Troubled Water," Simon later admitted, was written so quickly that he was uncertain where it had even come from. "It doesn't seem like me."

At the same time, it was unmistakably his work, all the way down to the subtle borrowing of a favorite old gospel record, the Swan Silvertones' "Mary Don't You Weep"—that song's pledge to be "your bridge over deep water if you trust in me" rang so strongly in Simon's mind that he not only acknowledged the debt in interviews but also invited the original song's composer, the Reverend Claude Jeter, to add falsetto vocals to "Take Me to the Mardi Gras," one of several hits pulled off Simon's *There Goes Rhymin' Simon* album in 1973.

If the song was easy to write, however, the remainder of its genesis was turbulent.

Garfunkel was absent from the early scheduled recording sessions. Work on his debut movie, *Catch 22*, was delayed and he was stuck in Rome, while Simon was back in New York, "ready and raring to work."

So he worked. "Baby Driver" is a solo performance by Simon in all but billing, and he mixed "The Boxer" alone, regardless of the fact that that was a process to which Garfunkel had always contributed a great deal.

Art is little more than a background presence on "The Only Living Boy in New York," a song whose lyric is effectively a message from Paul for "Tom" (as in "and Jerry") to hurry home from Mexico, one of the principle locations for the movie.

Even when Garfunkel was available, the pair worked together less than they ever had in the past, as Simon later revealed: "It's a Simon and Garfunkel record, but not really. And it became easier to work by

The rare reel-to-reel tape release of 1970's valedictory *Bridge Over Troubled Water*.

Author's collection

separating. There are many songs where you don't hear [us] singing together."

In fact, it's ironic that the session that went the furthest in recreating the duo's former sense of togetherness should produce what could easily be described as the most annoying track on the album: the slapstick "Cecilia."

Ensconced in the living room of the house on Blue Jay Way, in the Hollywood Hills, that Simon was then renting (the same address where George Harrison wrote the song "Blue Jay Way" in 1967), Simon and Garfunkel, together with Paul's brother Eddie on piano and guitarist friend Stewey Scharf, were effectively jamming around the riot of percussive effects that they were coaxing out of their instruments and anything else they could lay their hands on.

It was never intended as anything serious, but playing it back, all professed themselves astonished at the sounds they had created. Back in the studio with co-producer Roy Halee, further sounds were added to the tape—Simon hammering a xylophone, a bundle of drumsticks being dropped onto the floor, and so on.

Then, the initial minute-and-a-half track was doubled in length by the simple expedient of playing it through once again, and Simon all but ad-libbed the lyrics on top. It was indeed a bold experiment. But its presence on the finished album surely speaks more for an increasingly obvious lack of new material than it did for the album's cohesion.

That became even more obvious with the inclusion of a live recording of the Everly's "Bye Bye Love," while Garfunkel's refusal to allow Simon to include another rocker—the "Sweet Little Sixteen"-like "Cuba Si, Nixon No"—limited the album's contents even further.

From "Parsley" to "El Condor Pasa"

September 1966: "The Dangling Conversation"/"The Big Bright Green Pleasure Machine" (Columbia 43728)

November 1966: *Parsley, Sage, Rosemary and Thyme* (Columbia LP CS 9363)

"Scarborough Fair—Canticle"	"Cloudy"
"Patterns"	"Homeward Bound"

"The Big Bright Green Pleasure
   Machine"
"The 59th Street Bridge Song" (Feelin'
   Groovy)
"The Dangling Conversation"
"Flowers Never Bend with the Rainfall"

"A Simple Desultory Philippic" (or
   How I Was Robert McNamara'd Into
   Submission)
"For Emily, Whenever I May Find Her"
"A Poem on the Underground Wall"
"7 O'Clock News—Silent Night"

Produced by Bob: Johnston

November 1966: "A Hazy Shade of Winter"/"For Emily, Whenever I May Find Her" (Columbia 43873)

January 1967: "At the Zoo"/"The 59th Street Bridge Song" (Feelin' Groovy) (Columbia 44046)

July 1967: "Fakin' It"/"You Don't Know Where Your Interest Lies" (Columbia 44232)

October 1967: "Scarborough Fair—Canticle"/"April, Come She Will" (Columbia 44465)

May 1968: "Mrs. Robinson"/"Old Friends"/"Bookends" (Columbia 44511)

Musicians

Larry Knechtel—bass   Hal Blaine—congas and drums

May 1968: *Bookends* (Columbia LP KCS 9529)

"Bookends Theme" (Instrumental)
"Save the Life of My Child"
"America"
"Overs"
"[voices of old people]"
"Old Friends"

"Bookends Theme"
"Fakin' It"
"Punky's Dilemma"
"Mrs. Robinson"
"A Hazy Shade of Winter"
"At the Zoo"

Produced by: Simon, Garfunkel, and Roy Halee; production assistants: John Simon and Bob Johnston; arrangement ("Old Friends"): Jimmy Haskell

Musicians

Larry Knechtel—bass and organ
Hal Blaine—drums

May 1969: "The Boxer"/"Baby Driver (Columbia 44785)

Musicians

Fred Carter Jr.—guitar

Peter Drake—pedal steel guitar
dobro

Hal Blaine—drums

Charlie McCoy—harmonica

Hal Blaine and Buddy
Harmon—percussion

February 1970: *Bridge Over Troubled Water* (Columbia LP KCS 9914)

"Bridge Over Troubled Water"

"El Condor Pasa" (arrangement and
original lyric: Paul; arrangement of
eighteenth-century Peruvian folk
melody by Jorge Milchberg; musicians: Los Incas)

"Cecilia"

"Keep the Customer Satisfied"

"So Long, Frank Lloyd Wright"

"The Boxer"

"Baby Driver"

"The Only Living Boy in New York"

"Why Don't You Write Me"

"Bye Bye Love" (Felice and Boudleaux
Bryant)

"Song for the Asking"

Produced by: Simon, Garfunkel, and
Roy Halee

Musicians

Fred Carter Jr.—guitars

Hal Blaine—drums

Joe Osborn—bass

Larry Knechtel—keyboard

Jimmy Haskell and Ernie
Freeman—strings

February 1970: "Bridge Over Troubled Water"/"Keep the Customer Satisfied" (Columbia 45079)

May 1970: "Cecilia"/"The Only Living Boy in New York" (Columbia 45133)

October 1970: "El Condor Pasa"/"Why Don't You Write Me" (Columbia 45237)

June 1972: *Simon and Garfunkel's Greatest Hits* (Columbia LP KC 31350)

"Mrs. Robinson"

"For Emily, Whenever I May Find Her"

"The Boxer"

"The 59th Street Bridge Song" (Feelin'
Groovy)

"The Sound of Silence"

"I Am a Rock"

"Scarborough Fair—Canticle"

"Homeward Bound"/"Bridge Over
Troubled Water"

"America"

"Kathy's Song"

"El Condor Pasa"

"Bookends"

October 1972: "America"/"For Emily, Whenever I May Find Her" (Columbia 45663)

Simon, however, had more tricks up his sleeve—even if Garfunkel, again, seemed determined to sabotage them.

"Bridge Over Troubled Water" was another of the songs Simon wrote and demoed on Blue Jay Way. Originally, it was a guitar ballad, which he then rearranged for piano to make it easier for Garfunkel to sing. The vocal on Simon's original demo even aped his partner's angelic tones.

Garfunkel didn't want to do it. The song was not right for him, he insisted; Simon should sing it, and he should use that same near-falsetto as well. And besides, it was in the wrong key for Garfunkel, G major.

Co-producer Roy Halee weighed in. The song was too short; Simon had written just two verses, and he and Garfunkel agreed that it demanded three.

The song was written for Simon's wife, Peggy, and was the tenderest declaration of love and support that said as much as it needed to. Simon knew that, but he agreed to write that third verse anyway, basing it upon Peggy's recent discovery of her first gray hairs—"sail on silver girl."

He still considered that extra verse to be extraneous, though. In his introduction to *The Songs of Paul Simon*, he mused: "I always felt you could tell [that verse] was added later, as it never really fit the first two in style. Also, I couldn't think of another 'down' rhyme, so the metaphor 'I will lay me down' is discarded in the last verse and 'I'm sailing right behind' is substituted."

"This weakness" still rankled.

Nevertheless, his critics were silenced, with Garfunkel's other objections being salved after arranger Jimmie Haskell transposed the song into the key of E-flat major. Finally, work could begin.

The actual arranging, rearranging, recording—the very construction—of the finished "Bridge Over Troubled Water" reads like an epic task because that's what it was. But few can deny that the song, in its original released form, remains one of the most peerlessly arranged records of the age, and it remains so today.

Woody Woodmansey, years later the drummer for the solo Garfunkel, recalls: "On other tracks like 'Cecilia' and 'The Sound of Silence,' Art let me be creative, so I did things like taking the conga part from the original version of 'Cecilia' and incorporat[ing] it into the song with a new drum beat, which gave a new approach that worked whilst staying true to the original recording."

On "Bridge Over Troubled Water," however, Woodmansey took a different approach, saying: "I had to duplicate exactly the drums and percussion parts that were on the original. Doing anything else felt wrong, and tended to stick out even when the parts fitted musically."

The song's other interpreters have been less rigid, however, and here we see the sheer resilience of the composition. "Bridge Over Troubled Water" has been taken back to its gospel roots, forward into rock 'n' roll, and sideways into almost any other genre you can imagine.

R&B singer Linda Clifford transformed it into a pulsating disco number, complete with a ten-minute dance mix, and the song didn't turn a hair. Artists for Grenfell, an aggregation of twenty-first-century stars brought together to raise funds for victims of the terrible Grenfell fire disaster in 2017, inserted a rap into the song without it losing an iota of its emotional punch. Elvis rendered it a masterpiece of emotion, Stevie Wonder piled on the soul, and Byron Lee and the Dragonaires made it reggae.

Small wonder that even Simon, despite his own tendency to rank among his own greatest critics, conceded, "I think 'Bridge' is my strongest melody to date, even if not my best lyric."

Although he could not resist the temptation, in 1972, to add, "I think my next songs will be better."

7

Kingston, Jamaica

Throughout his career, Simon had evinced an interest in what would later be called "world music," but which, at the time, was simply evidence of his fascination with disciplines and roots that had nothing to do with the sounds he grew up with—and everything in common with them, too.

The investigation of English folk music that took him to London in 1964, which saw him come close to becoming a permanent resident of the local music scene, was one example. Indeed, even after "The Sound of Silence" took off as a hit single in late 1965, he mused that he'd enjoy its success while he could and then go back to his career in the United Kingdom once it was over.

In Paris, he so fell in love with Latin American stylings that he would later introduce them to the Anglo-American pop audience via a new set of lyrics performed over Jorge Milchberg's arrangement of the eighteenth-century Peruvian folk melody "El Condor Pasa," and in 1970, discussing his future plans with Columbia chief Clive Davies, he certainly gave the older man a surprise when he said where he was intending to go next to record.

Nashville, maybe. Or Kingston, Jamaica.

Paul Simon's first visit to London fell during a very propitious time, not only for a young man with an ear for traditional music, or even one wanting to hear the latest Beatles and Stones 45s before his friends back Stateside. Travel outside of the world of mainstream pop, or even the folk and R&B undergrounds that were so vibrant at that point in time; delve even further below the surface, in other words, and you would inevitably come into contact with Jamaican music.

It permeated those London streets toward which a wave of West Indian immigrants had been funneled in the years following World War

Two; it became a part of the furniture in the pubs and coffee houses where they gathered; and it was utterly unavoidable at impromptu "shebeen" parties, which every other house seemed to host.

The music was nothing like the Jamaicans' neighbors had ever heard—tight and jerky, pulsating, almost hiccuping, an insatiable rhythm that emphasized beats that local players had never dreamed of leaning on, and sung of a world that they'd never imagined existed.

It was utterly alien, but it was equally contagious. There were only a handful of record labels, largely West Indian owned, that catered to this audience, either by licensing music from back home and then re-pressing it for the United Kingdom or by recruiting other immigrants to form their own groups in England. But the records that they made were both powerful and popular.

The Mod movement, dropping speed in nightclubs like the Flamingo, at the foot of Wardour Street, or the Roaring Twenties off Carnaby Street, heard this strangely syncopated "ska" music and made it their own. And it launched, in the process, a subculture that was as vibrant in its world as any other popular sound of the day was in its.

The music spread. Ross McManus—a popular bandman of the day but better known today as Elvis Costello's father—cut one of the first-ever English ska records, a neat little number called "Patsy Girl." R&B singer Chris Farlowe and the Beazers landed a club smash with "The Blue Beat," titled after the British name for the music. (Bluebeat was, in fact, the most popular of the aforementioned record labels.) The Migil Five went to number ten on the chart with the ska-flavored "Mockingbird Hill," and in North London, a white schoolboy outfit called the Soul Survivors were rehearsing with visiting Jamaican star Owen Gray. Soul Survivor later became "Everlasting Love" hit makers Love Affair.

Georgie Fame and his Blue Flames experimented with the ska sound and recorded with the great Prince Buster; the Spencer Davis Group enjoyed a pair of monster hits penned by another Jamaican superstar, singer Jackie Edwards.

Paul Simon heard it all, digested it all. As he would tell the UK magazine Sounds, in 1973: "Yeah. I like reggae [the successor, via sundry musical convolutions, to ska]. I was more into it no. I like it, no qualifications. I haven't been listening too much lately, but for a while I listened to it a lot."

Here Comes Syncopated Simon

It was not, he quickly realized, an easy music to replicate. Even Eric Clapton's mid-seventies cover of Bob Marley's "I Shot the Sheriff" (the record most frequently cited as that which paved the way for Jamaican music's eventual commercial breakthrough) is reggae by association alone. Clapton's actual performance barely hints at the syncopated power of the true reggae beat.

Simon's first deliberate experiment was no more successful. Recorded during the *Bridge Over Troubled Water* sessions in 1969, "Why Don't You Write Me" was Simon and the accompanying Fred Carter Jr., Hal Blaine, Joe Osborn, and Larry Knechtel striving for the elusive reggae sound but foundering within the sheer unfamiliarity of what they were expected to play.

PAUL SIMON

Two years seemed a long time to wait, but Simon's self-titled debut was worth the delay.
Author's collection

They captured the written sound, of course—musicians of that caliber can play whatever is placed in front of them. But reggae music, like so many other forms of non-rock and pop music, is less concerned with what is written on paper than it is with what is felt in the heart. Listening to the finished song, in fact, one is reminded of what bluesman Sonny Boy Williamson II once said about another of Eric Clapton's cross-cultural approximations: "These British want to play the blues so bad, and they play the blues so bad."

Simon knew it, too.

He did not pull his dream of recording a reggae song out of thin air, or even out of nostalgia for his London sojourn. The late 1960s saw several Jamaican performers make major inroads into both the British and, to a lesser degree, American markets. Desmond Dekker, who topped the UK chart with "The Israelites" in 1968, saw the same song reach the Top 10 in the United States; Jimmy Cliff—like Dekker, a Jamaican star since the early 1960s—was newly signed to Island Records, and scored with both "Wonderful World, Beautiful People" and "Vietnam," the latter of which was described by Bob Dylan as the best protest song he had ever heard.

Again in the United Kingdom, reggae records were becoming a more and more common sight in the Top 40, each one clambering into the daylight from the tiny clubs and local scenes wherein they had always dwelt, before spreading across an ever-increasing network of likeminded venues. Very often, songs like "The Liquidator," "Wet Dream," "Montego Bay," and "Double Barrel" were chartbound long before the regular outlets for top pop singles—radio, TV, and the music papers—were even aware they existed.

That, too, was a part of the appeal to Simon—a music whose very existence was so organic that it operated almost *despite* the efforts of the mainstream, not because of them. And, while it was doubtless foolish of him to even imagine he could replicate that in a plush Los Angeles studio, surrounded by some of the greatest session men the nation could offer him, the fact was, he tried. And he knew why he had failed.

He was determined to try again, but this time, he would do so far from the United States. Armed with a new song that he deemed suitable, Simon contacted Leslie Kong, who was at that time one of Jamaica's leading producers.

Desmond Dekker, the Pioneers, Toots and the Maytals, Bob Marley and the Wailers, and many more had each filed through Kong's Beverley Records setup and emerged with some stellar music. And he also oversaw the session at which Jimmy Cliff's "Vietnam" was recorded, and that was what Simon was interested in.

Simon wanted to know if Kong could put him in touch with the guitarist who played on that session. Of course Kong could.

Jimmy Cliff

Although he was barely into his teens when he was discovered by producer Derrick Morgan in 1962, Jimmy Cliff moved quickly up the echelon of local Jamaican stars. In 1964, Cliff was invited (alongside Prince Buster and Byron Lee) to represent Jamaica at the New York World's Fair, and it was there that he met Island Records chief Chris Blackwell, who was excitedly releasing Cliff's singles in the United Kingdom. Now Blackwell was desperate to bring the singer back to England, confident that his presence on the live circuit would break him wide open.

It didn't, but the experience was to prove invaluable. Cliff remained in London for three years, working with everybody from Millie Small to the Spencer Davis Group, while at the same time honing his own vibrant stage act to visual perfection.

This time, it worked. Jimmy Cliff would become reggae music's first international superstar when his "Wonderful World, Beautiful People" made the UK Top 10 in 1969. His critically acclaimed debut LP, *Hard Road to Travel*, followed, together with a string of further hits—"Viet-Nam," "Come Into My Life," "Many Rivers to Cross," and a cover of Cat Stevens's "Wild World"—while Cliff's own compositions were hits for Desmond Dekker ("You Can Get It If You Really Want It") and the Pioneers ("Let Your Yeah Be Yeah," "Give and Take").

Sensing Cliff's literate style was an ideal match for the then-burgeoning market for singer-songwriters, Island Records targeted his next few releases wholly at that market, and not always with success.

Nevertheless, Cliff maintained his edge with the lead role in Perry Henzell's *The Harder They Come* movie, destined to become not only one of the breakout hits of 1972 but a touchstone for generations of reggae fans to come.

The title track alone is now rated among the most frequently covered songs in Jamaican musical history.

That success in turn paved the way for a career that, more than four decades on, is still going strong. The mid-1980s saw Cliff cut a live album with legendary Rolling Stones producer Andrew Oldham; in 1993, his version of Texan Johnny Nash's ska classic "I Can See Clearly Now" became an international hit on the back of the *Cool Running* movie, and into the 2010s, an album recorded with Tim Armstrong of Rancid brought a fresh wave of interest, and an entirely new generation of fans, firmly into Cliff's camp.

He and Simon, meanwhile, have remained friends and occasional collaborators. Cliff joined Simon at his 1976 benefit for the New York Public Library system (see chapter 17), and in July 2012, he appeared as a special guest at Simon's concert in Hyde Park (see chapter 18).

The headliner's set was already underway when Cliff was introduced. He walked out to wild applause for a brief two-song set of his own, "The Harder They Come" and "Many Rivers to Cross," before Simon returned to the stage and they launched into the songs that started it all—for Simon, at any rate—a medley of Cliff's "Viet-Nam" spinning into "Mother and Child Reunion."

In a concert packed with highlights, that was one of the most remarkable.

Welcome to Kingston

Lynford "Hux" Brown was best known as guitarist with Toots and the Maytals. However, he was also a key element of the house band at Dynamic Sounds in Kingston, Jamaica.

Originally known as the West Indies Records Limited and owned by Edward Seaga, a future President of Jamaica, Dynamic was now operated by Byron Lee, whose own band, the Dragonaires, was one of Jamaica's most successful.

With Leslie Kong agreeing to organize a suitable backing band, Simon booked three days in the studio. He got there to find Hux Brown joined by rhythm guitarist Wallace Wilson, organist Neville Hinds, bassist Jackie Jackson, drummer Winston Grennan, and percussionist Denzil Laing—

a team that, between them, had played on more hit records than any of them could count.

Simon later admitted he made the journey with some trepidation, feeling a little like a thief in the night, come to spirit away Jamaica's patent sound. At the same time, however, he was also relishing the freedom he had suddenly discovered as a solo artist, not least of all, as he confessed to *Rolling Stone*, the knowledge that he "didn't have to write a Simon and Garfunkel follow-up to *Bridge Over Troubled Water*." That, he was sure, would have been "an inevitable letdown for people."

One emotion balanced the other, with the former finally tipping the scales when he discovered, like so many British and American musicians in later years (the Rolling Stones checked into Dynamic in 1972, lured at least partially by the success of Simon's sojourn), nothing but warmth and welcome when he arrived at the studio.

A solo Simon makes the coveted cover of *Rolling Stone* magazine.   *Author's collection*

So much, in fact, that he was even able to overlook the (by American standards) primitive surroundings in which he was to work.

There was no monster mixing desk and high-tech equipment at Dynamic—just a serviceable eight-track recorder, basic soundproofing, old microphones and amps, and the most electrifying, and least antiseptic, atmosphere of any studio he had ever spent time in.

Simon introduced himself and then introduced his song. The musicians stared at him. Finally, one of them told him, "That's ska. We don't play ska, we play reggae."

Simon stared back. He hadn't realized there was any difference, although he quickly learned. "Ska is basically very simple," he told Sounds. "Reggae, I can't define." But he was happy to accede to their wisdom, regardless. The song was on its way.

There was one thing he didn't understand, however—why the mood in the room began to change as he led the musicians through the song and put a few exploratory takes onto tape. The longer the session lasted, with still just the one song being tried and tried again, the more the musicians seemed unhappy.

March 1972: *Paul Simon* (CK 30750)

"Mother and Child Reunion"
"Duncan"
"Everything Put Together Falls Apart"
"Run That Body Down"
"Armistice Day"
"Me and Julio Down by the Schoolyard"
"Peace Like a River"
"Papa Hobo"
"Hobo's Blues" (Simon/Stephane Grappelli)
"Paranoia Blues"
"Congratulations"

Recorded in: Jamaica, Paris, New York, Los Angeles, and San Francisco
Produced by: Simon and Roy Halee

Musicians

David Spinoza—guitars
Mike Manieri—vibes
Jerry Hahn—electric guitar
Ron Carter—bass
Hal Blaine—drums

Airto Moreira—percussion
Fred Lipsius—horns
John Schroer—horns
Russel George—bass
Victor Montanez—drums

Joe Osborn—bass
Charlie McCoy—bass harmonica
Stephane Grappelli—violin
Stefan Grossman—bottleneck
Steven Turre—horns
Hux Brown—lead guitar
Wallace Wilson—rhythm guitar
Neville Hands—organ
Jackie Jackson—bass

Winston Grennan—drums
Denzil Laing—percussion
Larry Knechtel—piano
Cissy Houston, Renelle Stafford, Deirdre Tuck, and Von Eva Sims—singers
Los Incas—charango, flutes, and percussion

March 1972: "Mother and Child Reunion"/"Paranoia Blues" (Columbia 45547)

May 1972: "Me and Julio Down by the Schoolyard"/Congratulations (Columbia 45585)

August 1972: "Duncan"/"Run That Body Down" (Columbia 45638)

Finally, Simon was put out of his misery. Unlike in New York or London, where every session unfolded along those lines, Jamaican musicians were accustomed to banging out track after track, rarely more than a couple of takes apiece. And that was how they got paid, by the completed track. To their eyes, the idea of spending an entire day playing with the same tune wasn't simply anathema, it was also financially ruinous.

Simon gathered them around him. He would pay them three times their usual rate per day—a three-day session would leave each of them close to $100 apiece better off, as much as if they'd recorded *nine* songs.

The mood immediately lifted and, by the time Simon returned to New York City, he had the backing track he required. Only Larry Knechtel's piano needed to be overdubbed—that and the lyrics, of course, which he had not yet written.

But "Mother and Child Reunion" came together quickly, and it swiftly rewarded Simon's efforts, as well as becoming, among his fans, one of his most patiently analyzed songs—theories range from a response to, again, Jimmy Cliff's "Viet-Nam" to the successful outcome of a child custody case. (The reunion, we are told, is "only a motion away.")

One of the most memorable hits of 1972, "Mother and Child Reunion."

Author's collection

Simon apparently enjoys the speculation. His few comments on the origins of the song include the aforementioned credit to a Chinese restaurant for serving the meal that inspired the title and a vague reference to the death of a beloved pet dog.

What is not in doubt is the status of "Mother and Child Reunion" as the most successful, and most visible, stab at white reggae yet released anywhere in the world—a status it would retain until (and, perhaps, even after) Eric Clapton's "I Shot the Sheriff."

It also confirmed to Simon that if you truly wanted to touch the soul of music, you needed go to where the music came from. Because it would never come to you.

Live Rhymin'—In Concert 1973–1980

In these days when it sometimes feels as though any live show given anywhere in the world is all but guaranteed to appear, at least in part, on an internet video channel within hours, and when even the most professionally produced modern concert movie will itself be interspersed with the sight of the audience raising their own cameras to the stage . . . in an age like this, it seems impossible that there was ever a time when somebody or other did *not* film, or at least record, *every* concert.

A lot of people did, of course, particularly during the 1970s, as bootlegging became one of the music business's most unwelcome growth industries, and cassette recorders contrarily became small enough to smuggle in under your coat. And today, thanks to the internet, many of them are available to whosoever might seek them out—a trove, in Paul Simon's case, that reaches as far back as the Santa Monica Civic Center show on May 19, 1973, two weeks into his first-ever solo tour of America, and forward to the last show of his last-ever tour in September 2018.

The sound quality cannot always be expected to be pristine, although if you ever wondered how it felt to be halfway back in an echoing auditorium, with an overenthusiastic drunk yelling "whoooo" on one side and a couple discussing their day at work on the other, while Paul Simon held court half a football field away, you would have come to the right place.

Occasionally, however, it all comes together—not as all-consumingly as it does with today's technology, but certainly enough to be happily listened to.

A bootleg CD from Simon & Garfunkel's 1966 US concerts.   *Author's collection*

Live in the Sixties

Track further back in time, however, to the 1960s, and it's a very different story. Those same internet emporiums offer up barely a half-dozen genuine live recordings featuring Simon and Garfunkel, and that includes their less than stellar performance at the Monterey Pop Festival in 1967.

The performances that have survived, however, testify to the sheer electricity of the duo's personal chemistry—uncaged from the studio, unfettered by lifestyle, released, in fact, to do what they had always done best: sing and play together.

They had not been shy of revealing this side of their partnership, of course. With the exception of 1967, Simon and Garfunkel undertook tours both at home and abroad in every year between 1965 and 1970, and if their itineraries were sparse during the first couple of years, by 1968 they were subject to outings as immense and exhausting as any multi-instrumental rock 'n' roll band.

It was not an experience that either especially looked forward to. Simon later confessed that he existed on the road in a permanent state of "semi-hypnosis," to the point where he effectively stopped thinking about what he was expected to do and just did it. Arrive in town, go to the venue, run through the soundcheck, change his guitar strings, look at the guest list, hunt down a restaurant for the after-show meal. Everything was regimented, everything was rote.

But the time they spent on stage was magical.

The earliest complete live concert to have been granted at least a quasi-legal release appeared in the mid-1980s, as various European labels located a possible loophole in existing copyright laws and flooded the market accordingly.

Sound of Silence Live was recorded in late 1966 in New York and features: "Sparrow," "Homeward Bound," "You Don't Know Where Your Interest Lies," "A Most Peculiar Man," "Red Rubber Ball," "The Dangling Conversation," "The 59th Street Bridge Song," "Richard Cory," "Benedictus," "Blessed," "A Poem on the Underground Wall," "I Am a Rock," "Anji," "The Sound of Silence," "For Emily, Whenever I May Find Her," "The Church Is Burning," and "Wednesday Morning, 3 A.M."

It's a glorious snapshot of their period repertoire, as the duo placed the more overt manifestations of their "protest" period behind them. However, they were more than willing to return to it as the occasion demanded, a point proven by their performance at the New York Philharmonic Hall on January 22, 1967, released decades later as the very sensibly titled *Live from New York City, 1967*.

It illustrates a repertoire informed by each of their albums to date, opening with a naked "He Was My Brother," ending with a rare performance of "A Church Is Burning" and "Wednesday Morning, 3 A.M.," and in between these times, rounding up what the casual modern purchaser,

"American Tune" was one of the highlights of Simon's first solo tour.
Author's collection

knowing the duo only from the full expanse of their catalog, might regard as an especially obscure set list.

"Homeward Bound," "I Am a Rock," and "The Sound of Silence" are all featured, of course. So are "You Don't Know Where Your Interest Lies," the strangely arrogant (not to mention misogynistic) B-side to the "Fakin' It" single; the instrumental "Anji"; the Latin language "Benedictus"; and a couple of songs which, rightly or wrongly, are probably better remembered today for latter-day cover versions than for their significance during Simon and Garfunkel's career.

"Hazy Shade of Winter" became an early-eighties hit for the California girl band the Bangles; "Richard Cory" was an unexpected addition to Paul McCartney's 1975 American tour and an equally surprising highlight of the attendant *Wings Over America* triple album. Indeed, there are few more joyful moments in the ex-Beatle's recorded live catalog than the apparently ad-libbed omission of Cory's name from the song's "I wish that I could be" hook, and its replacement with "John Denver." A substitution, needless to say, that Simon and Garfunkel never made.

Yet the album is very much a frozen moment in time. The concert took place a few months shy of the dawning of the Summer of Love, but already 1967 was shaping up to be a "groovy" year. The Beatles had just released "Strawberry Fields Forever"; Jimi Hendrix had issued "Hey Joe." In London, Pink Floyd were getting ready to record their first single; in San Francisco, Jefferson Airplane and the Grateful Dead were preparing for their second albums.

All of which must have felt a universe away from the comfortably upholstered seats and staid ornate decoration of the Philharmonic Hall, from its uniformed ushers and smartly dressed patrons.

For sure the concert was open to all who wanted to attend, but the Philharmonic Hall is far removed from any venue Simon and Garfunkel might have played in even recent months—Johns Hopkins University in Baltimore, the Marquee Club in London, Melodyland in West Corina, the Yale Bowl in New Haven.

The Philharmonic Hall was establishment; it was the music industry welcoming Simon and Garfunkel into the very heart of its diamond-toting, tuxedo-wearing elite. No wonder, years later, that critic Robert Christgau would describe Simon's vocals, at least, as "studied wimpiness." From the outside, Simon and Garfunkel made white bread look coarse.

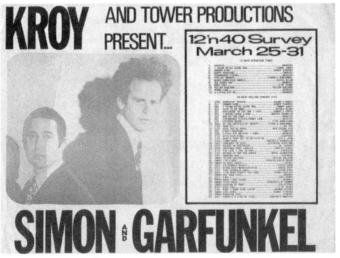

A *Sacramento* magazine ad for an upcoming Simon & Garfunkel show.
Author's collection

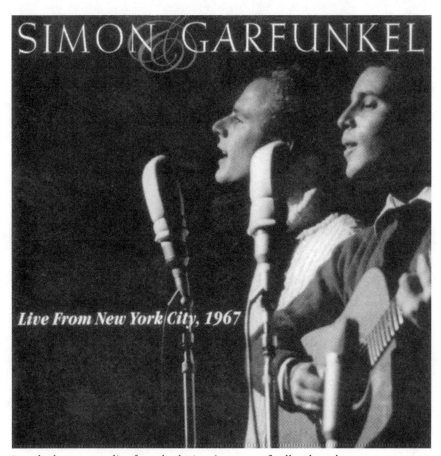

Decades later, a recording from the duo's 1967 tour was finally released.

Author's collection

But how did they repay the Philharmonic's largesse? With one song about a murdered activist and another about racial cleansing in the South. With a condemnation of capitalism and the suicide of a capitalist—how many Richard Corys had sat out in those same seats in the months and years beforehand?

They lionized street graffiti ("A Poem on the Underground Wall") and glorified social vapidity ("The Dangling Conversation"). Brick by brick, song by song, they utterly dismantled the very fabric of the world that traditionally called that venue its home, and they did it with such angelic voices, such rhapsodic harmonies, such aching sweetness and purity that barely a soul even noticed.

The Airplane, the Dead, the Fugs, and the Doors—with hair hung like sloths from the sides of their heads and ragged, tie-dyed clothes that looked like they'd been loaded into a blunderbuss and aimed in their general direction—might have been the squalling, finger-pointing focal point of American rock's uprising against the staid conformity of late-sixties society.

But it was Simon and Garfunkel—respectably dressed, smartly groomed, and singing like choirboys in search of their supper—who took the fight to the doors of the capitol.

It would take thirty-five years for that recording to be released.

Recorded with a view to releasing a live album as an instant follow-up to *Bridge*, Simon and Garfunkel's second live album, *Live 1969*, captures a very different animal.

They were still prone to broadcast their political opinions from the stage; indeed, as they toured America's colleges during 1967–68, the duo frequently ended concerts by inviting the audience to stay behind and discuss civil rights, resulting in lengthy rap sessions that could last as long as the concert.

"The college circuit is ideal for us," Simon told *Record Mirror*. Audiences were a manageable size, the available equipment was adequate. But most important of all: "There are no distractions. We can talk to those audiences and communicate. You see, although teenage pop kids buy my records, I find it a little hard to communicate with them. We don't have that much in common."

But embarking upon what would prove to be their final tour together until the eighties brought their first reunion, and previewing several songs from the as-yet-unreleased *Bridge Over Troubled Water*, Simon and Garfunkel were now a well-oiled showbiz machine.

The set is very different to that of two years previous. There is no subtle insurrection in the set list, no uncomfortable truths or discomforting accusations. No rap sessions. Richard Cory lies undisturbed; the burning church has been extinguished.

They could have been performing a greatest hits album, and though it surely is coincidence, that is almost exactly what they were doing. When, in 1972, Columbia released *Simon and Garfunkel's Greatest Hits*, no less

Another deeply posthumous album, this time from 1969.   *Author's collection*

than nine of its twelve tracks replicated titles that were performed this evening, and several of them were recorded live during this very tour.

The performance, of course, is exquisite. Again, Simon and Garfunkel are singing for the love of it, and the liner notes to *Live 1969* make a point of remarking that there is "interestingly no trace of the acrimony that was thought to have accrued as they neared their breakup."

"Interestingly?" Why? Again, the live environment, that hour or so they spent on stage together, was one of the few occasions when Simon and Garfunkel could be Paul and Artie, old friends doing what they'd done when they were young and would probably still have been doing if fame and expectation had not come along as well.

Unfortunately, however, they did, and less than nine months after the show was recorded, Simon and Garfunkel played their last concert together at Forest Hills Tennis Stadium on July 18, 1970.

A tape exists of that performance, as well. Sadly, it sounds as though it were recorded from underwater—a quagmire of distortion and extraneous scuffling sound (just a guess, but was the taper's microphone concealed in a pocket?) that requires a lot of dedication to get through.

What it reveals, however, is—there was nothing to reveal. The duo was still having fun and still singing for the love of it. Why else would they have exhumed "Rambler Gambler" from their days exploring the folk canon? Returned to their teens with "Teenager in Love"? And added one more Everly Brothers cover to the already sizable canon they had covered in the past—and not even an especially well-known one?

"Put My Little Shoes Away," from 1958's *Songs Our Daddy Taught Us* collection of Appalachian songs, might even be more obscure than the same LP's "That Silver Haired Daddy of Mine," which was also aired during this last burst of live shows. At least the latter had once been a hit for Gene Autry.

Of course, there would be further performances, even after the breakup: at the Grammys in March 1971, when "Bridge Over Troubled Water" swept all before it; at Madison Square Garden in June 1972, when they reunited to headline a benefit concert for Senator George McGovern, Democratic candidate in the upcoming Presidential elections (see chapter 17); in 1975 for *Saturday Night Live*; and two years later at the Britannia Music Awards in London.

But they were one-off special occasions alone. Both artists' solo careers were now underway, and both had their own solo concerts to play.

Simply Simon

Simon made his solo concert debut at the Summer Concert for Peace at Shea Stadium on August 6, 1970 (see chapter 17). He then opted not to tour his first solo album, 1972's *Paul Simon*, confining his live appearances to some television and the McGovern benefit concert.

But the success of the following year's *There Goes Rhymin' Simon* made an outing inevitable—and besides, Simon was keen to get back on the road even if he wasn't quite certain whether he even remembered how to carry a show on his own.

Of course, he would not *be* on his own. Gone were the days of one night stands, suitcase and guitar in hand. He knew (and record label chief Clive Davis reminded him of the fact on at least one occasion) that *Paul Simon* would have been a far bigger record if he had taken it to the people; and he also knew that the best reason he'd had for *not* touring it, the fact that he only had forty minutes worth of solo songs to perform, would no longer carry water.

He was well aware that the Simon and Garfunkel songbook would have to be given some kind of airing when he performed; he was never so arrogant as to believe that he could satisfy an auditorium full of fans without giving them at least a handful of oldies. But he had no intention of filling the set with the things.

In the event, the set list that he settled upon as the first rehearsals approached would have satisfied all but the most stubborn oldies fan. It kicked off with a lone voice-and-guitar-only "Me and Julio Down by the Schoolyard," the second hit single to be drawn from Paul Simon.

He moved on through "Run That Body Down" and "Was a Sunny Day" but dropped both "Cecilia" and, on some nights, "The 59th Street Bridge Song" into the first half a dozen numbers. "American Tune" received an always lovely airing.

Urubamba (formerly Los Incas), the long-running Argentine/Uruguayan band—whose members Simon first met in Paris almost a decade before and who provided the accompaniment to the studio versions of both "El Condor Pasa (If I Could)" and "Duncan"—rejoined him for those numbers and then took over for a couple of numbers of their own.

Simon returned with "The Boxer" and "Mrs. Robinson," and then it was into a confident run of both new and old material—"Congratulations," "Kodachrome," "Homeward Bound," "Something So Right," and a spectacularly rearranged "Mother and Child Reunion," with the Jessy Dixon Singers plying the song's original reggae stylings with a heavy dose of gospel and then following suit with a similarly and magnificently reimagined "The Sound of Silence."

The Jessy Dixon Singers now took the spotlight for their own two-song set before Simon reemerged to join them for the closing straight: a lengthy, impassioned "Bridge Over Troubled Water," "Loves Me Like a Rock," and, finally, "America."

The tour opened at the Boston Music Hall on May 6, 1973, and the sold-out audience included *Rolling Stone* critic Jon Landau. His praise for the show—particularly the gospel portion at the end—went a long way toward assuaging any nerves Simon may have entertained before the tour began and a lot of the uncertainty that, perhaps, audiences felt.

Simon in the Seventies

May 1973: *There Goes Rhymin' Simon* (Columbia LP KC 32280)

"Kodachrome"

"Tenderness"

"Take Me to the Mardi Gras"

"Something So Right"

"One Man's Ceiling Is Another Man's Floor"

"American Tune"

"Was a Sunny Day"

"Learn How to Fall"

"St. Judy's Comet"

"Loves Me Like a Rock"

Produced by: Paul Simon; co-producers: Phil Ramone, the Muscle Shoals Sound Rhythm Section, Paul Samwell-Smith, and Roy Halee

Musicians

Pete Carr—guitar

Jimmy Johnson—electric guitar

David Hood—bass

Roger Hawkins—drums

Barry Beckett—keyboard

Cornell Dupree—guitar

Gordon Edwards—bass

Paul Griffin—piano

Rick Marotta—drums

The Dixie Hummingbirds—vocal group

Allen Toussaint—horns arrangement

Rev. Claude Jeter—falsetto voice

Onward Brass Band—horns

David Spinozza—guitar

Alexander Gafa—guitar

Bob Cranshaw—electric bass

Richard Davis—acoustic bass

Grady Tate—drums

Bobby James—keyboard

Bobby Scott—piano

Don Elliot—vibes

Quincy Jones—strings

Del Newman—strings

Airto Moreira—percussion

Maggie Roche—vocals

Terre Roche—vocals

Jerry Pucket—guitar

Vernie Robbins—bass

James Stroud—drums

Carson Witsett—organ

July 1973: "Kodachrome"/"Tenderness" (Columbia 45859)

September 1973: "American Tune"/"One Man's Ceiling Is Another Man's Floor" (Columbia 45900)

October 1973: "Loves Me Like a Rock"/"Learn How to Fall" (Columbia 45907)

April 1974: *Live Rhymin'* (Columbia LP PC 32855)

"Me and Julio Down by the Schoolyard"

"Homeward Bound"

"American Tune"

"El Condor Pasa" (If I Could) (D. Robles / J. Milchberg / Paul Simon)

"Duncan"

"The Boxer"

"Mother and Child Reunion"

"The Sound of Silence"

"Jesus Is the Answer" (A. and S. Crouch)

"Bridge Over Troubled Water"

"Loves Me Like a Rock"

"America"

Musicians

Urubamba and the Jessy Dixon Singers

December 1975: *Still Crazy After All These Years* (Columbia LP PC 33540)

"Still Crazy After All These Years"

"My Little Town" (duet with Art Garfunkel)

"I Do It for Your Love"

"50 Ways to Leave Your Lover"

"Night Game"

"Gone at Last" (duet with Phoebe Snow)

"Some Folks' Lives Roll Easy"

"Have a Good Time"

"You're Kind"

"Silent Eyes"

Produced by: Paul Simon and Phil Ramone

Musicians

Barry Beckett—electric piano

David Hood—bass

Roger Hawkins—drums

Mike Brecker—saxophone

Bob James—woodwind and string arrangements

Pete Carr—electric guitar
Ralph McDonald—percussion
Dave Matthews—horn arrangements
Joe Beck—guitar
Jerry Friedman—guitar
Tony Levin—bass
Steve Gadd—drums
Sivuca—accordion and vocal solo
Ken Asher—electric piano
Hugh McCracken—guitar
John Tropea—guitar;
Valerie Simpson—vocals

Patti Austin—vocals
Toots Thielans—harmonica
Richard Tee—piano
Gordon Edwards—bass
Grady Tate—drums
Jessy Dixon Singers—vocals
Dave Sanborn—sax
Eddie Daniels—sax
Phil Woods—sax
Leon Pendarvis—piano
the Chicago Community
    Choir—vocals

October 1975: "Gone at Last"/"Take Me to the Mardi Gras" (Columbia 10197)

December 1975: "50 Ways to Leave Your Lover"/"Some Folks' Lives Roll Easy" (Columbia 10270)

May 1976: "Still Crazy After All These Years"/"I Do It for Your Love" (Columbia 10332)

December 1977: *Greatest Hits, Etc.* (Columbia LP JC 35032)

"Slip Slidin' Away"
"Stranded in a Limousine"
"Still Crazy After All These Years"
"Have a Good Time"
"Duncan"
"Me and Julio Down by the
    Schoolyard"
"Something So Right"

"Kodachrome"
"I Do It for Your Love"
"50 Ways to Leave Your Lover"
"American Tune"
"Mother and Child Reunion"
"Loves Me Like a Rock"
"Take Me to the Mardi Gras"

Produced by: Various

Musicians

See albums above plus (tracks 1, 2, 11) Ralph McDonald—percussion
Anthony Jackson—bass
Steve Gadd—drums
Richard Tee—piano
The Oak Ridge Boys—vocals

Gordon Edwards—bass
Randy Brecker—trumpet
Marvin Stamm—trumpet
Irvin Markowitz—trumpet

Michael Brecker—sax   Richard Sortomme—violin
David Sanborn—sax   Janet Hamilton—Cello
Lou Delgado—sax   Alfred Brown—Viola
Kathy Kienke—violin

December 1977: "Slip Slidin' Away"/"Something So Right" (Columbia 10630)

February 1977: "Stranded in a Limousine"/"Have a Good Time" (Columbia 10711)

The *There Goes Rhymin' Simon* album had already acquainted audiences to Simon's penchant for musical shifts, as it twisted through gospel ("Loves Me Like a Rock") and Dixieland ("Take Me to the Mardi Gras"), horns by New Orleans legend Allen Toussaint ("Tenderness") and strings by Quincy Jones ("Something So Right"). The live show would simply broaden that palette even further.

The band lineup was the first eye-opener, as Simon recruited Urubamba and the Jessy Dixon Singers to the stage—a far cry, as he admitted, from past outings. He told the UK newspaper Sounds: "All I've ever worked with is one other voice and a guitar and this is great, I love it. I get off easy because I have a group to play with, people to sing and play with."

Neither would the tour run according to the traditional schedule of concurrent dates. Rather, it was broken into three separate bursts of action, each one followed by a sizable break before heading back onto the road. So a string of American shows in May and June was swiftly followed by a brief European sojourn and two trips to London, first to headline the Palladium, and then the Royal Albert Hall. Another round of American shows, this time concentrating on colleges, occupied much of October and November. And it all wrapped up with Simon's first-ever shows in Japan in April 1974.

The tour would also be preserved, for those listeners who lose patience with the lo-fi hum of so many bootlegs, on the *Live Rhymin'* album, released in March 1974 and recorded for the most part at Nassau Veterans Memorial Coliseum in New York on July 10, 1973.

Unfortunately, for those who thrilled to the full ninety-minute, twenty-four song set that awaited concert goers, the album gave space to

Paul's first Japanese tour was headline news in the local music press.   *Author's collection*

just twelve songs (two more were added to its CD reissue)—and not necessarily all of the highlights, either. The two songs that Simon performed with Urubamba, and his full performance with the Jessy Dixon Singers were intact—indeed, the latter consumed the entire second side of the album.

But the guests' own performances were shorn, and there was no space, either, for "Run That Body Down," "Mrs. Robinson," and more. Indeed, at a time when double and even triple live albums were becoming the industry norm, and with the mega success of Peter Frampton's *Comes*

Alive album less than eighteen months away, it seems remarkable that an artist of Simon's stature, heading up a performance of so much versatility, should be denied a double of his own.

The result, while exhilarating, is nevertheless a disappointment.

Still Crazy in Concert

It would be 1975 before Simon returned to the record-release racks, with *Still Crazy After All These Years,* and just as long before he returned to the road.

He arranged a far more relaxed schedule this time, a few handfuls of shows at home and abroad, crowned in December by a four-night return to the London Palladium.

Paul's second solo album, released in 1975.

Author's collection

It was a slick show, tight and well rehearsed *too* well, according to one concert-goer at the latter venue. Penny Valentine, writing in the UK magazine *Street Life*, recalled: "One member of the audience thought it was all a bit too neat and careful. A note was thrown, a cry of 'read it' heard." Simon did so but did not appear happy with the words. "Will you play some different songs—not just prearranged?" Valentine continued, "There was a sharp intake of breath from the audience that sounded like a long disquieted hiss."

"How rude," said Simon as he put the note down. Then he asked, "Would it suffice if I re-arranged the pre-arranged songs?"

He looked, concluded Valentine, "like he was walking on broken glass in bare feet."

That tour preluded the longest performing silence of Simon's career so far, the four year hiatus that was finally broken by *One-Trick Pony*—his first for new label Warner Brothers—by which time, he had almost wholly turned his back on his sixties past.

The Performing Pony

"Me and Julio" still opened the set, and the Jessy Dixon combo was back. But the show was all but over before the familiar strains of "Bridge Over Troubled Water" disturbed an unbroken vista of solo numbers, and it would be the very end of the evening before "Mrs. Robinson," "The Boxer," and "The Sound of Silence" finally burst out. And then the lights went up and the evening had ended.

Following on the heels of both a less-than-lauded LP and a critical stiff of a movie, the *One-Trick Pony* tour was itself a tentative venture. Simon was joined by much the same band that he had recorded the album with—sometime Peter Gabriel sideman Tony Levin (bass), drummer Steve Gadd, guitarist Eric Gale, and pianist Richard Tee, a slimmed-back outfit compared to the sometimes sprawling aggregations that had accompanied him in the past, and a phenomenally tight unit, too.

But maybe they were too tight. Even at his most rehearsed, Simon had always succeeded in appearing at ease, as though every new song in the set was one that he had decided to play on the spur of the moment.

That sense was gone this time; even more so than in London on the previous outing, the show felt regimented and flat—faultless in so many departments that its very perfection felt uncomfortably slick.

By the time the tour reached its conclusion in London in November, for three nights at the Hammersmith Odeon, even Simon appeared bored with the familiarity—and, perhaps, disillusioned with the new material, the first damp squibs he had released since the days of Tom and Jerry.

His confidence was shattered. Worse than that, his songwriting had dried up. It wasn't the first time he had undergone a "dry spell," but this was a veritable drought. When he flew to Los Angeles to meet with the renowned psychiatrist Dr. Roderic Gorney, author of the recent *The Human Agenda*, Simon did not even realize he'd forgotten to bring the guitar that always accompanied him on his travels until the doctor asked him to write a song about how he felt.

Gorney lent him his, and Simon duly came up with "Allergies," a song whose very first line outlined his state of mind: "My hands can't touch a guitar string."

But Gorney's treatment worked. Simon told *Playboy*:

He was able to penetrate someone whose defenses were seemingly impenetrable. He was able to make me feel that I wasn't there to work just for the satisfaction of having a hit but that there was a contribution to be made. Of course, the reason I'd been blocked was that I felt what I did was of absolutely no importance. He was able to say, "I'm telling you that the way to contribute is through your songs. And it's not for you to judge their merits, it's for you to write the songs." For me, that was brilliant—and liberating.

Three or four days later, I went home. And I began writing.

Shortly after, Simon was in the studio with Warner Bros. staff producers Russ Titelman and Lenny Waronker, beginning work on a new album that once felt as though it would never be written.

It was still early in the sessions when Simon received a call from New York promoter Ron Delsener. The promoter was working with the city's parks commissioner on a new initiative to "clean up" Central Park—to rid it of its reputation as the murder and mugging capital of the city and return it to the people.

The Central Park Conservancy was a private nonprofit group set up to fund the clean-up and Delsener, in turn, was calling to ask whether Simon—whose own home overlooked the park—would be interested in playing a free concert there to raise awareness.

Simon agreed, but he was also concerned. As Delsener outlined the group's aims and the publicity that the concert would engender, it was clear this was going to be a mammoth event. Yet Simon's last album had been a (comparative) flop, and his movie a disaster.

Yes, people always came out for free concerts, but attendance figures weren't the be-all and end-all of such events. Perception and reaction mattered, too, and Simon knew that neither his last live show nor his current concert repertoire would cut it on what might well be the biggest stage he had ever appeared on.

He needed more.

This time, however, there would be no time to take stock. No matter that his own career was wallowing within an altogether unexpected slough, Art Garfunkel's entire life had sustained a massive blow.

In June 1979, at almost precisely the same time as his latest album, *Fate for Breakfast*, became his own first American flop, Garfunkel's long-term girlfriend, Laurie Bird, committed suicide—the singer was in Vienna at the time, shooting the movie *Bad Timing*.

Garfunkel withdrew completely. He stayed at home rereading Bird's diaries and took long vacations to Europe, riding a motorbike from city to city, falling in love again with art and architecture.

It would be 1981 before he resurfaced.

9

Simon and Art Reunion

During the making of *Bridge Over Troubled Water,* there were a lot of times when it just wasn't fun to work together. It became apparent by the time [Art's] movie was out, and by the time [the] album was out, that it was over."

Thus spake Simon in 1972, explaining to *Rolling Stone* why the most successful duo of the 1960s had sundered and was apparently destined to remain so. Indeed, with Garfunkel having ignited his career as an actor even before Simon and Garfunkel parted, it would be some three years before the singer even returned (albeit sporadically) to music.

Art Alone

By the time Art Garfunkel released his first solo album, *Angel Clare*, in 1973, Simon had already produced two platinum albums of his own, effortlessly following up the duo's earlier success and further confirming the critical impression that the duo was really all his own work.

Garfunkel fought back gallantly, however. *Angel Clare* remains one of *the* under-sung jewels of the early 1970s, a point that author Mo Daviau reinforces in her 2016 novel *Every Anxious Wave.*

The story's protagonists, Karl and Lena, are discussing music, and the latter brings up her love of Garfunkel: "Solo. Post Simon break-up. I think we can all agree that Simon had the writing talent, but Garfunkel had the under-appreciated vocal talent."

Daviau herself elaborates on that opinion.

I've been obsessed with the album Angel Clare for years. My mom played it in the car when I was little—we were very much a Simon and Garfunkel family, with equal opportunity for both Simon and Garfunkel.

I guess *Angel Clare* got stuck in the happy childhood memory center of my brain. It's such an odd album—radio-ready hits + murder ballads + covers of African pop songs. It would be a bold combination of songs by today's standards, such that I can't see a major label green lighting such a mishmash. I don't agree with the notion that Simon was the talent and Garfunkel was the also-ran. Garfunkel had the big voice—he was cantor at his own bar mitzvah, after all.

Angel Clare went Gold, and Garfunkel's follow-up, *Breakaway*, turned Platinum, one of the biggest albums of 1975 and still one of the most exquisite records he (or anyone else) has ever made. Even today, it is hard to conjure a more perfect moment in pop history than when, during his version of Beach Boy Bruce Johnston's "Disney Girls," Garfunkel unleashes all the joy and celebration in his voice with the line "Love—get up, guess what, I'm in love with a girl I found."

She's really swell and so's the entire LP—and, as if to add to the sense of occasion, it was recorded in the midst of a brief reunion with Simon.

The duo recorded one song together, Simon's nostalgia-draped "My Little Town," and Garfunkel later described the sessions as something of a chore. He recalled how Simon sidelined almost all his suggested contributions to the performance (which the pair were nominally co-producing) and still complained afterward that Garfunkel had spoken up too often. But it was a tremendous performance, so much so that while the track was originally intended for Art's album alone, it was then shoehorned into Simon's own latest (*Still Crazy*) at the record company's insistence.

In the battle of the sales sheets, though, Garfunkel streaked ahead. "My Little Town" was an inevitable hit, although not as huge as it perhaps ought to have been; it made number nine on the Top 100. It was elsewhere that *Breakaway* impressed, as Garfunkel's cover of the Flamingos' 1959 hit "I Only Have Eyes for You" topped the British chart; as the title track effectively launched the hit-making career of its writers, Gallagher and Lyle; and as Richard Perry's pristine production set a benchmark toward which the AOR boom of the mid- to late 1970s never tired of aspiring.

Simon had nothing but bile for *Breakaway*, publicly complaining that it lacked "bite," and Garfunkel acknowledged that the criticism hurt. But when Simon invited him to join him on *Saturday Night Live*, Garfunkel agreed, and when the British music paper *Melody Maker* asked whether this sudden burst of activity perhaps presaged a full-fledged reunion, Garfunkel seemed cautiously optimistic.

"Yes, it would seem to indicate that. There is a chance that we might get together to record an album, but I really can't say any more because there is no more answer."

By the end of the year, however, the partnership had again sundered, and when the duo appeared at the 1977 BRIT Awards ceremony to perform "Old Friends," most viewers reported that they scarcely looked at one another.

They did, however, make amends with a genuinely warm performance of the same song on Simon's 1977 television special (see chapter 10), and they also paired up for a lighthearted sketch, with Charles Grodin playing a director, and Simon—who wrote the piece—perhaps speaking more directly to Garfunkel than he had in a long time.

"It's so easy to sing with Artie," Simon had mused before the 1975 reunion soured. "It's something I'd done all my life." Now, he was to go even further.

"You know," Grodin tells the pair. "The sound of you and Artie singing together is so much better than the sound of either one of you singing alone that whatever petty differences you have had in the past, I strongly urge that you take a long, hard look at them."

Or perhaps he was simply parodying the attitude of the outside world—for example, the movie houses that, three years later, insisted on running Simon's *One-Trick Pony* as a double bill with Garfunkel's latest film, Nicholas Roeg's *Bad Timing*.

Breakaway was the peak of Garfunkel's seventies. His 1977 album *Watermark* was the follow-up in chronology alone, while *Fate for Breakfast* performed even worse, at least at home. Its UK success offered some solace, however, and Garfunkel was clearly in the process of picking himself up again, only for Laurie Bird's suicide to send him spiraling into darkness.

It was Paul Simon who pulled him back again. As Garfunkel put it, "It felt as if he was saying 'we can't leave Artie to waste away on his own.'"

Let's Go to the Park

Simon's suggestion that the pair of them reunite for a benefit concert in Central Park *was* an act of kindness, but it was not a gesture that either artist's advisors would have rejected, particularly at that point.

Offers for Simon and Garfunkel to re-form had been a regular part of their postbag for years, but they could always be held at bay by the success of the pair's solo careers. Even as *Fate for Breakfast* crumbled in America, it was a massive hit in the United Kingdom, going so far as to spawn a number one hit in the form of "Bright Eyes," the theme to the massively successful animated movie version of Richard Adams's novel *Watership Down*.

Onstage at the Central Park free concert.   *Photofest*

But it was also clear that both artists were, if only temporarily, some way removed from the golden pomp and circumstance that had once attended their every utterance—that radio, when it played a Paul Simon composition, was more likely to refer back to his sixties opuses than the majority of his seventies output. A reunion of what was still the single most successful duo in rock history could only be a victory all around.

Simon's initial approach to Garfunkel was intended to be tentative. Garfunkel, however, leaped at the prospect; not only that, but they talked, too, about the problems they'd experienced when trying to work together in the recent past and agreed to work around those as well.

Back when he was still considering trying to pull off a solo performance, Simon initially intended gifting Central Park with a solid greatest hits set and hoped that would be sufficient to assure a successful event. But mere hope was not enough. An event this massive required more than that.

The greatest hits set was still paramount in Simon's mind, but with Garfunkel involved, it became a very different proposition. Either he effectively admitted that his own material had less resonance with the duo's songs and performed a solo set first, before ushering on Garfunkel for "the climax," or he eschewed that notion, got the duo's set out of the way first, and then completed the show as a solo artist. In which case, he ran the risk of becoming an anticlimax.

It was his friend Lorne Michaels, of television's *Saturday Night Live*, who offered up the most obvious solution. Why not turn the entire show into a Simon and Garfunkel reunion?

It was only a one-off event, after all, and it was for a cause that Simon held dear. It would neither impact on the remainder of his solo career nor give future audiences false expectations. And, as Simon listened, he realized that it made the most sense.

More than that, it would be a historical milestone—their first full show together since 1970. It could be filmed (by Michaels's own production company) and recorded; a live album and a television special both seemed the least that the event could demand.

With all concerned vowing to keep the reunion secret, plans went ahead for the show to take place on September 19, 1981. Now it was down to Simon and Garfunkel to decide how they wanted to present themselves.

For Garfunkel, that was easy—two voices and a guitar, with a pianist waiting in the wings for the inevitable "Bridge Over Troubled Water." Simon, however, demurred. Calcium deposits in his fingers had temporarily rendered guitar playing a painful exercise for more than a few songs. A two-hour set would cripple him.

Plus, he also intended to perform half a dozen examples of his own solo material, and much of that was written with accompanying musicians in mind.

Garfunkel agreed to the expanded band but countered by introducing some of his solo work too.

The arguments continued. Simon wanted to use his regular musicians; Garfunkel wanted to use his. Simon had his ideas for song arrangements; Garfunkel again had his. Even as news broke of the upcoming event, with a full-page ad in the *New York Times* a week before the show, there were still disputes simmering beneath the surface of the rehearsals at the Beacon Theater.

But, finally, consensus was reached on the major points—and that included the lineup of the band: a pair of drummers, Steve Gadd and Grady Tate; two guitarists, Pete Carr and David Brown; bassist Anthony Jackson; pianist Richard Tee; synthesizer player Rob Mounsey; and a four-man horn section.

The Concert in Central Park (Warner Brothers LP 2BSK 3654)

Recorded September 19, 1981, Central Park, New York City

"Mrs. Robinson"

"Homeward Bound"

"America"

"Me and Julio Down by the Schoolyard"

"Scarborough Fair"

"April Come She Will"

"Wake Up Little Susie" (Felice and Boudleaux Bryant)

"Still Crazy After All These Years"

"American Tune"

"Late in the Evening"

"Slip Slidin' Away"

"A Heart in New York" (Benny Gallagher and Graham Lyle)

"Kodachrome"—Maybelline (Chuck Berry, Russ Fratto, Alan Freed)
"Bridge Over Troubled Water"
"50 Ways to Leave Your Lover"

"The Boxer"/"Old Friends"
"The 59th Street Bridge Song" (Feelin' Groovy)
"The Sound of Silence"

Produced by: Simon, Garfunkel, Phil Ramone, and Roy Halee

Musicians

Steve Gadd and Grady Tate—drums
Paul, David Brown, and Pete Carr—guitars
Anthony Jackson—bass
Richard Tee—keyboards

Rob Mounsey—synthesizer
John Gatchell and John Eckert—trumpets
Dave Tofani and Gerry Niewood—saxophones

Arrangements: Paul Simon, David Matthews, and Dave Grusin

May 1982: "Wake Up Little Suzie"/"Me and Julio Down by the Schoolyard" (Warner Brothers WBS50053)

With six days to go before the show, the New York City Department of Parks and Recreation announced it was expecting 300,000 people at the show. The day before, while Simon was telling the *New York Times* that they were "back from the boulevard of broken duos," that estimate was upped to half a million.

He even acknowledged the possibility of the show merely preluding a full-blown tour, just so long as everybody enjoyed themselves, musicians and audience alike. "Fun," he was adamant, "is the key to this whole thing."

A cloudy day did not deter the crowds; the first were gathering around the stage before first light had even broken, staking out the optimum roost for what promised to be a long day. By late afternoon, the streets outside were choked with later arrivals; by evening, one of the largest outdoor crowds New York City had ever seen had transformed Central Park into a city of its own.

New York City Mayor Ed Koch strode out onto a stage that looked for all the world like a classic city rooftop—asphalt, chimney, ventilation pipes, water tower—created by *Saturday Night Live* set designer Eugene Lee. After a quick introduction, a green door opened and out walked Simon and Garfunkel, the latter in the lead, fists raised high, and Simon grinning in his wake, clutching his guitar. He was already strumming the introduction to "Mrs. Robinson" as they arrived at their microphones.

"Homeward Bound," "America," a surprising duet through "Me and Julio Down by the Schoolyard," a gentle "Scarborough Fair." The band behind them had the lightest touch—all eyes and ears were on the duo.

Their every move chronicled on camera by Michael Lindsay Hogg, the director behind some of the most storied music videos and films of the seventies, they drifted through "April She Will Come" and then turned the clock back even further with a joyful "Wake Up Little Susie." Simon alone would sing "Still Crazy After All These Years," but Garfunkel was still on the stage, and it was he who opened "American Tune"—just as a few people, back when the song was first released, always said he should have.

"A Heart in New York" spun from Garfunkel's just-released *Scissor Cut*. Simon introduced a new song, "The Late, Great, Johnny Ace"—a reflection on, among other things, his time in London and the murder of John Lennon, just a few blocks away the previous December. "Kodachrome" turned into Chuck Berry's "Maybelline" and "Bridge Over Troubled Water" arrived a lot sooner than anyone expected—even before "50 Ways to Leave Your Lover"!

But the closing straight was flawless: "The Boxer," "Old Friends," "The 59th Street Bridge Song," and what else could they have ended with but "The Sound of Silence"? And what could they have encored with but one of the loveliest numbers from *One-Trick Pony*, "Late in the Evening"?

How did it go? Garfunkel was unhappy with the sound; Simon agreed that it could have been better. They hadn't failed, but they hadn't triumphed, either—or so they thought until the following morning's newspaper headlines hit the streets.

Had it really been the biggest concert audience since Woodstock? Was the show truly a cultural milestone? Had they really reawakened every positive spirit for which nostalgia now celebrated the sixties? That's what the headlines said had taken place, and it was certainly the most successful venture that either of them had been involved with since they parted company in 1970. Maybe they could do it again?

In perfect harmony at Central Park.   *Photofest*

Now the pieces fell into place. Simon contacted Mort Lewis, the duo's former manager, and asked him to get back on the horse. Simon and Garfunkel, after all, had never officially split up; therefore Lewis had never officially retired.

By the end of their first meal together, the trio were fervently discussing a two-year world tour that would kick off with their first-ever gigs together in Japan. The Central Park film would be given a full theatrical release. The live album would become a reality, released in the United States by Simon's current label, Warner Brothers, and elsewhere through Garfunkel's continued relationship with Columbia.

Simon was even reconsidering that album he had started with Lenny Waronker and Russ Titelman (see chapter 8). Rolling Stone interviewed him shortly after the Central Park show and, asking Simon about his latest compositions, must have been gratified to hear his reply. "The songs are more like stories now. They're like Simon and Garfunkel songs." Shortly after, Garfunkel was in the studio with Simon adding his vocal to one of the new numbers.

Simon and Garfunkel returned to the road in early May 1982, with five nights in Japan—two in Osaka, three in Tokyo. Then it was on to Europe, with an even more expansive repertoire than that which so thrilled Central Park (see sidebar), and an onstage rapport that had completely overcome any first-night nerves that either had been prey to in New York City. Now both looked and felt like "the real thing."

Simon and Garfunkel were back.

European Tour 1982

"Mrs. Robinson"

"Homeward Bound"

"America"

"Me and Julio Down by the Schoolyard"

"Scarborough Fair"

"My Little Town"

"Wake Up Little Susie"

"Still Crazy After All These Years"

"Bright Eyes"

"Late in the Evening"

"Slip Slidin' Away"

"El Condor Pasa" (If I Could)

"Late in the Evening"

"50 Ways to Leave Your Lover"

"American Tune"

"The Late Great Johnny Ace"

"Kodachrome"

"Bridge Over Troubled Water"

"The Boxer"

"Old Friends"

"The 59th Street Bridge Song" (Feelin' Groovy)

"Cecilia"

"Sound of Silence"

"All I Have to Do Is Dream"

They continued work on that new album, too. Most of the basic tracks had already been completed when the reunion got underway;

now, Warners were readying themselves to unleash a full-fledged Simon and Garfunkel album, tentatively titled *Think Too Much* and scheduled to be released on the eve of the American leg of the tour the following summer, 1983.

It would not be completely locked into the past. With Titelman and Waronker already aboard as producers, Simon would not allow Garfunkel his customary role of co-producer; in return, he agreed that his partner could write and arrange his own harmonies.

But the studio was where things started to go awry. Sources claim that Garfunkel began turning up late in the studio, and when he did arrive, he would unleash new ideas and harmonies that he had never discussed with the song's composer.

Whether he was trying to sabotage the session, or simply assert his own equal share of the album, was unclear to anyone. But the mood slowly began to shift, from open cooperation to jealous possessiveness. No matter that his contributions invariably improved the performances and added entirely new dimensions to the music. Simon could never countenance such blatant hijacking of his own vision.

He admitted to *Playboy* that he'd had doubts "from the start," going on to say: "At first I thought, I really can't do it: These new songs are too much about my life to have anybody else sing them." (He later described the lyrics as the best he'd ever written.)

At first he tried to see things Garfunkel's way. No, the songs didn't deal with events in his own life, but he could understand the emotions behind them. He knew what it meant to be in love and pain. "I'm a singer," he told Simon. "I'm able to interpret. That's what I do."

Simon agreed but insisted that he would have final say over what the final tracks sounded like. Garfunkel's response? "You're dampening my enthusiasm because of your ambivalence."

Garfunkel was smoking heavily and that, too, slowed down the sessions, as his voice became so weakened that he needed days, even weeks, between studio dates to allow it to recover. Sessions that had been expected to be over before Christmas were still incomplete in the New Year. But the final straw came when Garfunkel announced that he needed to take some time off on his own.

He had recently been smitten by the walking bug, setting out on treks that would see him traverse entire countries on foot, albeit a week or so at a time. He would walk until he'd had enough, fly home, and then, when he was ready to resume, return to the point he'd last visited and continue on from there.

His latest quest was to walk to the Pacific coast from his apartment on Fifth Avenue, and his only concession to the schedule was that he'd work out all his harmonies while he did so. But, apparently, he didn't.

Think Too Much was never going to make its springtime debut; the tour would have to go ahead without it. As the American dates got under-way in Akron, Ohio, however, a number of the songs intended for the new album were in the show, regardless. The title track—"Allergies"—"Cars Are Cars," "Song About the Moon," "René and Georgette Magritte with Their Dog After the War," and, as expected, "The Late Great Johnny Ace" all made appearances during the outing, although new material was gener-ally confined to just three or four songs per evening.

The remainder of the set had been shuffled, too: "Cecilia" now opened the show before bleeding into "Mrs. Robinson," and the old Danleers' hit "One Summer Night" (1958) had been added to the show to celebrate its title being commandeered to name the tour itself.

Finally, "I Only Have Eyes for You" had replaced "Bright Eyes" as Garfunkel's sole solo contribution to the show—the latter, after all, had made sense in Europe where it was by far his biggest hit ever. But in the United States, it was still the old *Breakaway* favorite that was regarded as his opus, often receiving even more applause from audiences than many of Simon's seventies efforts.

The nature of the venues that they were visiting saw the arrange-ments, too, shift away from the more genteel approach that had won so many hearts at Central Park and toward a rockier, punchier outing that was especially noticeable on Simon's solo material.

Indeed, it seems strange, given the sheer breadth of material that was available to the duo and the still-breathing hopes for a future between them, that Simon should continue to insist that fully one-fifth of the set should comprise songs associated with him alone. Almost as if he knew, deep down inside, that the partnership was destined to fall apart once again, and he needed to continue preparing for a solo future.

Not that there were any other outward manifestations of such pessimism. The stage show was tremendous, with video screens conveying the onstage action to the furthest reaches of the gigantic stadiums in which the duo were playing.

There was a state-of-the-art sound system and, again, designer Eugene Lee's city rooftop stage set. In fact, the entourage was carrying two identical stages around the country; while one was in use at one show, the other would already be getting assembled at the next venue.

The tour itself was successful. Audiences were as ecstatic as the venues were full, and reviews overflowed with love for the duo. "I sang great, Artie sang great" was a typical Simon comment to the media when he was asked how a particular show had gone.

Behind the scenes, however, all was not well. *Think Too Much* was still far behind schedule, and Garfunkel was showing no more interest in completing his share of the work than he had been before he set out on his walking tour.

Finally, Simon had to concede defeat, meeting with Warners (where Waronker was now label president) to tell them there was no way the project could continue.

Nothing about the album felt right; nothing that Garfunkel brought to the sessions meshed with Simon's own vision of what he had increasingly come to realize was an especially personal set of songs.

He knew that a lot of people would be disappointed—not least of all Waronker, Titelman, and the ever-faithful Roy Halee; in those innocent days when superstar reunions were considerably less epidemic than they are today, Simon and Garfunkel's re-formation was probably as big as such an event could get—particularly now, because of Lennon's death, that the dream of the Beatles was off the table.

It was an age, too, when mainstream pop felt more superficial and facile than it ever had in the past—a consequence of any number of outside factors, but the twin demons of MTV-style pop videos and increasingly aggressive studio technology were certainly among them. It felt, sometimes, as though it was impossible to switch on the radio without being assailed by this drum sound, that keyboard sound, this vocal effect, that production technique, as though every musician was suddenly working from the same everything-but-the-kitchen-sink phrasebook, and some were throwing in the kitchen sink as well.

A Simon and Garfunkel reunion might not have proven an actual antidote to all of that, but it would have offered an alternative. The handful of *Think Too Much* songs that could be called nearly complete, although nobody outside of the studio would ever get to hear them, were exquisite—a recounting of all that had made Simon and Garfunkel so peerless in the past yet in no way beholden to that past. It had taken thirteen years, but they were finally on their way to creating the follow-up record that *Bridge Over Troubled Water* had always required.

The official double LP release of the central Park concert.   *Author's collection*

Now Simon was knocking it on the head. Onstage a few nights later, he would introduce what would have been its title track, "Think Too Much," and admit, "We both did it this time."

He was unrepentant, and immovable, too. He wiped all his vocals from the tapes and would be completing the album alone. It would be released in the fall as a Paul Simon solo record.

The tour was still underway at the time.

Simon's own mood lifted considerably once the deed was done; it was raised, too, by his marriage in his New York apartment on August 16, 1983, to longtime girlfriend Carrie Fisher, the subject of many of the new album's songs. (Dashingly, Simon proposed to her during a baseball game.)

In Houston, the first show after their nuptials, Fisher even joined her husband onstage to sing, and Simon was positively beaming through the remainder of the tour—something he'd not been able to do onstage for a long time.

He joked about his demeanor. "The 59th Street Bridge Song (Feelin' Groovy)," he announced one evening, "[was written] one day when I was in a good mood. And today here again. Two good moods! Two decades!"

Whether that glee would be long-lived, however, was an altogether different question. Robbed of what had been one of the most eagerly anticipated records of the year, the public turned against its "replacement," *Hearts and Bones*, with unforgiving bitterness.

The single "Allergies" collapsed at number forty-four; the album halted at number thirty-five. Even among the people who did buy it, but who had heard at least part of its contents on the road in recent months, it was impossible to escape a soupçon of bewilderment and the sense that they had been cheated.

This could have been a once-in-a-generation LP. Instead it was just another Paul Simon record, albeit one featuring guest appearances from Philip Glass and Chic.

The collapse of *Hearts and Bones* effectively marked the end of an era that had never truly been given the chance to begin. And more than one pop prophet smiled smugly when the news was announced, as if to remind the world "I told you so."

They Thought Too Much

December 1983: *Hearts and Bones* (Warner Brothers 9 23942-1)

"Allergies"

"Hearts and Bones"

"When Numbers Get Serious"

"Think Too Much" (b)

"Song About the Moon"

"Think Too Much" (a)

"Train in the Distance"

"René and Georgette Magritte with Their Dog After the War"

"Cars Are Cars"

"The Late Great Johnny Ace"

Produced by: Paul Simon, Russ Titelman, and Roy Halee; tracks 1, 5, 10 co-produced by: Lenny Waronker

Recorded in: North Hollywood and New York City

Musicians

Dean Parks—guitar

Al Di Meola—guitar

Anthony Jackson—contrabass guitar

Steve Gadd—drums

Steve Ferrone—drums

Greg Phillinganes—Fender Rhodes

Rob Sabino—synthesizer

Rob Mounsey—synthesizer, vocoder

Airto Moreira—percussion

Dave Matthews—horn arrangements

Richard Tee—Fender Rhodes

Michael Mainieri—vibes and marimba

Eric Gale—guitar

Anthony Jackson—contrabass guitar

Tom Coppola—synclavier

Marcus Miller—bass

Nile Rodgers—guitar

Bernard Edwards—bass

Jeff Porcaro—drums

Jess Levy—cello

Peter Gordon—french horn

Mark Rivera—alto sax

Wells Christie—synclavier

The Harptones—background vocal

George Delerue—orchestral arrangements

Sid McGinnis—guitar

Michael Boddicker—synthesizer

Philip Glass—orchestration

Michael Reisman—synthesizer

Carol Wincenc—flute

George Marge—bass clarinet

Marin Alsop—violin

Frederick Zlotkin—cello

Jill Jaffe—viola

Back for More

Few people would have expected the duo to bounce back from the traumas of *Think Too Much*, but they would. In 1989, Simon and Garfunkel were nominated for inclusion in the Rock and Roll Hall of Fame—still an infant at the time, but one whose authoritative stance on who matters, and who doesn't, in the annals of pop history was growing increasingly strident.

On this occasion, at least, one of the most common complaints about the Hall of Fame's induction policy—that one act was voted into the hall ahead of the one that most influenced them—could not be applied; Don and Phil Everly were there among the Hall's first-ever intake, alongside Chuck Berry, Fats Domino, Elvis Presley, Buddy Holly, and Simon and Garfunkel's equally beloved Alan Freed.

The Beatles and the Rolling Stones were in there, too, and the previous year saw Bob Dylan enter the annals. Now it was Simon and Garfunkel's turn, in the first year in which they were eligible (the twenty-fifth anniversary of their "official" launch under that name), and on January 18, 1990, they took their place alongside fellow newcomers Louis Armstrong, the Who, the Platters, the Kinks, the Four Tops, Holland-Dozier-Holland, and Simon's old demo partners, Carole King and Gerry Goffin.

James Taylor welcomed the duo to the podium, and anybody who had wondered whether the pair would be able to maintain civil relations for the time they were on stage may have received a little justification from the odd sense of distance that appeared to separate them from one another.

Garfunkel stepped onto the podium and fiddled with the microphone. "It's mic height," he explained. "That's what broke up this group." Then he stepped aside for "the person who has most enriched my life by putting these great songs through me, my friend Paul, here."

Simon took the microphone. "Well, Arthur and I agree about almost nothing," he began. "But it's true. I have enriched his life quite a bit, now that I think about it."

But then he ventured down memory lane, recalling the music that had inspired their teenaged dreams, the DJs and the radio stations, the singer and the stars. All, he said, prompted them to "use our imaginations to figure out what were the connections. [Music] became the dominant interest in our lives, and to this day it's still fascinating all this time in my life I've never been bored."

It was a glorious evening. Future relations would, however, remain frosty. When Simon organized a concert of his own in Central Park in August 1991, just shy of the tenth anniversary of his last appearance there (see chapter 12), he turned down all of Garfunkel's overtures to transform it into another reunion.

As the *New York Times* put it: "Mr. Garfunkel did not disguise the hurt. 'I'm not good enough to be invited,' he told a reporter before leaving town."

10

That's Me on the TV

Amerian *American Bandstand* had only been on the air for a couple of months when Tom and Jerry made their debut on it on November 22, 1957. It had already established itself as the go-to show for American teenagers, however.

Launched on August 5, and airing for ninety minutes every afternoon, *American Bandstand* both made and displayed the biggest stars of the day. Some 200 different performers appeared on the show during its inaugural five-month run, and even a partial list reads like a who's who of the music that mattered at the time: the Everly Brothers, Buddy Holly, Gene Vincent, Jackie Wilson, Chuck Berry, Bill Haley and the Comets, Sam Cooke, Paul Anka, Jerry Lee Lewis, Bobby Darin, Frankie Avalon.

And Tom and Jerry, one in a long line of unknowns who were invited along to lip-synch through their latest single, in the hope that the performance might launch them to stardom. Well, it worked for Danny and the Juniors!

More than sixty years on, footage of that historical event remains one of the holy grails of music television archaeology, reminding us that it was as late as the 1980s before many television production companies realized that there was a market for "vintage" programming—that it was possible to monetize those shelves full of old tapes that were gathering dust in the basement. And only then, too, that the public became aware of just how much historical television footage had been "lost," which then turned out to be a polite way of saying wiped so that the tape could be reused.

We have no way of knowing precisely what befell the November 22, 1957, *American Bandstand*, with its precious footage of Tom and Jerry, Billy and Lily, Jerry Lee Lewis, and the remainder of the afternoon's performers. But sixty years on, the search is still underway.

A decade later, of course, and there were occasions when Simon and Garfunkel appeared to be all over the television. In the United States alone, they appeared on everything from the *The Ed Sullivan Show* to *The Kraft Music Hall*, *The Fred Astaire Show* to *The Smothers Brothers Comedy Hour*, *The Red Skelton Hour* to *Eenie Meenie Minee Schmo*, the national sensation *Hullabaloo* to the LA variety program *Shivaree*, and beyond. In fact, it was *Shivaree* that caused the pair to be thrown off an episode of Ed Sullivan!

As Simon explained to the *New Musical Express* a few weeks later: "There is a barring clause [in the *Ed Sullivan* contract] which says you must not have appeared on any other national TV show three weeks before *Sullivan*. We rehearsed on the Saturday, got through all the taping and that night *Shivaree* used a tape we had made for them two months ago! That meant we were off *Sullivan*. Now we refuse to do any teenage TV shows."

Overseas, the list of shows grows even longer—*Let's Sing Out* in Canada, Music Hall in France, *Twien* in the Netherlands, *Top of the Pops* in the United Kingdom, and more. British television's Granada franchise even gave the duo a thirty-minute television special in 1966, and that performance does still exist. The footage is a little foggy, but the sound quality is as spectacular as either of the "official" live recordings that have been released of the duo in their prime; and, of course, it was earlier than either of them.

The peak of Simon and Garfunkel's television work, however, is *Songs of America*.

Better remembered today for the convoluted controversy that surrounded its making and broadcast than for its actual content and quality, *Songs of America* now feels seems impossibly dated. How could anybody get so hung up about a bunch of recent news reels set to pop songs? Especially songs so generally unobjectionable as those of Simon and Garfunkel?

But maybe that's what gives this film its impact—and one deploys the present tense because it is still a breathtaking vision, half a century after its creation. Like the footage of war casualties appended to "Happy Xmas (War Is Over)" on John Lennon's *Lennon Legend* DVD anthology, *Songs of America* blisters because the songs are so sweet.

Art Garfunkel, thoughtful on the phone during *Songs of America*.
Photofest

Combining live performance with prefilmed footage cut through with conversational snippets that puncture the cuddliness even further, matching Vietnam to Woodstock, and allowing both Simon and Garfunkel to question the nature of fame and the point of life, *Songs of America* is usually summed up as "the one where they debuted 'Bridge Over Troubled Water.'" In fact, that's the least of its virtues.

Songs of America was originally commissioned, by CBS-TV, as a prime-time fifty-two minute special designed to coincide with the release of Simon and Garfunkel's then-gestating fifth album—the set that would eventually become *Bridge Over Troubled Water*.

Delays in that record's completion, of course, pushed the schedules far apart, but as early as their first meeting with filmmaker Robert Drew, the duo appear to have decided that a documentary about the mere making of a record was far down on their list of priorities.

Ten Key US TV Performances

1957: *American Bandstand* (Tom and Jerry)
"Hey, Schoolgirl"

1966: *The Ed Sullivan Show* (Simon and Garfunkel)
"I Am a Rock"

1966: *Hullabaloo* (Simon and Garfunkel)
"Homeward Bound"

1967: *The Smothers Brothers Comedy Hour* (Simon and Garfunkel)

"Cloudy"   "Overs" (two episodes)
"Homeward Bound"

1968: *Kraft Music Hall: Trio for Tonight* (Simon and Garfunkel)

"A Poem on the Underground Wall"   "The Sound of Silence"
"For Emily, Whenever I May Find Her" "The 59th Street Bridge Song" (Feelin'
"Overs"   Groovy) (with Victor Borge and
"Anji" (with Eddie Simon)   Nancy Wilson)
"Patterns"

1969: *The Bell Telephone Hour*/*Songs of America* (Simon and Garfunkel)

"America"   "The 59th Street Bridge Song (Feelin'
"So Long, Frank Lloyd Wright"   Groovy)"
"Bridge Over Troubled Water"   "Mystery Train"
"At the Zoo"   "For Emily, Whenever I May Find Her"
"Scarborough Fair"   "The Boxer"
"El Condor Pasa (If I Could)"   "Homeward Bound"
"Punky's Dilemma"   "America"
"Mrs. Robinson"   "Sound of Silence"
                                      "Song for the Asking"

1971: *Sesame Street*
"Me and Julio Down by the Schoolyard"/"El Condor Pasa" (If I Could)

1977: *The Paul Simon Special*

"Bridge Over Troubled Water"   "The Boxer"
"Still Crazy After All These Years"   "Slip Slidin' Away"
"Old Friends" (with Art Garfunkel)   "Something So Right"
"Loves Me Like a Rock"   "I Do It for Your Love"

1980: *The Muppet Show*

"Scarborough Fair"   "50 Ways to Leave Your Lover"
"El Condor Pasa (If I Could)"   "Baby Driver"
"Long Long Day"   "Loves Me Like a Rock"

1993: *MTV Unplugged*

"Born at the Right Time"   "Bridge Over Troubled Water"
"Me and Julio Down by the
    Schoolyard"   "Something So Right"
"Graceland"   "Boy in the Bubble"
"Still Crazy After All These Years"   "Late in the Evening"
"Mrs. Robinson"   "Homeward Bound"

They had, after all, been given carte blanche as far as the special's content was concerned. Like those other establishment figures who simply listened to the duo's music and appreciated it for its melodic gentleness, CBS (and sponsors AT&T) appear to have had no concept whatsoever that there might be any kind of subversive viper lurking within either Simon's or Garfunkel's breast.

But their commitment to the anti-war movement, and the general sense of antiestablishment fervor that dominated their generation's thinking, would never allow them to put their names to an anodyne hour of sweetness and light, and Robert Drew both knew and welcomed that.

His own background included the 1960 documentary about the Democratic primary race between John F. Kennedy and Hubert Humphrey in West Virginia, a production that has been cited as the birth of documentary vérité.

However, realizing that it was Simon who would be calling the conceptual shots here, he ultimately accepted the role of executive producer, handing the more direct role to actor Charles Grodin—untried as a director but a firm friend of the duo and a fellow supporter of the causes they wanted to illustrate.

The result, in the eyes of any conventional television executive, was chaos liberally peppered with racism, war, poverty, and pollution. The riots that shook American cities the previous year lined up alongside the political assassinations that robbed a generation of three of its leading figureheads—JFK, Bobby Kennedy, and Martin Luther King Jr.

It was polemic, plain and simple—a muddled, monstrous collage of modern news clips intercut with images of the lost world of America's bygone innocence.

But it worked—not, perhaps, as the slice of prime-time family entertainment that its creators' paymasters had dreamed of, nor as the kind of thing any average corporate executive would happily put his name to. But as an object lesson in the world as American liberal youth saw it, *Songs of America* was in turn witty, poignant, moving, and horrifying.

AT&T took one look and demanded all trace of political grandstanding be excised from the program. Simon and Garfunkel refused, so the grand old telephone company walked and took their $700,000 or so of sponsorship money with them.

CBS didn't lose faith; they had a contract to fulfill, after all. They also had Robert Redford to introduce the special with the words, "We think you'll find the next hour to be both entertaining and stimulating."

But Alberto-Culver, the beauty products manufacturer that stepped in to replace AT&T, may not have shared their acceptance even after they landed the sponsorship for a fraction of what AT&T had paid. By the time *Songs of America* arrived at its first commercial break, over a million viewers had changed the channel.

There was plenty of music, much of it performed specifically for the cameras, and much, too, making its public debut—a band rehearsal of "So Long, Frank Lloyd Wright"; "Bridge Over Troubled Water" playing out over footage of the assassins' bullets; "Cuba Si, Nixon No."

Viewers saw the duo in the studio, in hotel rooms, on and off the road. But they also saw starving children, weeping mourners, burning villages, bemused soldiers, body bags; and they heard both Simon and Garfunkel make remarks that, in all fairness, still feel faintly incomprehensible today. "The chaos of what the hell is the whole thing is a violent screaming reaction to the confusion of what is this thing?" was one of Garfunkel's choicest zingers.

Songs of America would never be rebroadcast, and within six months of its airing, Simon and Garfunkel were no more.

Paul Simon's solo television career began during his London sojourn. He was a guest on *Stramash*, a Scottish music show that aired during 1965–66, and performed "I Am a Rock" on *Ready Steady Go*, British TV's legendary Friday night music show—compulsory viewing at the time, and still regarded as one of the peaks of broadcast pop. "The weekend starts here," the show's opening credits insisted, and for many people, it did.

A lone Simon also appeared on *Dick Cavett* in April 1970, but of course Simon and Garfunkel was still officially a going concern at that time—that much is obvious from the studio band's insistence on playing a jaunty "The 59th Street Bridge Song (Feelin' Groovy)" as Simon walked onto the set.

Over the course of the twenty-minute interview, Simon broke down the writing of "Bridge Over Troubled Water" (the broadcast took place toward the end of his time teaching at NYU), discussed Garfunkel's movie career, chatted about baseball ("I used to be known as the spunky little left-hander"), and played a rocking "Mrs. Robinson."

But he did bat away some questions about the state of his relationship with his partner, although there would be plenty more to come when he returned to late-night TV the following June, for an appearance alongside Muhammad Ali and author William Peter Blatty, on Johnny Carson's *The Tonight Show*. (His performance that night of "Papa Hobo," sadly, is another that appears to be lost.)

He also made a wonderful appearance on *Sesame Street*, his intended solo rendering of "Me and Julio Down by the Schoolyard" accompanied by a little girl who insisted on singing her own lyrics—largely comprising "everybody dance"—to the music.

Live from New York

A handful of chat show appearances notwithstanding, Simon's most significant television broadcasts of the 1970s were probably his appearances on *Saturday Night Live*, which, in turn, set the stage for the eponymous TV special that he hosted in 1977.

Simon and the show's producer, Lorne Michaels, were introduced by Edie Baskin, the photographer Simon was dating at the time. Michaels was still working toward the fall 1975 launch of what was then called

Garfunkel (left) and Simon (right) with Chevy Chase on the *Saturday Night Live* set, 1975.
Photofest

NBC's Saturday Night, and he had hired Baskin as the venture's chief photographer.

Simon quickly became a familiar face around the *Saturday Night* office. He and Michaels had become immediate friends, and he was soon a part of the entire family too—writers Chevy Chase, John Belushi, Dan Aykroyd, and Rosie Shuster swiftly grew accustomed to him being present at meetings and even meals, with Aykroyd later admitting that if he was working on a joke, Simon was usually the best judge of its efficacy. "It's hard to get Paul to laugh [so] when he start[s] to snort, I said, 'Man, I got something.'"

There was talk that Simon would be the perfect host for the show's debut episode on October 11, 1975. Michaels, however, demurred—Simon could take the second show; George Carlin would handle the first, and so it transpired.

Nevertheless, a lot of media attention was focused upon Simon's upcoming appearance—and all the more so when it was announced that the show would also bring Simon and Garfunkel back together for the first time in three years.

That in itself was exactly the kind of publicity the newborn show required. However, as planning for the broadcast developed, a sense of unease set in among the show's regular cast. Very early into the show's gestation, it had been agreed that each week's musical guests, whether they were hosting the show or not, would have a couple of performance spots of their own but would otherwise be treated like any other visitor.

Simon and Michaels, however, had decided to completely up end that scenario. The reunion was only the icing on the musical cake—both Simon and Garfunkel would also be performing solo, and soon it was difficult not to sympathize with John Belushi when he complained, loudly, that "the folksinging wimp" hadn't simply taken over; he had torn up everything Saturday Night was supposed to be.

And so it transpired. Broadcast on October 18, the show opened with a solo Simon singing "Still Crazy After All These Years." (The album was on the very eve of release.) Chevy Chase squeezed in the "Live from New York, it's Saturday Night!" announcement, and then Simon returned, this time with the Jessy Dixon Singers for "Loves Me Like a Rock."

Randy Newman was next, singing his own "Sail Away," and while what we would now consider normal service was immediately resumed with the Weekend Update segment, it was followed by an overlong sketch revolving around Simon playing one-on-one basketball against the towering form of the Philadelphia 76ers' Connie Hawkins, with Simon saying: "I'm spotting him a one-foot, four-inch advantage. I gotta admit that's gonna be a factor in this game. He's got me on shooting ability, but I just have to play my game as I usually play it [and] stay with my strengths. Basically singing and songwriting."

And, at last, it was time for the reunion.

> Simon: "So Artie, you've come crawling back."
>
> Garfunkel: "It's very nice of you to invite me onto your show. Thanks a lot."
>
> Simon: "Movies are over now?"
>
> Garfunkel: "Yeah."
>
> Simon: "A little two-part harmony?"
>
> Garfunkel: "I'll try it again. See if it works this time."

If the opening exchange felt a little forced, however (not to mention, in places, a little spiteful, too), the music was flawless—first "The Boxer," which led into "Scarborough Fair," just their voices and guitars in the same perfect harmony they had always been, and then "My Little Town," the duet that would appear on both of their upcoming albums, and it was as if they both, simultaneously, were hit with the realization of exactly what was happening.

Simon and Garfunkel on a national television show, performing a brand new song together, for the first time in half a decade.

That October night was the first of (at the time of writing) eighteen performances Simon would make on *Saturday Night Live*. Most have been thoroughly enjoyable, a few have been memorable, and several have been positively historic.

There was the night in November 1976 when he duetted a couple of numbers with George Harrison. Lorne Michaels had famously offered the Beatles $3,000 (a ludicrously paltry amount, even then) to re-form for the show, and according to legend, Lennon and McCartney, who were watching the show together at Lennon's New York apartment, seriously considered taking him up on it.

They didn't, and even Michaels's offer of an extra $200 (!) did not persuade them. But when George Harrison guested on the show seven months later, he did jokingly ask for his $3,000—only to be informed that that was the offer for all four of them. His share would be $750.

The Beatle and the boy from Queens actually performed four songs together that night, but only two—Simon's "Homeward Bound" and Harrison's "Here Comes the Sun"—were broadcast. Decades later, *Guitar World* recalled the performance with all the fanfare it deserves: "There's something intimate and beautiful about the performances; pay close attention to Simon's harmonies on 'Here Comes the Sun,' Harrison's ethereal lead vocals on 'Homeward Bound' and his smooth little pentatonic lick at the very end of the clip (we also dig the phantom 7th chord heard during the last chorus of 'Homeward Bound'). And let's not forget those groovy sweaters."

There was the time Simon allowed himself to be dressed up as a turkey to sing "Still Crazy After All These Years" for that same 1976 Thanksgiving episode.

There was his appearance on October 13, 2018, with his farewell tour still fresh in the memory, now bidding farewell to the show he loved. With the yMusic combo behind him, he performed two songs, "Can't Run But" and, so movingly, "Bridge Over Troubled Water," to remind us, as *Consequence of Sound* remarked, "not only of what a profound talent Simon is but also what a unique contributor to the pop-culture world he's been for all the years that *Saturday Night Live* has been on the air." But even that paled alongside the night he performed "The Boxer" in the aftermath of 9/11 to the first responders who witnessed that awful day just a couple of weeks earlier.

"For me, Paul singing that song," Lorne Michaels reflected, "would capture the strength of the city and the emotion." And he was correct.

You cannot play favorites with events of such magnitude, but perhaps even more than his breathtaking performance at the Concert for America, that rendition of "The Boxer" remains among Paul Simon's most devastatingly beautiful, and meaningful, performances ever.

Simon Night Live

October 11, 1975 (filmed cameo)
October 18, 1975 (host and musical guest)
November 20, 1976 (host and musical guest)
October 29, 1977 (musical guest)
March 15, 1980 (musical guest)
May 10, 1986 (cohost [with Robin Williams] and musical guest)
November 22, 1986 (musical guest)
December 19, 1987 (host and musical guest)
November 17, 1990 (musical guest)
December 8, 1990 (cameo)
May 15, 1993 (musical guest)
October 22, 1994 (musical cameo)
November 4, 2000 (musical guest)
September 29, 2001 (musical cameo)
May 13, 2006 (musical guest)
May 14, 2011 (musical guest)
February 18, 2012 (cameo)
March 9, 2013 (cameo)
October 13, 2018 (musical guest)

The Less-Than-Special Special

It was early into his run of *Saturday Night Live* appearances, in 1977, that Simon and Michaels hatched the television spectacular that would become *The Paul Simon Special*. It was written by Simon, together with a host of more familiar comedy writers—SNL's own Chevy Chase, Al Franken, and Lily Tomlin were numbered among the crew, alongside Charles Grodin and Lorne Michaels himself—and was effectively a satirical look at the making of the special itself.

Grodin played the Lorne Michaels role, and turned in a tremendous performance—one of the highlights has to be his concern that some other Paul Simon, the artist, perhaps, or maybe the politician, might also be granted a TV special around the same time as this one, and they needed, therefore, to pinpoint Simon's identity for the audience. He suggests retitling the show *The Paul "Bridge Over Troubled Water" Simon Special*.

With Art Garfunkel making a surprise appearance (they delivered a terrific "Old Friends") and Simon turning in some similarly powerful performances, *The Paul Simon Special* is, it must be confessed, something of a time capsule as regards what late 1970s network television found funny, but no more so than *Saturday Night Live* itself.

Paul in the run-up to the release of *One-Trick Pony*.
Author's collection

Neither was it especially successful. Viewing figures were low, reviews lukewarm. In its wake, it would be three years before Simon resurfaced as a performer.

The eighties, however, would see him swiftly make up for lost time. A stunning appearance on *Midnight Special* in 1980 left many viewers wishing that *One-Trick Pony* had been released not as a studio album and movie but as a live recording—a mood that was only born out by the release that same year of Simon's first ever VHS tape, a film of his recent Philadelphia show.

He cohosted an edition of *Solid Gold* with Andy Gibb, and on April 25, 1981, he became the latest star to surprise the faithful with an appearance on *The Muppet Show*—in fact, he would be the last guest to be invited to perform the show's opening number. This is the episode, incidentally, in which Gonzo decides he wants to become a songwriter—a dream that Simon himself inspired.

But there would be no flashback to Simon's days teaching songwriting at NYU here. Not when his star pupil turns in lyrics the caliber of:

> For yooooouuuuuuu I'd wash my hair with stinky glue,
> I'd fry my legs and eat them too,
> I'd put a spider in my shoe—for yooooouuuuuuuu!

For his flabbergasted mentor, it probably comes as a relief when Gonzo's chickens arrive and spirit him away, sparing him from further torment at the hands of his pupil. It then transpires that Gonzo's ambitions were but a passing fancy—by the time Simon returns to his side, Gonzo has abandoned songwriting for a whole new obsession. Asparagus.

Simon remained, and remains, a television ubiquity—a familiar face in documentaries and a ready participant in charitable events (see chapter 17). He is always, it seems, turning up at awards events—usually to receive another addition to what must be a seriously overpopulated trophy cabinet; and, of course, he remains a reliable guest on television chat shows.

In just the last decade or so, he has shown up alongside Stephen Colbert, Jimmy Fallon, Charlie Rose, Oprah Winfrey, David Letterman, Michael Parkinson, Ellen DeGeneres, and more.

He appeared in a sketch for comic Louis C. K.'s 2016 web series *Horace and Pete*, portraying an alcoholic, and he wrote the show's theme music, too. And, of course, he has made a string of oft-lauded appearances on different music shows—among them, a breathtaking rendition of "Graceland" for the BBC's *Later with Jools Holland* in May 2006.

Here Comes *Graceland*

Graceland takes pride of position, too, almost every time Paul Simon's fans gather to discuss their own favorite television performance of all those that he has ever given, just as the album ranks high among his most important records. And, not surprisingly, it is another *Saturday Night Live* appearance, from 1986, that they choose.

Simon performed three songs that night: "The Late, Great Johnny Ace" was his closing number, following on from a buoyant "The Boy in the Bubble." But it was "Diamonds on the Soles of Her Shoes" that took the breath away.

Graceland was still some weeks shy of release at the time; what little that people knew of it was more hearsay and speculation than it was any actual awareness of the music. *Saturday Night Live*, then, was effectively its introduction to America—and, alongside that, the introduction of what many viewers would perceive as a whole new musical form.

The performance opened with the camera panning across the ten-strong lineup of the Ladysmith Black Mambazo choir, nearly identically dressed in matching orange shirts and white shoes. Behind them, Simon's South African band were hunched with their instruments; in front was Simon in a dark suit, clutching his guitar.

The choir began to chant; Simon began to sing. For a full minute, they continued a cappella before a moment's pause as the band crept in, a lilting ballad to which the choir now danced.

The rhythm was irresistible, the pace relentless. It didn't matter, even, that "Diamonds on the Soles of Her Shoes" is scarcely one of Simon's most accomplished creations as a song.

The arrangement, the visuals, the sheer dynamism of the performance—that's what made it matter, and almost twenty-five years later, Lorne Michaels still referred to the occasion as "a revolution in taste" in the United States.

"It was the synthesis of two cultures, and the obvious affection they had for Paul, and that Paul had for them. It was the perfect moment."

11

Graceland

If *Bridge Over Troubled Water* is universally acclaimed to be Simon and Garfunkel's masterpiece (and *Breakaway* is Art Garfunkel's), *Graceland* is far and away Paul Simon's most adored and considered solo release—all the more so since, before even a note of music had been heard outside of the studio, it was also on course to become one of the most controversial records of its age.

South Africa, in the seventies and especially the eighties, was an international pariah, and its all-white government's unapologetic policy of apartheid was condemned across the globe.

Engineered by the United Nations Anti-Apartheid Committee and encouraged by Artists Against Apartheid (an organization formed by South African media personality Dali Tambo, and Jerry Dammers of the band the Specials), embargoes and boycotts alike set the country adrift from the remainder of the "civilized" world. Sports organizations refused to visit; entertainers turned down the most lucrative invitations to play.

The UN General Assembly itself, in December 1980, passed Resolution 35/206, demanding "all states prevent all cultural, academic, sporting and other exchanges with South Africa," and insisting that "writers, artists, musicians and other personalities" boycott the country.

Sun City, the luxurious leisure resort built to cater for the tourists who never came, itself was the subject of scorn and ire; 1985 even saw producer Arthur Baker and E Street Band member Steven Van Zandt organize Artists Against Apartheid, a sprawling conglomeration of musicians united in the musical insistence "Ain't Gonna Play Sun City": reggae stars Jimmy Cliff and Big Youth; rappers Kool DJ Herc, Afrika Bambaataa, Kurtis Blow, Run DMC, and Grandmaster Melle Mel; funkateers Herbie Hancock and George Clinton; veteran rockers Bob Dylan, Lou Reed, Ringo Starr, Keith Richards, and Ronnie Wood; soul singers Bobby

Onstage at *Under African Skies*, 2012.   *Photofest*

Womack, Nona Hendryx, David Ruffin, and Eddie Kendricks; eighties superstars Pat Benatar, Peter Gabriel, Bob Geldof, Bono; punk rockers Stiv Bators and Joey Ramone and more.

It was a phenomenal turnout and an impassioned call, one which caught the ear even of people who might never have given a second thought to the true nature of affairs in South Africa.

But not, perhaps, those who believed that the solution to South Africa's ills lay not in boycotts and abandonment but in positive engagement; in lifting apartheid's *victims* out of their appointed role as victims and showing them for what they really were—a vibrant culture, a living society, human beings like everybody else. What is a boycott anyway, asked the isolationists' opponents, if not a self-congratulatory extension of the old "ignore it and it'll go (hopefully) away" canard?

This was the side upon which Paul Simon found himself. His past record, and records, proved that he was no friend of racism in any form. But he questioned whether "the Ramones saying, 'We ain't gonna play Sun City' means anything, because nobody ever asked them," and on a more serious note, he couldn't help but wonder, "What gives [governments] the right to wear the cloak of morality, [if that] morality comes out of the barrel of a gun?"

That in itself was a courageous stance to take. As with so many of society's most emotive issues, it is very easy to take sides—either you support a solution or you oppose it. The option to step into the middle ground is rarely volunteered, particularly once that solution transcends the ranks of the people who understand it, or experience it, and becomes simply another slogan to wear on a T-shirt.

When Simon let it be known that he intended to travel to South Africa to see the situation for himself, and work with local black musicians—who, after all, were numbered among the intended beneficiaries of the watching world's concern—the condemnation was both swift and, in its own mind, righteous.

Simon was not, in fairness, in an altogether innocent position. Twice in the past—in 1964, when he traveled to London and came home with a Child Ballad in his pocket, which he and Garfunkel then proceeded to claim as an original joint composition in the credits to the duo's third album, and again in 1971, when he visited Jamaica and then flew back with an "authentic" reggae song—he had placed himself wide open to accusations of cultural appropriation *at the very least*. Drop by, pick up a rhythm, and then bring it home and make a mint.

It's a damning accusation, but it's also a very conditional one. Most rock 'n' roll (and many other twentieth- and twenty-first-century musical forms) is built upon that very same foundation. The classics, vaudeville, the blues, jazz, rock, pop—all have borrowed and have been borrowed from. That is how new sounds are developed, fresh genres created.

Simon himself addressed that topic in a 2016 interview with writer Tshepo Mokoena, quoting jazz trumpeter Wynton Marsalis who, in turn, was quoting his father, pianist Ellis Louis Marsalis Jr.

"Music is not a competition. It's an idea." So you can't steal some-one's idea, it's out there. Everyone participates in the idea, you can enhance that idea, you can look at it from another angle, people may say "I prefer the way you look at it," "No I don't like the way you look at it" But the idea is there. This discussion about "You stole this or that" is a waste of time, it's not true. Either you col-laborate in a way that makes something people like, something that's enjoyable, or you don't.

In 2006, too, recalling another example—the mock-Latin stylings of "Me and Julio Down by the Schoolyard"—Simon touched upon the topic in an interview with *Performing Songwriter*'s Bill DeMain: "When I was doing *The Capeman*, Ruben Blades said to me, 'You can't imagine what it was like to hear coming out of America—and you were living in Panama—a song about a guy named Julio.'"

Nevertheless, the controversy lingered (and still lingers) on. If a rocker lifts a lick from a blues song, he is simply taking an influence from a musical form that is already a part of his vocabulary. That is very differ-ent to purposefully visiting another land, or culture, in order to re-create, wholesale, a sound that has never previously (or at least, so deliberately) been a part of your own popular culture.

The Peter Gabriel Show

At the same time, however, Simon was hardly stepping into the musical unknown. There is, of course, no such thing as "African music"—how could there be, in a continent comprising fifty-plus separate nations, and many times that number of cultures?

Ever since 1929, however, when anthropologist Laura C. Boulton returned from the Straus West African Expedition's latest field trip with a collection of recordings of indigenous singers and musicians, their styles *had* infiltrated the west.

Several volumes of Boulton's recordings were released that same year under the title *Rhythm in the Jungle*, and since that time, western ears had been beguiled by the highlife sounds of Nigerian Fela Ransome Kuti and his Koola Lobitos, the pan pipes of Morocco that so entranced Rolling Stone Brian Jones, the "African heritage" fusion of the London-based rock band Osibisa, the Royal Drummers of Burundi, and much more.

Such influences were pervasive. Several of the hottest bands of the early 1980s existed within a tribal framework that aficionados of African rhythm would certainly have recognized—indeed, Peter Gabriel would later complain that "most people who haven't seen the Drummers of Burundi are still a bit cynical about them because of all the hipness of Adam and the Ants and Bow Wow Wow."

The Return of the Giant Slits, the second album by the Slits, seamlessly interwove reggae and African beat influences into its soul; Echo and the Bunnymen performed live with the Burundi drummers; even Stewart Copeland, the drummer with the Police, was looking abroad for inspiration and would soon be off to Africa, where he conceived the startling *The Rhythmatist* solo album.

And then there was, again, Peter Gabriel.

In 1980, five years on from his departure from the band Genesis, Peter Gabriel released his third solo album, *Peter Gabriel*—and the performer who, more than any other of the time, was to bring "world music" to the fore stepped fully formed into the spotlight.

Rhythms were drawn from across the musical spectrum, atmospheres from even further away. Within a year, Gabriel was preparing to stage the WOMAD (World of Music and Dance) Festival—a vastly ambitious enterprise that he spread across four days near his home in Shepton Mallet, England, and which cross-fertilized many of the non-Anglo-American musical strains that would continue developing over the next few years.

"I think a lot more musicians are now working in this area," Gabriel predicted during a British TV documentary celebrating the festival, "and there will be a [corresponding] style of music to emerge in the 1980s which I think will be very important and influential."

He was correct, too. But of all the records that would emerge from the fusion, one Gabriel song in particular caught the imagination.

"Biko," from that third eponymous album, was a lament for the South African state-sponsored murder, three years earlier, of the black activist and journalist Steven Biko.

A founder, in 1972, of the Black People's Convention, Biko remained politically active even after being placed under a banning order by the South African government. His life was constantly threatened, he was regularly detained by state security services, and he was condemned as a subversive. It was in the course of another of these arrests, in August 1977, that Biko was beaten to death by members of the security forces. At his funeral the following month, a crowd of over 20,000 people turned out, while the murder made headlines round the world.

"Biko" itself was funereal, dark and protracted, reflective and condemning. More than any other song, whether on its parent album or in the canon of other musicians, "Biko"'s blend of rock sensibility and indigenous chant and rhythm ably set the scene for the World Music explosion that was about to descend—and *Graceland* is just one of many albums that conceivably took their lead from the six-or-so minutes that closed *Peter Gabriel* with such chilling finality.

Indeed, in 2010, Simon was granted the opportunity to repay that debt when Gabriel invited him aboard what would become his And *I'll Scratch Yours* album—a self-styled tribute record on which artists whom Gabriel had covered on his last record, *Scratch My Back*, covered Gabriel in return. Simon would cover "Biko."

Simon's performance does not—perhaps surprisingly, but probably wisely—venture into the musical territory that might have been expected. Rather, "Biko" becomes a wistful ballad, haunted by viola and spectral backing vocals, while Simon's vocal is as forceful as any he has ever committed to tape.

Back in the mid-1980s, however, Paul Simon was not Peter Gabriel, and a visit to South Africa was not a trip to Nigeria, Burundi, or Morocco. The apartheid state's very name and reputation pressed very different buttons in the Western mind, and Simon was perhaps a little naive when he questioned some of the criticisms that were thrown in his direction once his intentions became clear: "The intensity of the criticism really did surprise me, [and] part of the criticism was, 'Here's this white guy from New York, and he ripped off these poor innocent guys.'"

Whereas a major part of his intention was to help them—to give their music an international platform so vast that their government would no longer be able to enact the prohibitions that had previously held back native black entertainers (not to mention sportsmen, artists, and many others) from any form of recognition.

In Simon's mind, if the world was calling out for a South African group to tour America, the South African government would need to find a very good reason to refuse them permission, and simply saying "they can't because they're black" would not fit the bill.

From there, it was easy to slip to the other side of the coin—that the anti-apartheid lobby's refusal to countenance a white musician's decision to visit South Africa was, in some ways, no different to the apartheid regime's refusal to allow a black musician to visit America. But, in other ways, it was a threat to all that the movement had achieved so far.

As Dali Tambo told the *New York Times*: "We were fighting for our land, for our identity. We had a job to do, and it was a serious job. And we saw Paul Simon coming as a threat because it was not sanctioned by the liberation movement."

August 1986: *Graceland* (Warner Brothers CD 9 25447-2)

"The Boy in the Bubble"
Words: Paul Simon; music: Paul Simon and Forere Motlobeloa

Original sessions
Recorded at Ovation Studios, Johannesburg, South Africa, February 1985
Assistant Engineer: Peter Thwaites

Musicians

Forere—accordion	Vusi Khumalo—drums
Baghiti Khumalo—bass	Makhaya Mahlangu—percussion

Overdubs
Overdubs recorded at The Hit Factory, New York, April 1986
Assistant Engineer: Mark Cobrin

Musicians
Adrian Belew—synthesizer guitar
Rob Mounsey—synthesizer

"Graceland"

Original sessions recorded at Ovation Studios, Johannesburg, South Africa, February 1985

Assistant Engineer: Peter Thwaites

Musicians

Baghiti Khumalo—bass

Vusi Khumalo—drums

Makhaya Mahlangu—percussion

Ckikapa "Ray" Phiri—guitar

Demola Adepoju—pedal steel

Overdubs

Overdubs recorded at Amigo Studios, Los Angeles

Assistant Engineer: Steven Strassman

The Everly Brothers—vocals

"I Know What I Know"

With General M. D. Shirinda and the Gaza Sisters

Words: Paul Simon; Music: Paul Simon and General M. D. Shirinda

Original sessions

Recorded at Ovation Studios, Johannesburg, South Africa, February 1985

Assistant Engineer: Peter Thwaites

The Gaza Sisters—vocals

Overdubs

Recorded at The Hit Factory, New York, April 1986

Assistant Engineer: Mark Cobrin

Paul Simon—Synclavier

"Gumboots"

With the Boyoyo Boys

Words: Paul Simon; music: Paul Simon, Jonhjon Mkhalali, and Lulu Masilela

Recorded at Ovation Studios, Johannesburg, South Africa, February 1985

Assistant Engineer: Peter Thwaites

Musicians

Jonhjon Mkhalali—accordion

Lulu Masilela—tambourines

Daniel Xilakuzi—lead guitars and rhythm

Petrus Manile—drums

Barney Rachabane, Mike
   Makhalemele, and Teaspoon
   Ndlela—saxophones

Overdubs

Recorded at The Hit Factory, New York, April 1986
Assistant Engineer: Mark Cobrin

Musicians

Paul Simon—synclavier and back-   Diane Garisto—background vocals
   ground vocals   Michele Cobbs—background vocals
Ralph McDonald—percussion

"Diamonds on the Soles of Her Shoes"

Intro by Paul Simon and Joseph Shabalala
Recorded at The Hit Factory, New York, April 1986
Assistant Engineer: Mark Cobrin

Musicians

Chikapa "Ray" Phiri—guitar   Assane Thiam—percussion
Baghiti Khumalo—bass   Earl Gardner—trumpet
Isaac Mtshali—drums   Leonard Pickett—tenor sax
Youssou N'Dour—percussion   Alex Foster—alto sax
Babacar Faye—percussion   Ladysmith Black Mambazo—vocals

"You Can Call Me Al"

Co-arranged with Chikapa "Ray" Phiri
Recorded at The Hit Factory, New York, April 1986
Assistant Engineer: Mark Cobrin

Musicians

Paul Simon—six-string electric bass   Ronald E. Cuber—bass sax and bari-
   and background vocals   tone sax
Chikapa "Ray" Phiri—guitar   John Faddis, Ronald E. Brecker, and
Baghiti Khumalo—bass   Lewis Michael Soloff—trumpet
Isaac Mtshali—drums   Alan Rubin—trumpet
Ralph McDonald—percussion   David W. Bargeron—trombone
Rob Mounsey—synthesizer   Kim Allan Cissel—trombone
Adrian Belew—guitar synthesizer   Morris Goldberg—pennywhistle solo

"Under African Skies"

Co-arranged with Chikapa "Ray" Phiri

Original sessions

Recorded at The Hit Factory, New York, April 1986

Assistant Engineer: Mark Cobrin

Musicians

Chikapa "Ray" Phiri, Adrian Belew,   Isaac Mtshali—drums
    and Paul Simon—guitars   Ralph McDonald—percussion

Baghiti Khumalo—bass

Overdubs

Recorded at Amigo Studios, Los Angeles

Assistant Engineer: Steven Strassman

Linda Ronstadt—vocals

"Homeless"

With Ladysmith Black Mambazo

Words and music: Paul Simon and Joseph Shabalala

Recorded at Abbey Road Studios, London, October 1985

Assistant Engineer: Andrew Fraser

Joseph Shabalala—lead singer

"Crazy Love, Vol. II"

With Stimela; co-arranged with Chikapa "Ray" Phiri

Original sessions

Recorded at Ovation Studios, Johannesburg, South Africa, February 1985

Assistant Engineer: Peter Thwaites

Musicians

Chikapa "Ray" Phiri—guitar   Isaac Mtshali—drums

Lloyd Lelose—bass

Overdubs

Recorded at The Hit Factory, New York, April 1986

Assistant Engineer: Mark Cobrin

Musicians

Morris Goldberg—soprano sax   Adrian Belew—guitar synthesizer

"That Was Your Mother"

With Good Rockin' Dopsie and the Twisters
Recorded at Master-Trak Enterprises, Crowley, Louisiana
Assistant Engineer: Mark Miller

Musicians

Alton Rubin Sr. (Dopsie)—accordion
Alton Rubin Jr.—drums
David Rubin—washboard
Alonzo Johnson—bass
Sherman Robertson—guitar
Johnny Hoyt—saxophone

"All Around the World or the Myth of Fingerprints"

With Los Lobos
Recorded at Amigo Studios, Los Angeles
Assistant Engineer: Steven Strassman

Musicians

David Hildago—vocals, guitar, accordion
Cesar Rosas—vocals, guitar
Louie Perez—drums
Steve Berlin—saxophone
Conrad Lozano—bass

Overdubs

Recorded at The Hit Factory, New York
Assistant Engineer: Mark Cobrin

Musicians

Steve Gadd—additional drums
Produced by: Paul Simon
Engineer: Roy Halee
Ralph McDonald—percussion

The Journey Begins

It was Lorne Michaels who, in his capacity as former producer of the television comedy *The New Show*, set Simon off on his journey. Following the short-lived show's cancellation, he introduced Simon to Heidi Berg, the program's band leader. Michaels was preparing to return to *SNL*, and Berg was looking for work. Perhaps Paul Simon would be able to suggest something?

In fact, she discovered Simon was himself looking for something. The collapse of the *Think Too Much* reunion with Garfunkel and the failure of its *Hearts and Bones* revamp had left him reeling. For the first time in his career, he was forced to face up to the fact that he would always be one half of Simon and Garfunkel and that the public, given the choice, would always take the duo.

Had *Think Too Much* been completed according to the initial plan, Simon would probably now have been celebrating one of the biggest, and most acclaimed, hits of his entire career. Instead, the exact same songs, performed by (almost) the exact same musicians, had been released to little fanfare, few sales, and no action. Now he was socked away in his office, a few doors down from the old Brill Building, wondering what, if anything, he could do next.

If his career was in tatters, his personal life was scarcely any improvement. His friendship with Garfunkel was, it seemed, irrevocably compromised. His marriage to Carrie Fisher was over, little more than a year after they wed. Heidi Berg didn't know what to expect when she knocked on his door for their prearranged meeting. For Simon, the very fact that somebody wanted to meet with him was probably the highlight of the day . . . if not the entire week.

The purpose of the initial meeting was to allow Simon to hear some of the songs Berg was writing. Intrigued, he then agreed to produce an album for her, and in the course of several subsequent meetings, the conversation turned to the kind of sound she was looking for.

She responded by handing him a homemade cassette compilation of South African *mbaqanga* ("township jive") music recorded in Soweto, a raucous, joyous mix of guitars, sax, accordions—any instruments that the players could lay their hands on.

Simon listened to it in the car—he was having a beach house built in Montauk, at the far end of Long Island, and it proved the ideal companion for the nearly-three hour drive, "very good summer music," as he told *Rolling Stone* in 1986. It reminded him, he continued, of "very early rock and roll black, urban, mid-fifties rock and roll." If he closed his eyes, he could almost visualize the old red-and-black Atlantic Records label spinning around, spitting the sound. At first, he said, he was simply playing it for the joy of the sound. It was only as time went by, and the sounds

Graceland graces the cover of *Rolling Stone*.   *Author's collection*

refused to let him go, that he found himself creating his own melodies over the rhythms. And, "even then, I wasn't making them up for the purpose of writing. I was just singing along with the tape, the way people do."

But he wanted to know more about the music's origins.

His first call was to Lenny Waronker at Warners, who in turn put him in touch with Hilton Rosenthal, the white South African producer whose MINC label introduced the band Juluka—South Africa's first commercially successful mixed-race act—to the world.

He was able to identify one of the tracks on the tape, an old (1970s) Boyoyo Boys instrumental written by Jonhjon Mikhali and Lulu Maslela, and just one of a multitude of tracks that the Soweto-based band released on a series of *Gumboot* cassettes during that decade.

Simon was fascinated. Thinking back to "El Condor Pasa (If I Could)" and how he had added his own melody and lyrics to an already existing performance, he mused on the possibility of purchasing the rights to the song. Rosenthal asked him, why stop at one? He should record an entire album in the same spirit.

Berg was sidelined. All talk of Simon producing her album ended, while his own tour that summer ensured she rarely even had the opportunity to talk to him. Finally, she buttonholed him backstage at one of the shows, where Simon told her of his intentions.

Years later, in 2013, the change of plans still hurt. Commenting on a Boyoyo Boys track on YouTube, Berg wrote: "I was put [with Simon] to be produced, as he said. So I played my music, spilled all my best ideas, influence, poetry, conversations, [and] they made it onto his album—it was a creative robbery as he presented himself as my producer."

Nor, she alleged, did Simon stop at buying the rights to just the one track. "Paul Simon bought rights to all Boyoyo Boys *Gumboots* series . . . [and] made sure those LPs/cassettes all disappeared from Earth."

Neither did she appreciate what she considered to be her gradual airbrushing from the history of what she called "Paul Simon's last good idea that he stole": "I was on the first sentence of [the original album's] liner notes. I got moved to [the] end of page six in his 10th anniversary [release] and then his $250 '25th anniversary' he doesn't mention [Heidi Berg] at all."

Simon began planning his trip to South Africa. He had no songs prepared—he believed that once he was in the studio with the right musicians, all he needed would come to him there, and so it proved. As he told *National Geographic* in 2012, "I learned pretty early on if you want to get the music right you should probably travel to where it's being played, as opposed to asking musicians who are not familiar with it to copy it."

He knew he was taking a chance, setting himself up against some very powerful anti-apartheid lobbies—not only the United Nations and Artists Against Apartheid but also individual governments and even many of his own fans. The vitals of his conscience, however, remained ungnawed by their opprobrium. His determination to record what he wanted, where he wanted, and with whom he wanted was placing him so far out on a limb that it could easily have spelled the downfall of his entire career. And he didn't care.

Even when calypso singer Harry Belafonte offered to mediate and at least try and secure the blessing of the African National Congress, South

Africa's anti-apartheid opposition party, Simon would not change his plans. He wanted to get to work, and in February 1986, he and Roy Halee flew to Johannesburg to meet up with Hilton Rosenthal. It was he who was going to make things happen.

Recording *Graceland*

The team sequestered themselves in Ovation Studios, and Rosenthal got to work, booking musicians to come in and play. And that is all they did—they played, with Simon adding to the sense of adventure and enthusiasm by *tripling* even the hourly rates he would expect to pay New York session musicians.

Effectively, Simon and Halee would record the musicians as they jammed, not even thinking about "songs" at this point in the process. As Simon told the *New York Times*, "My typical style of songwriting in the past [was] to sit with a guitar and write a song, finish it, go into the studio, book the musicians, lay out the song and the chords, and then try to make a track."

This time, he reversed the process.

Just as had happened in Jamaica more than a decade before, the backing tracks preceded the songs. Then, with the band effectively jamming around him, he would search for the melodies and words that "fit the scale they were playing in."

The cream of the mbaqanga scene filed through the studio—Tau Ea Matsekha, whose "Ke Ikhethetse E Motle" would ultimately become Simon's "The Boy in the Bubble"; General M. D. Shirinda and the Gaza Sisters, accompanied by sundry other family members, created what became "I Know What I Know," with the Sisters' distinctive vocals ringing out in their native Shangaan language. "It's different," explained singer Sonti Mndebele, "because it's like you're singing out of tune sometimes, but that is how it should sound."

Of course the Boyoyo Boys were there to perform the song that started the entire odyssey; another local hit band, Stimela, would appear on "Crazy Love," one of the first of his own songs Simon wrote for the project. (Elsewhere, writing credits would be assigned to both Simon and the composers behind the original songs.) And the only time the mood soured was as evening approached and the reality of apartheid hit home—the need for the musicians to be off the streets before dark.

In a 2012 interview with NPR, Simon recalled one particular example: "I was putting a saxophone on 'Gumboots' with Barney Rachabane and I wanted him to play a harmony to a part that he wrote. He said, 'I have to go. I don't have a permit to be in Johannesburg after five o'clock. And if I don't have a permit, I could be arrested.' So in the middle of the euphoric feeling in the studio, you would have reminders that you're living in incredibly tense racial environment, where the law of the land was apartheid."

Nevertheless, within little more than a week, Simon and Halee had pieced together the basic lineup of musicians who would accompany them through the remainder of the process: the trio of Stimela's Chikapa "Ray" Phiri on guitar; Isaa Mthsli on drums; and Bakithi Kumalo, of Tau Ea Matsekha, on bass. Other players came and went as the sessions progressed, and in the course of just one more week, he and Halee had no less than eight tracks with which to work once they returned to New York City.

Now, however, the real work began: piecing together actual songs from the hours of jams that Simon and Halee had captured—a project that might never have been possible a few years earlier, before digital recording and editing became a reality.

Painstakingly, every note of music was listened to and then listened to again; riffs and rhythms were separated out from the original tape and exported to a fresh one. Only then, once something resembling a conventional backing track had been completed, could Simon seriously settle to writing the lyrics.

The album would not be devoted wholly to the fruits of the Ovation Studios sessions; in fact, only five complete tracks were culled from that exercise.

"You Can Call Me Al," featuring such a distinctive bass line from Baghiti Khumalo that Simon included it played both forward and backward, was cut at The Hit Factory; "Under African Skies" traveled from New York to Los Angeles so Simon could record a duet with Linda Ronstadt; "That Was Your Mother" took him to Crowley, Louisiana, to record with the magnificently named Good Rockin' Dopsie and the Twisters; "All Around the World or the Myth of Fingerprints" was another Los Angeles session, this time with Los Lobos; "Homeless" was taped at Abbey Road in London, with the choir Ladysmith Black Mambazo.

"Graceland" itself was recorded in South Africa, but the song was originally written with Willie Nelson in mind and overdubbed with exquisite harmonies from the Everly Brothers. Almost thirty years after he rewrote one of their songs, the brothers were now realigning one of his.

And "Diamonds on the Soles of Her Shoes" almost didn't make the album at all. Warner Brothers' original plan was to release *Graceland* in June 1986, so when Simon and Ladysmith Black Mambazo performed the song on *Saturday Night Live,* they did so more out of excitement for a new, as-yet-unrecorded song than because they were dutifully plugging the upcoming album.

The epochal *Graceland* LP changed the popular face of World Music.
Author's collection

Vinyl or CD?

Graceland was Paul Simon's first new release of the CD age—the first to come along during that brief interlude when the two formats, the new fangled digital coaster and the old fashioned vinyl scratch-magnet, were still battling it out for supremacy.

Simon knew firmly which side of the fence he fell on. He was the offspring, he told *Mojo* in 2000, of a world in which "you made [records] for a listener with an attention span of about twenty minutes [per side of vinyl]." He went on to say: "Now, either we got used to that because we're an album generation, or that's a natural attention span, I don't know. Anyway, it was right."

Years passed, vinyl shriveled, and the CD became the dominant force, both in the marketplace and in the minds of the artists recording them. Suddenly twenty minutes was no longer enough; now albums were being stretched to an hour or more, anything to fill up the available space (seventy-eight minutes initially, eighty later) that a CD offered.

A collection of songs that would once have required four sides of vinyl, and the attendant grand status of a double album, could now be fit into precisely the same amount of shelf space as a single LP. And some artists made the most of the freedom.

Others, however, simply made fools of themselves. And audiences, perhaps, got bored.

Simon: "When the required attention span more than doubled for a CD, I think people stopped listening to CDs as a piece of work."

Purposefully, then, he has timed each of his subsequent solo albums (soundtracks and live albums notwithstanding) to clock in at, or in the immediate vicinity of, that magical twenty minutes per side.

"I tried to [take] into account what an attention span is. So, it had to do with a certain flow, and ebb of energy. I had to make an album that's so interesting on first listening that someone will listen again and fall in love. And if I don't, no one's gonna listen, because everybody's stopped listening."

And After All That

Graceland's new late-summer release date reprieved the song. Immediately after the television broadcast, Simon, the choir, Senegalese percussionist Youssou N'Dour, and the ever-loyal Phiri, Kumalo, and Mtshali returned to the Hit Factory to record what would become the album's signature hit single.

And after all the fuss, all the controversy, all the finger wagging and so on, *Graceland* emerged—a triumph. From the low points of his last two albums, Simon had completely, and quite unexpectedly, revitalized a career that had indeed felt increasingly disconnected from everything else that was going on in eighties rock.

Simon's best-received album at least since *Still Crazy After All These Years* a decade previous, *Graceland* received almost unanimously favorable reviews—indeed, once past the continued political fallout (which nothing could have stilled), the only cloud over its reception was, ironically, what might ordinarily have been the least controversial aspect of the entire affair—the involvement of Linda Ronstadt.

Ronstadt told the *Guardian*: "I was in Tucson visiting my dad. Paul called and said he was writing a song for us to sing together, and could I give him some kind of a geographic point, something that was around Tucson? I loved this mission that was built in the early 1700s. It's a beautiful little building, built by pagans, and on the Indian reservation. It was kind of my spiritual home, so I told him about that."

Three years previous, however, Ronstadt brought a firestorm of rage down around herself when she agreed to perform at Sun City, stepping in as a last-minute replacement for Frank Sinatra.

She did not knowingly break the boycott. Apparently, the promoters were more than a little economical with the truth when they explained where Sun City was actually located. The shows went ahead. Ronstadt was roundly castigated; in fact, she was one of the offenders who were personally named in "Ain't Gonna Play Sun City"—one reason why Paul Simon turned down his own invitation to appear on that record. She was a friend of his before she went to South Africa, and she was still a friend now.

But writer Robert Christgau, in the Village Voice, spoke for many when he puzzled over the sheer dichotomy with which Simon had presented the world: "Even if the [song's] lyric called for total US divestiture, Ronstadt's presence on Graceland would be a slap in the face to the world anti-apartheid movement. A deliberate, considered, headstrong slap in the face."

Still the album was a success, both musically and commercially, but also politically. It forced people to look again at their most entrenched attitudes toward a cultural exchange with South Africa. And, more than that, it fostered dialogue, reminding even the regime's most resolute opponents that it was not the white government alone that suffered from the boycotts and bans. The black citizens, too, missed out on so much.

Graceland didn't just place the musicians and their music into the international spotlight; it also illuminated their culture, causing outsiders to question not only South Africa's political stance but also its insistence on burying such a vibrant and thrilling sound.

What else were they keeping out of sight, people wondered. How many other joys were being buried, not only by the country's own leaders but also by the boycott?

A few observers complained that Simon did not address the political system in his lyrics, but he did not need to. The sound of the record spoke louder than any earnest polemic ever could, and he knew it.

"I never said there were not strong political implications to what I did," he told *Rolling Stone*. "I just said the music was not overtly political. But the implications of the music certainly are. People get attracted to [it], and once they hear what's going on within it, they say, 'What? They're doing that to these people?'"

Nevertheless, there were ramifications. The United Nations added Simon's name to its much-feared list of the boycott's violators, while the militant black radical Azanian People's Organization (AZAPO) apparently placed him at the top of their hit list.

But when apartheid finally crumbled in the early 1990s and the African National Congress swept into power under President Nelson Mandela, who was among the first western performers to be invited to play in South Africa following the lifting of the cultural boycott in December 1991?

Paul Simon. He played five shows in the country the following month, launched with a formal reception, fronted by Mandela, in Johannesburg on January 9, 1992.

Graceland Revisited

Graceland has remained the key component within Simon's solo career, the one album that seemingly everybody knows, most people love, and, when he tours, all are keen to hear.

A full in-concert performance of the album was among the highlights of his 2012 appearance at the Hard Rock Calling Festival in London's Hyde Park (see chapter 18), and six years on, in the midst of his 2018 farewell tour, Simon released *Graceland—The Remixes*, a full reenvisioning of the original album.

The timing was not, perhaps, ideal. Less than a year earlier, in July 2017, *Graceland* guitarist Ray Phiri passed away at the age of seventy.

Tributes were swift to follow, including Simon's heartfelt recollection: "[Phiri was] a beautiful, masterful guitarist and an inventive musician. He will be remembered as a patriot who used his music to fight apartheid and brought that message to the world."

Phiri would have been proud. What he would have made of *Graceland—The Remixes*, on the other hand, may best be left unconjectured.

With the task of pulling the entire beast together entrusted to "project curator" Michael Gaiman, this new album would see some of the dance scene's most respected and best-known remixers—say hello to the likes of Paul Oakenfold, Thievery Corporation, MK, and Joris Voorn—"reimagine" the album with what most critics would swiftly condemn as mixed results.

The esteemed Super Deluxe Edition website, for example, insisted Richey Ahmed's vision of "The Boy in the Bubble" "should have been dubbed the 'give me a headache, immediately' mix." But Groove Armada's "Dub Redemption" mix of "You Can Call Me Al" fared even more poorly, being described as "absolutely horrendous," with the reviewer claiming, "So devastating is the level of destruction that the existence of the original song could only be confirmed by reference to its dental records."

Groove Armada's Andy Cato remained unperturbed. The Armada had stubbornly resisted any number of calls to "remix a classic" in the past, but this was different. *Graceland*, explained Cato, "was an album . . . which had opened our ears to a new world of sound." Even more alluring was the fact that they could choose the song they would work with—they opted for "You Can Call Me Al" because they had been deploying its horn riff in their live set for the last thirty years! "We tried it at Fais Do-Do's Ballroom in LA back in 1998 and it created an electric moment of dance-floor unity. So the remix wrote itself and our ace-in-the-pack Horn Drop is now public property."

June 2018: *Graceland—The Remixes* (Legacy 19075846602)

For original musician credits, see Graceland

"Homeless"
Joris Voorn Final Remix

"Gumboots"
Joyce Muniz Remix

"I Know What I Know"
Sharam's Motherland Mix

"Crazy Love, Vol. II"
Paul Oakenfold Extended Remix

"The Boy in the Bubble"
Richy Ahmed Remix

"You Can Call Me Al"
Groove Armada Dub Redemption

"Under African Skies"
Rich Pinder/Djoko Vocal Mix

"Graceland"
MK's KC Lights Remix

"That Was Your Mother"
Gui Boratto Remix

"Diamonds on the Soles of Her Shoes"
Thievery Corporation Remix

"All Around the World or the Myth of Fingerprints"
Photek Remix

"Homeless"
Joris Voorn Kitchen Table Mix / The Duke of New York's Edit

Executive Producer: The Duke of New York, Jeff Kramer

Perhaps the most hostile response, however, was that delivered by New Zealand's Off the Tracks website.

"Paul Simon approved this. He's also approved far too many live albums, Simon & Garfunkel reunions and around 87 unnecessary Greatest Hits compilations. But let's just be clear, those other mild transgressions are what happens when a gifted songwriter receives far too many orders and offers across the desk. You make a few mistakes.

"But this, this is fucking criminal. This is murder regardless of whether it ever makes it onto the dance floor.

"To give your work over to these animals, these unfeeling bastards, is to simply say 'I'm retired: Go fuck yourselves!'"

Remix projects have always been contentious, whether it is George Martin's son giving the universally beloved *Sgt. Pepper* an anniversary once-over, or another well-meaning studio maven trying to "update" some past classic in a bid to show what the artist might have achieved had they been granted modern technology.

Some fans approve and applaud all concerned for their efforts; others shift uncomfortably and wonder why the original could not have been left in peace.

That latter was the company into which *Graceland—The Remixes* fell. No less than eleven disparate remixers were granted license to range at will across *Graceland* (Joris Voorn was offered two songs), to concoct a disc that ranged, likewise, across a wealth of stylistic dance grooves. Which, in turn, disrupted the listening experience even further.

No club DJ could ever have gotten away with blending so many different styles into one evening's set, so why anybody thought it would work as an album is one of those questions that might never be answered. But it has certainly been frequently asked.

Impressively, *Graceland—The Remixes* debuted at number three on *Billboard*'s specialist Dance/Electronic Album Sales chart (June 16, 2018). Perhaps less impressively, it needed to sell just one thousand copies to do so, and it surely remains destined to become the lowest-selling and least loved album of Simon's entire career.

A career which, even as this album attracted some of the worst reviews of his entire life, was itself wrapping up on the stages of America in the form of Simon's Homeward Bound farewell outing.

12

The Music of the World

For a decade and a half, beginning in 1970, the world was waiting for Paul Simon to produce a second *Bridge Over Troubled Water.* Instead, he delivered a first *Graceland*, perhaps the most significant album released by any so-called sixties survivor throughout the entire span of the 1980s.

All around him, after all, his peers were tumbling. Dylan followed up the controversy of his so-called Christian trilogy (*Slow Train Coming*, *Saved*, and *Shot of Love*) with a sequence of fresh LPs that barely hinted at commanding the respect he had once deserved. Neil Young was all over the place, with every new album apparently testing a new, even less palatable direction than the last. The Rolling Stones seemed more intent on in-fighting than recording. The surviving Beatles were either dropping off the Top 40 altogether or desperately clinging to it with anodyne ditties. Other heroes seemed to lose any semblance of interest in making good music.

It wasn't age. Almost without exception, each of the veterans who struggled through the bulk of the eighties would celebrate their end with a genuine return to form—Dylan's *Oh Mercy*, the Stones' *Steel Wheels*, David Bowie's *Tin Machine*. There really is no other explanation—the eighties had literally sucked the joy and creativity out of all of them, and only now that the decade was breathing its last did it relax its stifling grip.

Only Paul Simon was immune. Perhaps it was because he had already experienced his darkest hour, with the one-two-*three* punch of *One-Trick Pony*, the abortive reunion with Garfunkel, and *Hearts and Bones*. Perhaps it was because he'd stopped not caring, but competing. He had spent so long creating music that was instinctively in tune with the hearts and minds of his audience that, when that audience suddenly moved away, he had no alternative but to make it for himself.

Whatever the cause, and whatever cultural zeitgeists it may unknowingly have tapped into, *Graceland* not only shook off the torpor that his own muse had been laboring beneath, but it revitalized the mid-eighties themselves. It proved that there was an alternative to the increasingly faceless, feckless nonsense that MTV was pushing into everyone's face—that overpermed hair metal, soulless dance pop, and rent-a-quote country were not all that we had to look forward to.

A New Genre

Graceland did not *invent* world music the rest of the world did that. But it opened eyes and ears to its possibility, and it was astonishing how quickly the change was wrought.

Record stores that once filed non-domestic music by genre—English folk, Jamaican reggae, and so on, with an "international" category for everything else—refiled them by country of origin. Suddenly, Bob Marley was racked up under Jamaica, Steeleye Span under England, Jacques Brel under France.

It was clumsy, and it was also frustrating. No longer was it enough to know the name of the singer of that oddly-accented song you heard on the radio; you now needed to know their place of birth as well. Nevertheless, the change was wrought. Within five years of *Graceland*, world music was itself a definable musical genre, with acclaimed labels like Putumayo (formed 1991) and the World Music Network's Rough Guide series (launched 1994) both encou*raging and enhancing the curious listener's explorations.

Again, *Graceland* was not wholly responsible. More credit, perhaps, is owed to the loose conglomerate of musicians, label heads, and other interested parties who gathered in London in late June 1987 to organize a concerted drive to market (and indeed name) World Music outside of the specialist stores that had hitherto sold such esoteric goods.

But they, too, acknowledged that it was the success of *Graceland* and, to a lesser degree, Peter Gabriel, which had brought the music home to a mainstream Anglo-American audience. All they needed do now was maintain the momentum.

If, however, *Graceland*'s role in popularizing World Music must be shared equally with the marketing men, the album's effect on Simon himself is less contradictory. Essentially, it completely reversed his fortunes.

Prior to 1986, in the eyes of the critical cognoscenti, Paul Simon was heading toward irrelevance, a drifting reminder of a previous era and, in the minds of more politically aware commentators, a cultural liability, too—the breaking of the boycott remained a very sore point, and the sheer majesty of *Graceland*'s music, and the weight that its success would bring to bear on the anti-apartheid movement, did not change everybody's mind on that latter point.

But it was futile to disagree with that impact, to attempt to argue that *Graceland* did more harm to the cause than good; and, in the vivid glare of that reality, it was pointless to continue claiming that Paul Simon had no relevance to the modern, mid-1980s music scene. The man had just reshaped it in his own image, and even more importantly than that, he had redesigned the political climate, too.

Not to immediate effect. The South African regime still had another six years to live. But how uncomfortable were those six years, and how bruised were apartheid's apologists by the time those six years were up? A pop record cannot change the world. But it can influence the people who could.

"*Graceland* was never just a collection of songs," wrote Andrew Leahy in *American Songwriter*. "It was a bridge between cultures, genres and continents."

Perhaps it was mere coincidence that in August 1986, just as *Graceland* was released, the US Senate passed an early version of a hitherto fiercely contested anti-apartheid bill—what became the Comprehensive Anti-Apartheid Act later in the year. But a bill is just a bill. It requires public pressure, as well as political pressure, to truly effect change, and *Graceland*—with six million sales worldwide within just nine months of its release—was instrumental in bringing that to bear.

A number one album in the United Kingdom and Canada (it made number three in the United States), *Graceland* also ruled the roost as far afield as the Netherlands, France, Australia, and Switzerland.

It became South Africa's second-biggest-selling album of the decade so far (Michael Jackson's *Thriller* was uncatchable in that department), while

"You Can Call Me Al" became Paul Simon's first major South African chart hit since the early 1970s, when "Mother and Child Reunion" and "Take Me to the Mardi Gras" gave him two chart-toppers in succession. In fact, it only narrowly missed out on that same position itself—the single peaked at number two and spent eighteen weeks on the chart.

Counting the Hits

The success of *Graceland* even spawned a new Paul Simon "greatest hits" album, and this time, there was no need to append that title with any suspicious qualifier; a decade earlier, Columbia issued Simon's first *Greatest Hits* and then added "etc." to the title to excuse the fact that he'd not yet enjoyed a full album's worth of contenders.

This new set intended to remedy that. Released in November 1988, *Negotiations and Love Songs, 1971–1986* was neither wall-to-wall hit singles nor a full accounting of Simon's successes. But it came close to both.

We can pick fault with its investigation of the hits. "Take Me to the Mardi Gras" and "Stranded in a Limousine" were dropped in favor of their B-sides, "Something So Right" and "Have a Good Time." "Duncan," "Gone at Last," and "American Tune" were absent; "St Judy's Comet" was a surprising inclusion.

Only "Late in the Evening" survived from among the 45s released from *One-Trick Pony*; and, from *Hearts and Bones*, "Train in the Distance" was never a single; and "René and Georgette Magritte with Their Dog After the War" saw action only as a promotional disc for the media. Indeed, it would be thirty years more before we were offered another reason for that song's inclusion, when Simon revisited it for *In the Blue Light*—a collection of favorite songs that were never given a fair hearing at the time of release.

But still that left "Mother and Child Reunion," "Me and Julio Down by the Schoolyard," "Loves Me Like A Rock," "Kodachrome," "50 Ways to Leave Your Lover," "Still Crazy After All These Years," "Slip Slidin' Away," "Diamonds on the Soles of Her Shoes," "You Can Call Me Al," and (exclusive to the vinyl release) "Graceland" to populate the album's fifteen-year span with chart hits and radio memories, and the biggest surprise would be the album's almost absolute commercial failure. It peaked at number 110 on the *Billboard* chart, Simon's worst performance ever. Graceland sold its first million in a month. *Negotiations and Love Songs, 1971–1986* took six years.

Meanwhile, we still await the true Paul Simon single-disc hits collection:

Paul Simon's Every US Hit

1972: "Mother and Child Reunion" #4
1972: "Me and Julio Down by the Schoolyard" #22
1972: "Duncan" #52
1973: "Kodachrome" #2
1973: "Loves Me Like a Rock" #2
1973: "American Tune" #35
1975: "Gone at Last" #23 (with Phoebe Snow)
1975: "50 Ways to Leave Your Lover" #1
1976: "Still Crazy After All These Years" #40
1977: "Slip Slidin' Away" #5
1978: "Wonderful World" (with James Taylor, Art Garfunkel) #17
1980: "Late in the Evening" #6
1980: "One-Trick Pony" #40
1983: "The Blues" (with Randy Newman) #51
1983: "Allergies" #44
1986: "You Can Call Me Al" #23
1986: "Graceland" #81
1986: "The Boy in the Bubble" #86
1990: "The Obvious Child" #92

Graceland in Concert

Graceland retains its cachet today. Fresh repackages to mark its tenth and twenty-fifth anniversaries have kept the music alive for successive generations, while its twenty-first birthday in 2007 was marked by the album being added to the National Recording Registry, the official reposi-tory for music that is considered "culturally, historically, or aesthetically important."

It even found its way into an episode of *Beavis and Butt-Head*. Paul Simon, Beavis knowledgeably proclaimed, is "that dude from Africa that used to be in the Beatles."

The album would also become the subject of a riveting 2012 documen-tary. *Under African Skies* was Joe Berlinger's portrait of the artist return-ing to the scene of the triumph to reunite with people he'd met when he was recording, and encounter again Dali Tambo.

He recalls his fears that Simon's presence in the country might give the outside world the impression that the government of the day had some "legitimacy." He explained: "It wasn't the ideal form of cultural exchange. [The musicians] weren't free people."

"Then why did they say [I could] come?" Simon shot back. "Do you think they were all so selfish that they did it for three times union scale? We didn't have anything to do with color, race—it was purely music."

Live, too, *Graceland* would make its mark. With the same core of musicians that had been retained throughout the album sessions, along-side Ladysmith Black Mambazo and guests Hugh Masekela (trumpet) and Miriam Makeba (vocals), both of whom ranked among black South Africans best known musical exiles, Simon would undertake a six-month *Graceland: The African Concert* tour, culminating in Zimbabwe (the closest it could come to South Africa without further angering the anti-apartheid lobby), where the entire event was captured by the cameras of director Michael Lindsay Hogg.

It was in Zimbabwe, incidentally, at a concert where "blacks and whites were about 50/50 in the audience a very unusual situation," that one of Simon's most endearing live traditions was born.

He had just finished a raucous version of "You Can Call Me Al," and, as he told NPR's David Greene: "The place was really up and dancing and really cheering! They just kept cheering, you know? So I started to count off the next number, and Hugh Masekela said to me, 'No, they want you to play it again.' And I said, 'Yeah, I know they want me to play it again, but I'm going on to the next number now.' He said, 'You don't understand.

They want you to play it again.' So we did. And after that, we used to do it twice in a row."

Controversy did, of course, ensue, even after Simon was able to convince the UN to remove his name from the list of boycott violators, and arrange for a number of shows to become benefits for a variety of African and African American causes. (It was even hoped that they could play a free concert at the UN headquarters itself, although that did not ultimately materialize.) Several of the gigs, including a six-night stand at London's Royal Albert Hall, would be marred by anti-apartheid protests.

Nevertheless, the tour rolled on, seeing a packed house wherever it touched down, and when Simon collected his Album of the Year award at the Grammys, just a week after the Zimbabwe concert, he made it clear to whom he believed he owed his success—the musicians who inspired the entire project in the first place.

"They live, along with other South African artists and their countrymen, under one of the most repressive regimes on the planet today, and still they are able to produce music of great power and nuance and joy.... I find that just extraordinary, and they have my great respect and love."

The following year, he was back at the Grammys, this time to collect a Song of the Year award for the album's title track. The year after that, 1989, *Graceland: The African Concert* was taken across Europe; and the year after *that*, following ANC leader Nelson Mandela's so-long-overdue release from the prison cell where he'd spent the past twenty-seven years, Simon and Ladysmith Black Mambazo were onstage in front of Mandela himself when he visited Los Angeles that summer.

A New Rhythm

There comes a time, however, in every artist's career, when even the most successful album they could ever make demands a follow-up.

It's not as immediate of a process as it used to be. In the sixties and seventies, one album, even two, a year was the norm for many; Simon and Garfunkel—with the eighteen-month gaps between *Parsley, Sage, Rosemary and Thyme* and *Bookends* and then between *Bookends* and

Bridge Over Troubled Water—had absolutely broken the mold, which was one reason why their next album, in early 1971, would have been a live set.

That conveyor belt had broken down considerably since then—and again, Simon, with his own supremely leisurely approach to new releases, had played a part in that. Two- or three-year gaps between new albums were increasingly becoming the norm.

Nevertheless, it seemed incredible that, *twenty years* after he launched his solo career, Simon had released just six new albums (seven if you also included *Live Rhymin'* and eight if you added *The Concert in Central Park*, but that really would be stretching it).

Six albums. Sixty-two new songs. Simon and Garfunkel had recorded and released almost as many in six years. It was time to start thinking about a new project, in the knowledge that this time, more than ever before in his life, the ears of the world were awaiting it.

Two arguments come to mind here. On the one hand, there were those observers who felt he should follow the *Graceland* formula (which, of course, had never been a formula in the first place) and seek out some other cruelly repressed indigenous musical form to raise up on a much-merited pedestal. And on the other, there were those who believed he should step back from the pioneering role, allow *Graceland* to remain a solitary, unsullied statement, and return to the simple singer-songwriter medium he had pursued in the past.

Or there was a third alternative, and that was to follow his heart. Again.

Simon's love of Latin and South American music was nothing new. He'd been talking about it since that trip to Paris in the sixties, where he first met the musicians of Ulumbara; he had flirted with it across his redeployment of "El Condor Pasa."

But it was not the modern sounds, or their pre-Columbian forebears, that fascinated him. It was the elements that arrived on the continent with the slave ships that he wanted to trace. The rhythms and the drums.

A call from Quincy Jones had set him on his way—back in 1987, Jones was recording in Los Angeles with Milton Nascimento, one of Brazil's biggest stars, and he invited Simon along to duet with the star. ("O Vendedor De Sonhos" appears on Nascimento's album *Yauaretê*.)

In the course of conversation, Simon mentioned to Nascimento and his producer, Marco Mazzola, that he was interested in working with some Brazilian percussionists. A few weeks later, with his flight to Rio de Janeiro already booked, Simon called Mazzola again and asked him to arrange some studio time and some musicians.

"This album is about drums, about West African drumming," Simon told Paul Zollo of *SongTalk*. But it was also about how that drumming, and the culture and religion that it was a part of, were brought to the new world; how the world of the Yuruba people "was exported with the African Diaspora because of slavery." There, he continued, the deities that the people brought with them were "syncretized" with the Catholocism that they discovered when they reached their destination, until every West African deity had its own "corresponding

Catholic saint. So when the slave-master came in and said, 'I told you guys not to be playing drums,' because the drum was forbidden, especially the holy drum, the bata, they would say, 'This is not about Chango, this is about Santa Barbara.' So it became an Afro-Catholic religion."

The album's eventual title, *The Rhythm of the Saints*, came from there, the saga of "West African drumming as it is expressed through Brazilian pallms."

Roy Halee and producer Phil Ramone accompanied Simon on the trip; the party then made their way to Salvador, in the north of the country, to link up with Banda Olodum, a fourteen-strong percussion group operating out of the cultural center they established in the town's Pelourinho Square.

A recording session was mooted, with Simon offering the same kind of arrangement as he had in Johannesburg—that he pay the musicians well for their work, and in return he owned all the rights in their music. They agreed.

The session would be recorded live in Pelourinho Square itself, with a portable eight-track recorder capturing some forty minutes of music. Back in New York City, this would be distilled into what became the gestating new album's opening track, "The Obvious Child."

"Olodum take their name from the Yoruba name for God," Simon told *The Observer* newspaper. "The West African religions have a colorful pantheon of gods, and when they merged with Roman Catholicism, the result

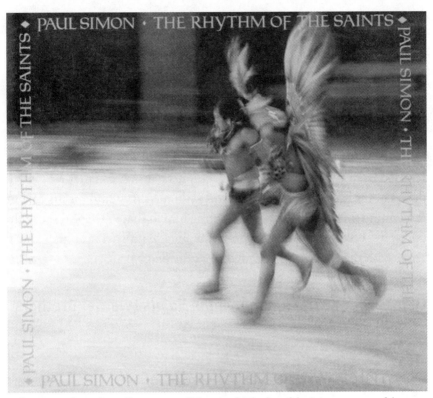

Following on from the stellar success of *Graceland*, *Rhythm of the Saints* was one of the most eagerly awaited albums of the eighties.   *Author's collection*

was this syncretic religion called Kandomble. The kind of massed drum sound that Olodum create was originally used in African religious ceremonies to induce a trance state, so that the worshipper could be inhabited by the grisha or deity. Even after decades of secular use, they still have that effect."

Another set of sessions, some months later, paired Simon with cellist Marco Antônio Guimarães's Uatki instrumental combo—a combo with a difference. Their instruments were handmade from "found objects," everything from PVC pipes to pieces of rubber. "Can't Run But" resonates with the ensuing magic.

Other sessions drew in other players; ultimately, Simon would make four trips to Brazil, recording in the main at either Transamerica Studios or Impressao Digital Studios in Rio. Then it would be back to The Hit Factory where, under many of the same conditions that attended the creation of *Graceland*, the sound would be sliced, diced, sampled, and molded into usable backing tracks.

American session men overlaid the recordings, players the caliber of Michael Brecker, Adrian Belew, J. J. Cale, and Steve Gadd. (Amusingly, the credits to the 2004 remaster add Beatles drummer Ringo Starr to the lineup and award him a guitar playing role as well. In fact, it's a typo; the actual player was the West African Rego Star.)

Ladysmith Black Mambazo, Ray Phiri, and Bakithi Kumalo were recalled from *Graceland*; zydeco accordionist Clifton Chenier was introduced to the party; and Simon repaid Milton Nascimento for his role in fermenting this latest journey by inviting him to share the vocal spotlight on "Spirit Voices"—a song Simon wrote, incidentally, about his experiences with the Amazonian psychotropic *ayahuasca*!

October 1990: *The Rhythm of the Saints* (Warner Brothers 26098)

"The Obvious Child"
Recorded at Pelourinho Square, Salvador, Bahia, Brazil
Musicians
Grupo Cultural Olodum (directed by: Antonio Luis Alves de Souza [Neguinho do Samba])—drums
Recorded at The Hit Factory, New York
Overdub Musicians
Kim Wilson—harmonica; Michael Brecker—Akai EWI synthesizer; Briz—background vocal

"Can't Run But"
Recorded at Transamerica Studios and Impressao Digital Studios, Rio de Janeiro, Brazil
Musicians
Uakti (Marco Antônio Guimarães, Paulinho Santos, Decio Ramos, Arthur Andres)—percussion
Nana Vasconcelos—percussion
Mingo Araujo and Remy Kabocka—talking drum
Mingo Araujo—triangle and castinet
Mazzola—chicote

Paulo Santos—chicote

Basic track arranged by Marco Antonio Guimaraes

Recorded at The Hit Factory, NYC.

Musicians

J. J. Cale—guitar   Steve Gadd—drums

"The Coast"

Words by Paul; music by Paul Simon and Vincent Nguini
Recorded at Transamerica Studios, Multi Studios, and Impressao Digital
Studios, Rio de Janeiro, Brazil, and The Hit Factory, New York

Musicians

Vincent Nguini—guitars   Charles Doherty—alto sax
Bakithi Kumalo—bass   Clifton Anderson—trombone
Nana Vasconcelos—gourds and voice   Errol Ince—trumpet
Michael Brecker—Akai EWI   Clyde Mitchell—trumpet
   synthesizer   Ladysmith Black Mambazo, Karen
Mingo Araujo—African bells and   Bernod—vocals
   shaker   Myrna Lynn Gomila—vocals
Greg Phillinganes—synthesizer   Kia Y. Jeffries—background vocals
Jude Bethel—tenor sax

"Proof"

Recorded at Studio Guillhaume Tell, Paris; Impressao Digital Studios, Rio de
Janeiro, Brazil; and The Hit Factory, New York

Musicians

Georges Seba—guitar   Mingo Araujo—talking drum, cymbal,
Martin Atangana—guitar   bass drums
Andre Manga—bass   Alain Hatot—saxophone
Bakithi Kumalo—bass   Phillipe Slominski—trumpet
Justin Tchounou—synthesizer   Jacques Bolognesi—trombone
Steve Gadd—drums   Jimmy McDonald—accordion
Ya Yo de la Nelson—chakeire   Florence Gnimagnon—vocals
Sidinho—water bowl   Djana'd, Elolongue Mbango
Dom Chacal—bongo   Catherine—vocals
                               Briz—vocals

"Further to Fly"

Recorded at Transamerica Studios and Impressao Digital Studios, Rio de Janeiro, Brazil, and The Hit Factory, New York

Musicians

Vincent Nguini—guitar
Rego Star—guitar
Vincent Nguini—bass
Rafael Rabello—classical guitar
Sidinho—bongos
Dom Chacal—congas
Sidinho—congas
Mingo Araujo—percussion
Dom Chacal—bata
Nana Vasconcelos—gourds

Jorginho, Marcalzinho, Wilson das Neves, Canegal, Beloba, Luna and Pedro Sorongo—additional percussion effects
Greg Phillinganes—synthesizer
Dave Bargeron—euphonium
Randy Brecker—trumpet
Hugh Masekela—flugelhorn
Michael Brecker—Akai EWI synthesizer

"She Moves On"

Recorded at Impressao Digital Studios, Rio de Janeiro, Brazil, and The Hit Factory, New York

Musicians

Vincent Nguini—guitar
Ray Phiri—guitar
Armand Sabel-Lecco—bass
Sidinho—conga
Dom Chacal—bongo
Mingo Araujo—conga
Gordinho—sordu
Wilson das Neves—cowbell

Pedro Sorongo—scraper
Michael Brecker—saxophones
Randy Brecker—piccolo trumpet
Florence Gnimagnon—vocals
Charlotte Mbango—vocals
Djana'd—vocals
Elolongue Mbango Catherine—vocals

"Born at the Right Time"

Recorded at The Hit Factory, New York; Impressao Digital Studios, Rio de Janeiro, Brazil; and Studio Guillhaume Tell, Paris

Musicians

Vincent Nguini—guitar
J. J. Cale—guitar

Armand Sabel-Lecco—bass
Bakithi Kumalo—bass

Felix Sabel-Lecco—drums
C. J. Chenier—accordion
Ya Yo de la Nelson—chakeire
Sidinho—bass drum, conga, bottles
Dom Chacal—conga
Mingo Araujo—conga

Mingo Araujo—go go bells
Florence Gnimagnon—vocals
Charlotte Mbango—vocals
Djana'd, Elolongue Mbango
    Catherine—vocals

"The Cool, Cool River"

Recorded at Transamerica Studio, Rio de Janeiro, Brazil, and at The Hit Factory, New York

Musicians

Vincent Nguini—guitars, bass
Greg Phillinganes—synthesizer
Mingo Araujo—conga and triangle
Ya Yo de la Nelson—chakeire
Nana Vasconcelos—berimbau and
    gourd
Asante—box drum

Uakti—percussion effects
Michael Brecker—Akai EWI
    synthesizer
Charles Doherty—tenor sax, alto sax
Clifton Anderson—trombone
Errol Ince—trumpet
Clyde Mitchell—trumpet

"Spirit Voices" (Portuguese lyrics by Milton Nascimento)

Recorded at The Hit Factory, New York, and at Impressao Digital Studios, Rio de Janeiro, Brazil

Musicians

Milton Nascimento—vocals
Vincent Nguini—guitars, clave
Bakithi Kumalo—bass
Armand Sabel-Lecco—bass
Sidinho—tambourine, congas
Francisco Aguabella—congas
Giovanni Hildago—congas
Anthony Carrillo—bongo

Dom Chacal—gourd
Nana Vasconcelos—triangle, congas,
    and gourds
Mingo Araujo—bass drum
Michael Brecker—Akai EWI
    synthesizer
Adrian Belew—guitar synthesizer

"The Rhythm of the Saints"

Recorded at Transamerica Studio and Impressao Digital Studios, Rio de Janeiro, Brazil, and at The Hit Factory, New York

Musicians

Kofi Electrik—guitar
Vincent Nguini—guitar
Tommy Bilson-Ogoe—guitar
Armand Sabel-Lecco—bass
Joao Severo da Silva—accordion
Produced by: Paul Simon
Engineered by: Roy Halee

Uakti—percussion
Nana Vasconcelos—percussion and
   berimbau
Armando Macedo—baiana guitar

A million dollars later, *The Rhythm of the Saints* was complete—a lurid, liquid album whose musical roots, if anything, are even closer to the surface than they appeared on *Graceland*, and just as true to their origins.

Or it was almost complete. At the last moment, however, Simon had a change of heart, not about the contents of the album itself but the order in which those contents would appear. And that can be just as important.

In Simon's original vision, the album would open with "The Coast" and would then continue on as follows: "She Moves On," "Proof," "Born at the Right Time," "The Cool, Cool River," "The Obvious Child," "Can't Run But," "Spirit Voices," "Further to Fly," and, finally, "Rhythm of the Saints."

On the revised version, only the title track remains in its originally ordained place; only two songs ("Can't Run But" and "The Cool, Cool River") follow on from the songs they were initially intended to succeed. Across the entire album, it was a radical change. But it would appear also to have been the correct decision. The album hangs together better in its revised form.

As an opening track, "The Obvious Child" in particular drags listeners to their feet, its irresistible rhythm still echoing from the walls and balconies of Pelourinho Square, just as "Can't Run But" and "The Coast" echo with the noises of the jungle—a creeping, slithering sensation whose closest musical relative might easily be one of the young Dr. John's early *gris gris ju ju* conjurations, and a reminder, of course, that the music that informs the musicians of Brazil would also make its way across the Caribbean, and into the Creole quarter of New Orleans.

Moment for moment, it would not be as memorable an album as the best of *Graceland*, but neither, as its predecessor did, would it meander off point for a few of the songs. More than before, Simon melded his melodies to those that his accomplices concocted—there would be no "You Can Call Me Al" here, and no sideways glance towards Los Lobos and co.

But the same sense of gleeful exuberance permeated the record, and the public response was scarcely less enthused than it was four years earlier. *The Rhythm of the Saints* gave Simon a second album chart-topper in the United Kingdom and elsewhere, and in reaching number four in the United States, it slipped only marginally behind *Graceland*.

Another Concert in the Park

Reviews, unhindered by any sense of political controversy, were almost unanimously supportive; the *Born at the Right Time* tour that followed, in 1991, was easily oversubscribed, and astonishing, too, was the ease with which Simon blended old and new songs into a single celebration of his latest sound.

Even more satisfyingly, more than one critic was quick to point out that, for the first time in his solo career, Simon's "new" songs were receiving more rapturous applause, and more shouted requests as well, than anything from his past.

That must have been intensely satisfying for Simon. And, for the same reasons, one could excuse him if he believed that the climax of the tour might well have been the show that kicked it off, on August 15, 1991, on a cloudy day in Central Park.

November 1991: *Paul Simon's Concert in the Park* (Warner Brothers 26737)

"The Obvious Child" (special guests: Grupo Cultural OLODUM (Percussion) and Briz (vocals)

"The Boy in the Bubble"

"She Moves On"

"Kodachrome"

"Born at the Right Time"

"Train in the Distance"

"Me and Julio Down by the Schoolyard"

"I Know What I Know"

"The Cool, Cool River"

"Bridge Over Troubled Water"

"Proof"

"The Coast"

"Graceland"

"You Can Call Me Al"

"Still Crazy After All These Years"

"Loves Me Like A Rock"

"Diamonds on the Soles of Her
    Shoes"

"Hearts and Bones"

"Late in the Evening"

"America"

"The Boxer"

"Cecilia"

"The Sound of Silence"

Produced by Paul Simon. Musical supervision by Roy Halee. Engineered by Roy Halee, Stacey Foster, Jay Vicari, and Rich Travali. Remixed by Roy Halee at The Hit Factory, New York City. Assistant: Rich Travali.

Recorded live in Central Park, New York City, on August 15, 1991.

Musicians

Mingo Araujo, Cyro Baptista,
    Dom Chacal, and Sidinho
    Moreira—percussion

Chris Botti—trumpet

Michael Brecker—saxophone and EWI

Tony Cedras—keyboards and
    accordion

Steve Gadd—drums

Vincent Nguini, Ray Phiri, and John
    Selolwane—guitars

Barney Rachabane—saxophone and
    pennywhistle

Armand Sabel-Lecco—bass

Richard Tee—keyboards

The Waters (Julia, Maxine, and
    Oren)—vocalists

Again a free concert. Again an audience that shattered records—reports estimate around three-quarters of a million people crammed themselves into Sheep Meadow for the occasion. Again a magnificent live album, a fabulous concert film.

This time, however, he'd done it on his own. He still played the oldest songs, of course, and he still ended the show with "The Sound of Silence." But "Bridge Over Troubled Water" was relegated to somewhere around the middle of the set, and "Cecilia" was so dramatically reconfigured that it could have slipped off *The Rhythm of the Saints* itself.

It had taken twenty years, but the ghosts of Paul Simon's past had finally been laid.

So, of course, he reawakened them.

In May the following year, Simon and Garfunkel combined once more, this time to join another precious reunion, as comedic legends Mike Nichols and Elaine May regrouped to headline a benefit for cancer-stricken children. Three decades earlier, the pair's act was among the highlights of NBC's long-running *Monitor* variety show; a little more recently than that, it was Nichols who first introduced Simon and Garfunkel to Hollywood (see chapter 13).

Repeated across two nights at the Atkinson Theater in Manhattan, Simon and Garfunkel's set was short, just eight songs ("The Boxer," "Scarborough Fair," "Mrs. Robinson," "America," "Homeward Bound," "The Sound of Silence," "The 59th Street Bridge Song," and "Old Friends/ Bookends"), but it was also a rapprochement. The year 1993 marked the thirtieth anniversary of Simon and Garfunkel's emergence from the chrysalis of Tom and Jerry et al., and it was not an occasion that either intended overlooking.

Simon had already organized the release of a three-CD box set spanning his entire career to date (see sidebar). Garfunkel, even though his physical contributions to that career amounted to little more than one-third, was nevertheless an integral part of it. Simon determined to involve him in the celebration.

The Ultimate (For Now) *Paul Simon Anthology*

1964 / 1993 (Warner Brothers 9 45394-2)

Disc One

"Leaves That Are Green" (*The Paul Simon Songbook*)

"The Sound of Silence" (Simon and Garfunkel—*Sound of Silence*)

"Kathy's Song" (live) (Simon and Garfunkel—*Simon and Garfunkel's Greatest Hits*)

"America" (Simon and Garfunkel—*Bookends*)

"Cecilia" (Simon and Garfunkel—*Bridge Over Troubled Water*)

"El Condor Pasa" (If I Could) (Simon and Garfunkel—*Bridge Over Troubled Water*)

"The Boxer" (Simon and Garfunkel—*Bridge Over Troubled Water*)

"Mrs. Robinson" (Simon and Garfunkel—*Bookends*)

"Bridge Over Troubled Water" (demo)

"Bridge Over Troubled Water" (Simon and Garfunkel—*Bridge Over Troubled Water*)

"The Breakup" (Simon and Garfunkel—spoken word)

"Hey, Schoolgirl" (Tom and Jerry)

"My Little Town" (Simon and Garfunkel—*Still Crazy After All These Years*)

"Me and Julio Down by the Schoolyard" (*Paul Simon*)

"Peace Like a River" (*Paul Simon*)

"Mother and Child Reunion" (*Paul Simon*)

"Congratulations" (*Paul Simon*)

"Duncan" (*Live Rhymin'*)

"American Tune" (*There Goes Rhymin' Simon*)

Disc Two

"Loves Me Like a Rock" (*There Goes Rhymin' Simon*)

"Tenderness" (*There Goes Rhymin' Simon*)

"Kodachrome" (*There Goes Rhymin' Simon*)

"Gone at Last" (*Still Crazy After All These Years*)

"Take Me to the Mardi Gras" (*There Goes Rhymin' Simon*)

"St. Judy's Comet" (*There Goes Rhymin' Simon*)

"Something So Right" (*There Goes Rhymin' Simon*)

"Still Crazy After All These Years" (live in Dortmund, Germany, July 4, 1991)

"Have a Good Time" (*Still Crazy After All These Years*)

"Jonah" (*One-Trick Pony*)

"How the Heart Approaches What It Yearns" (*One-Trick Pony*)

"50 Ways to Leave Your Lover" (*Still Crazy After All These Years*)

"Slip Slidin' Away" (*Greatest Hits, Etc.*)

"Late in the Evening" (*One-Trick Pony*)

"Hearts and Bones" (*Hearts and Bones*)

"René and Georgette Magritte with Their Dog After the War" (*Hearts and Bones*)

"The Late Great Johnny Ace" (*Hearts and Bones*)

Disc Three

"The Boy in the Bubble" (*Graceland*)

"Graceland" (*Graceland*)

"Under African Skies" (*Graceland*)

"That Was Your Mother" (*Graceland*)

"Diamonds on the Soles of Her Shoes" (*Graceland*)

"You Can Call Me Al" (*Graceland*)

"Homeless" (*Graceland*)
"Spirit Voices" (*Rhythm of the Saints*)
"The Obvious Child" (*Rhythm of the Saints*)
"Can't Run But" (*Rhythm of the Saints*)
"Thelma" (*Rhythm of the Saints* outtake)
"Further to Fly" (*Rhythm of the Saints*)
"She Moves On" (*Rhythm of the Saints*)
"Born at the Right Time" (*Paul Simon's Concert in the Park*)
"The Cool, Cool River" (*Paul Simon's Concert in the Park*)
"The Sound of Silence" (*Paul Simon's Concert in the Park*)

The Concert Event of a Lifetime

Simon's modestly titled Concert Event of a Lifetime was originally intended to run for ten nights at the Paramount Theater in New York. However, the sheer demand for tickets ultimately saw that tally rise to twenty-one shows, with some one hundred thousand people paying up to $100 a ticket to witness it.

It was as ambitious as it was grandiose.

On each of those twenty-one nights, Simon would effectively oversee the re-creation of the box set on stage, with the evening effectively divided into three key parts.

First, Simon and Garfunkel would reconnect (both were careful not to describe the event as a reunion) to re-create at least a few of the highlights of their time together and deliver a handful of surprises as well. And so "Be Bop a Lula," "Black Slacks," and their own "Hey Schoolgirl" sidled in alongside the expected "The Boxer," "Mrs. Robinson," and "Homeward Bound"; and at the end of the evening, the pair would regroup again for "Bridge Over Troubled Water," "Cecilia," "Kathy's Song," and "The Sound of Silence."

In between times, though, Simon conjured an equally spellbinding dance through the twenty-plus years that followed that era, from "Me and Julio Down by the Schoolyard" to "You Can Call Me Al," a song that had taken on fresh resonance following the election of Al Gore to the vice presidency of the United States.

Guests proliferated—the Mighty Clouds of Joy re-creating the gospel qualities of "Loves Me Like a Rock," and Phoebe Snow conjuring liquid gold from the gorgeous "Gone at Last"; Ladysmith Black Mambazo reigniting the rhythms and passions of *Graceland*; comedian Steve Martin relishing the now-quaint irony of "The 59th Street Bridge Song (Feelin' Groovy)"; and Simon overseeing it all with an expression that at least in part echoed the same amazement that was etched on the face of every ticket holder in the room.

The idea, after all, was to re-create the original music in as exact a form as was possible. There would be no rock band pumping away behind "Scarborough Fair"—Simon and Garfunkel's set would be exactly what it ought to be, as Garfunkel purred to the *New York Times*: "I love working with Paul acoustically. That's the key to the whole thing. I really believe in Simon and Garfunkel as an acoustic act, and I have a lot of appetite for this."

So did the critics. "In past concerts, Mr. Simon's meticulousness has sometimes interfered with the groove," observed the *New York Times*. "He would end songs just as they were starting to lift off. But at the Paramount, with no loss of control, Mr. Simon and his band turned songs like 'Proof' and a South Africanized version of 'Me and Julio Down by the Schoolyard' into celebrations of rhythm and riffs. While both band and audience had the most kinetic fun with songs from Mr. Simon's last two studio albums Mr. Simon's intricately chromatic ballads from back in the 1970s still rang true."

Still denying they had reunited, Simon and Garfunkel also appeared at Neil Young's annual Bridge School Benefit Concert in November, before embarking upon a Japanese tour.

But that was it. Not only did the pair part, but they did so under what was surely the darkest and most damaging cloud they ever had—so dark that its true causes have never been discussed. But when the solo Simon was inducted into the Rock and Roll Hall of Fame in 2001, he could not resist a most singular barb.

"I regret the ending of our friendship. I hope that some day before we die we will make peace with each other." But then, after a pause, he finally said, "No rush."

13

Stage and Screen

I t was *Parsley, Sage, Rosemary and Thyme* that first brought Simon and
Garfunkel to comedian-turned-director Mike Nichols's attention.

He had recently acquired the film rights to *The Graduate*, Charles
Webb's novel about an affair between a more or less inert college kid
and a bored housewife (who is also a friend of his parents); and while he
would retain that premise, Nichols envisioned the movie as a lot more—a
commentary on the hypocrisy of modern American values, particularly
as they were practiced by the moneyed classes. But, still basking in the
success of his last movie—*Who's Afraid of Virginia Woolf?*—and with a
similarly successful Broadway streak behind him, Nichols had no intention of making things easy for himself.

His scriptwriter, Buck Henry, was all but unknown; his casting
scoured the theater rather than the silver screen; and where the novel
demanded an Adonis-like WASP as its hero, all blonde hair and buff
frame, Nichols chose Dustin Hoffman at a time when the diminutive
dark-haired Jew was still awaiting the release of his debut movie, *The
Tiger Makes Out.*

The parallels between a young man rejecting the mores of his parents'
generation and German Jew Nichols's own experiences as a first-gen-
eration immigrant struggling to accept (and be accepted by) American
reality were to be written loudly across the movie.

And, as if to emphasize the movie's identification with American
youth, Nichols required a soundtrack that was equally inwardly rebel-
lious. He was also aware that no "serious" Hollywood drama had ever
looked toward rock 'n' roll for its score. That, too, was a vital consideration.

His copy of Simon and Garfunkel's then (1966) latest album, *Parsley,
Sage, Rosemary and Thyme*, had been a gift from Nichols's younger
brother and, once he heard it, the filmmaker knew he had found the artists he was looking for.

Producer Larry Turman was instructed to make the first overtures, and although the duo was initially skeptical, they agreed to meet with Nichols and were immediately convinced.

Their schedule was tight, however. Columbia was crying out for the pair's next album, and they had a hectic tour schedule to manage. In addition, although they probably didn't mention this at the time, Simon was undergoing one of his periodic spells of writer's block and hadn't actually written what he considered a new song in some six months.

Any hopes Nichols may have had of extracting a full soundtrack from the duo, then, were dashed. But Simon agreed to supply three new songs while also opening up the back catalog to Nichols—"The Sound of Silence," "The Big Bright Green Pleasure Machine," "Scarborough Fair/Canticle," and "April Come She Will" would all be bookmarked for the movie's rushes at least, alongside half a dozen pieces composed by the more conventional soundtrack regular Dave Grusin.

Having got the artists he wanted, Nichols now became picky. The first two songs that Simon offered up for the movie, "Punky's Dilemma" and "Overs," were both rejected. It was not, he explained, because he didn't like the songs. He just didn't sense the mood he was looking for and pointed Simon back to the songs that were already being used. *That* mood. That sense of somebody barely holding things together, hanging on in quiet desperation in the hope that something might change.

And something a little more upbeat as well, please, to give the movie its theme song.

Simon promised to do his best; Garfunkel suspected he may already have accomplished it. Talking privately with Nichols later, he mentioned a fragment of a song that Simon had been toying with, ineffably buoyant, catchy, and commercial. He had a lyric, too, or a fragment of one, at any rate—"Here's to you, Mrs. Roosevelt"—which just happened to have the same number of syllables as the movie's *other* central character, Mrs. Robinson.

Nichols had his theme, and Simon had barely even written it yet; in fact, *The Graduate* was about to enter its final edit and Simon still only had the music completed—enough for Nichols to weave into his movie a percussive minute-long strum, accompanied by a few dee-dee-dees and a tentative attempt at the song's chorus, and a scarcely longer version that is more instrumental than anything else. The full song, the one that would become such a monster hit and is now so indelibly associated with the movie, would arrive later.

The soundtrack was not yet out of the woods, however. Piqued by the continued delay in the duo's next album (the *Bookends* sessions would not ultimately get underway until March 1968), Columbia was now pushing for an LP enshrining the duo's contributions to *The Graduate*.

The movie itself was regarded as an inevitable success (as indeed it would be). An accompanying soundtrack album, said the label, would doubtless do just as well, and the presence of a new Simon and Garfunkel song—even if it was little more than a demo—could only improve things further.

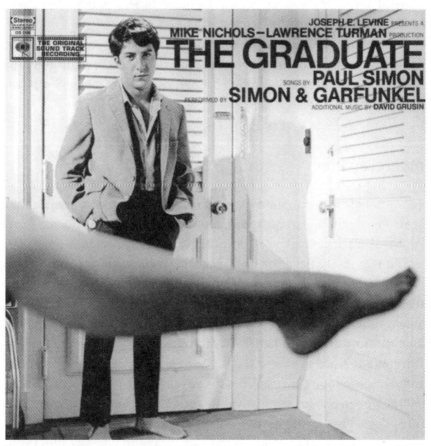

The hit "Mrs Robinson" ensured that the soundtrack to *The Graduate* would become a hit.

Author's collection

The duo demurred; they not only feared the ridicule that would normally accompany any "new" album that barely featured two minutes of fresh, unfinished music, but they were also unwilling to have anything on the market that might detract from their next "real" album.

But label head Clive Davies was persuasive. Just weeks after *The Graduate* opened to ecstatic reviews, its soundtrack was released and on the way to the top of the charts. Simon and Garfunkel had their first American number one album—and Simon needed only write two minutes of music to earn it.

Furthermore, any questions that may arise regarding the album's right to be described as a Simon and Garfunkel album (in terms of content, it is, after all, just half of one) were put to rest in 2014, when *The Graduate: The Original Sound Track Recording* was included in Simon and Garfunkel's boxed *Complete Albums Collection*.

Meanwhile, the highest-grossing film of 1967 went on to earn seven Academy Award nominations and scoop the Best Director gong for Nichols. It also introduced him to the star of his next movie, *Catch-22*. Art Garfunkel.

Monterey Pop

The Graduate was not Simon and Garfunkel's sole movie project that year. They would also be appearing in *Monterey Pop*, director D. A. Pennebaker's documentary of the festival of the same name.

The movie, like the event itself, was a sprawling affair.

Organized by a team that included John Phillips of the Mamas and the Papas, record producer Lou Adler, and Beatles publicist Derek Taylor, among others, the Monterey Pop Festival was rock 'n' roll's answer to the long-running Monterey Jazz Festival, staged at the Monterey County Fairgrounds since 1958, and the Big Sur Folk Festival, which had been running since 1964 and headlined every year by Joan Baez.

The lineup for the pop festival was somewhat more eclectic. Across three days, June 16–18, both the monsters of rock and their unknown siblings would take the stage—Jefferson Airplane and the Grateful Dead, at the height of their personal breakout years; British Invasion veterans the Who and the Animals; California folk-rock pioneers the Byrds; anti-war rabble-rousers-in-chief Country Joe and the Fish; one of the biggest names in soul and R&B, Otis Redding; Indian sitar maestro Ravi Shankar; bluesmen Paul Butterfield and Canned Heat; the fast-rising Steve Miller Band and Quicksilver Messenger Service; singer-songwriters Laura Nyro and Scott McKenzie; and playing his first-ever major American concert, a Seattle-born, London-based obscurity named Jimi Hendrix. He played the guitar, apparently.

Simon and Garfunkel would be headlining the Friday night bill.

The duo's involvement in the festival was, at least in part, a business decision. Earlier in the year, as the notion of the festival initially took hold of Phillips and Adler, Paul Simon was one of the first potential investors they contacted. Mounting any such event was an expensive proposition, but three days of the biggest names on the rock scene was going to be more than that.

Simon agreed to put up $50,000 and was elected onto the festival's board of directors alongside the likes of Paul McCartney, Mick Jagger and Brian Jones of the Rolling Stones, their manager Andrew Loog Oldham, and the Beach Boys' Brian Wilson. It was Simon, apparently, whose diplomatic skills persuaded San Francisco's Airplane and Dead to appear at an event they had previously viewed as Los Angeles attempting to steal some of their home city's musical fire.

Friday's bill was not, in fairness, the most exciting of them all. The Association were best known for the sugary-sweet hit "Windy"; Johnny Rivers, Lou Rawls, and Beverley weren't even known for that; and the Paupers were only on the bill because their manager, Albert Grossman, wouldn't allow any of his other acts to appear without them.

But the Animals, reconfigured around frontman Eric Burdon's insatiable appetite for the newborn psychedelic scene, promised to deliver an electrifying show, while backstage, Simon ran into the aforementioned unknown Hendrix, talked to him long enough to realize that it was only America that had never heard of him—in the United Kingdom, he was onto his third Top 10 single and had a monster hit album as well—and then sat and jammed with him on acoustic guitars.

Pennebaker's cameras weren't around for that. They did, however, catch Simon and Garfunkel's full set—abbreviated from their in concert norm but still producing a powerful seven-song showing.

Taking the stage at 1:00 a.m., the duo were introduced by John Phillips: "We'd like to introduce to you at this time, two very, very good friends of mine and two people who in the music business are respected by everyone, Paul Simon and Art Garfunkel."

They were dressed as they always dressed, turtle neck sweaters and slacks, and were clearly in a good mood. As the stage lights changed to a lush scarlet, Simon couldn't help remarking, "Ah, you dig the red lights . . . associated in my mind with, uh, for another good time. Very Pavlovian."

"Homeward Bound," "At the Zoo," "The 59th Street Bridge Song (Feelin' Groovy)" (the red light song!), "For Emily, Whenever I May Find Her," "The Sound of Silence," and "Benedictus" ("a blessing," Paul announced) all received rapturous applause, and for a moment, it sounded as though they were going to close with another favorite, "I Am a Rock."

Then Paul changed his mind and went, instead, into the *Graduate* reject "Punky's Dilemma," the first time it had ever been performed live.

The Monterey Pop Festival Lineup, 1967

Friday, June 16

The Association

The Paupers

Lou Rawls

Beverley

Johnny Rivers

Eric Burdon and the Animals

Simon and Garfunkel

Saturday, June 17

Canned Heat

Big Brother and the Holding Company

Country Joe and the Fish

Al Kooper

The Butterfield Blues Band
The Electric Flag
Quicksilver Messenger Service
Steve Miller Band
Moby Grape
Hugh Masekela
The Byrds
Laura Nyro
Jefferson Airplane
Booker T. and the MGs
The Mar-Keys
Otis Redding

Sunday, June 18

Ravi Shankar
The Blues Project
Big Brother and the Holding Company
The Group with No Name
Buffalo Springfield (with David Crosby)
The Who
Grateful Dead
The Jimi Hendrix Experience
Scott McKenzie
The Mamas and the Papas

The Monterey Pop movie appeared the following year, showcasing just fourteen of the acts that appeared at the event itself and confining the majority of them to just one single song. (The Mamas and the Papas, presumably by virtue of Phillips's role in organizing the festival, had two.)

Simon and Garfunkel's contribution was "The 59th Street Bridge Song (Feelin' Groovy)"—certainly the jauntiest of the numbers they performed but perhaps the most misleading, as well. A set that was characterized by its thoughtfulness probably shouldn't have been immortalized with its one concession to fluff.

Two further performances, "Homeward Bound" and "The Sound of Silence," would appear on the Criterion Collection reissue of the movie in 2002. However, when great swaths of the festival were released as a four-disc box set, with many of the bands granting permission for their entire performances to be included, Simon and Garfunkel moved in the opposite direction entirely and refused permission for a note of their music to appear. The sounds that delighted festival and moviegoers alike were apparently deemed unsuitable for CD.

Simon and Garfunkel's reluctance to throw themselves into the festival circuit that so marked out the last years of the sixties for many of their contemporaries ensured they would be absent from any of the other great live movies of the age—they were, apparently, invited to appear at Woodstock in 1969, but Garfunkel's movie commitments made that impossible, and a suggestion that they play August 1970's Isle of Wight Festival in England, which was to be filmed by Murray Lerner, was rendered academic by their breakup.

One-Trick Pony and Other Tales

Indeed, for the next decade, any fan hankering to catch either of the duo on the big screen needed to make do with Garfunkel's decidedly unmusical roles instead—following on from *Catch-22*, he went on to appear in two further big-screen enterprises, *Carnal Knowledge* (1971) and *Bad Timing* (1980), and one television movie, *Acts of Love and Other Comedies* (1973).

Simon, too, largely avoided the cameras until 1977 saw him invited to play the role of Tony Lacey, a greasy music producer in Woody Allen's upcoming *Annie Hall*. Allen even agreed to let Simon write his own lines—the latter had far more experience with this kind of character than the filmmaker, after all.

Simon's role was small, no more than two scenes, but he played it well—played it, in fact, with such perfection that more than one past (or even present) associate must have wondered precisely upon whom Simon based this open-shirted, hairy-chested, coke-spoon-toting slime ball. Perhaps they wonder still.

Art Garfunkel, as seen in *Carnal Knowledge*   *Photofest*

Annie Hall arrived at a propitious time, too, allowing Simon a hands-on experience in filmmaking at precisely the moment he was getting serious about what would simultaneously be seen as both his most ambitious solo project yet and, sadly, his most unsuccessful—a movie of his own. It was called *One-Trick Pony*.

In truth, few rock stars have ever truly negotiated the gulf that lies between a successful musical career and its translation into successful moviemaking—not even the Beatles, whose self-made *Magical Mystery Tour*, in 1967, became the first resounding flop of their entire career together.

Bob Dylan, too, foundered. In 1975–76, as he toured the United States with his Rolling Thunder Revue, the cameras followed him every step of the way, preserving the event for what would become *Renaldo and*

Clara—a four-hour movie that, though utterly enthralling and musically peerless, bombed long before Dylan edited it down to around half that length.

Neil Young, too, had tried his hand at moviemaking, but 1974's *Journey Through the Past* came and went from the theaters so quickly that many fans didn't get to see it until it was finally released on Blu-ray in 2009; and even as Paul Simon prepared to begin work on *One-Trick Pony*, Young was embarking on a four-year mission to complete *Human Highway*. He did it, too, but the movie sank without trace.

One-Trick Pony would soon be staking out its own special place on this ignominious butcher's list, beloved by the truly faithful, ignored by virtually everybody else.

Dave Marsh, in *Rolling Stone*, was one of the people who "got it." It was an "interesting rock movie," he wrote, if only because it looked at life from the bottom up. Most films of its ilk, after all, relish the glamor and glitz of a pop star's career. *One-Trick Pony* took the opposite tack—an approach, said Marsh, that said as much about its maker as its subject matter. "Remember the night he was guest host on *Saturday Night Live*, and he came out for the opening bit wearing a turkey suit? The joke was that though Simon might make any number of rational arguments about why a turkey costume was inappropriate, he would not simply rip it off and stomp away. *One-Trick Pony* is a movie filled with people who would rather wear the turkey suit than make too much fuss."

Although there are certainly similarities to be drawn between Paul Simon and Jonah, the character he created for *One-Trick Pony*—and that is certainly one of them—the story itself is less autobiography than it is a glimpse inside an alternate reality. One that could itself have been Simon's.

Like his creator, Jonah Levin is a mid-thirties singer-songwriter, estranged from his wife and son (Simon and first wife, Peggy, were parents to Harper, born in 1972), and still touring after all these years. Unlike Simon, he had one big hit in the mid-sixties, and since then, the cash registers have echoed only to the sound of silence.

Not a sniff of a follow-up hit has assailed his nostrils; instead, he just keeps on keeping on because there's nothing else he can do—least of all abandon music for the life of quiet, safe domesticity that his wife and son deserve.

Simon threw himself with abandon into examining not the failure but the life of the struggling older musician. His old friend Dave Van Ronk was one of the pioneers of the Greenwich Village folk scene back before even Bob Dylan, let alone Jerry Landis, set foot in his first coffee house.

The breaks hadn't gone his way, either. It was Van Ronk who came up with the revolutionary new arrangement of "The House of the Rising Sun" that highlighted Dylan's first album, but it was Dylan who received the plaudits; Van Ronk who came closest to joining Peter Yarrow and Mary Travers in what was expected to be a chart-topping new folk trio; but Noel Stookey who ultimately became the missing Paul. If anybody could offer Simon an insider's-eye view of a life lived outside of pop's mainstream, it was Van Ronk.

Plus, they had known one another way back when, and Van Ronk himself would admit, on occasion, that at least some of the disappointments that had held his career back were ones that he had purposefully engineered in the first place. Some people, despite their claims to the contrary, simply don't want to be recognized.

There were other thoughts on Simon's mind. With his Columbia deal nearing an end, he was keen to renegotiate at a far more advantageous rate. But his old friend Clive Davis no longer headed up the company; he had been replaced by the bullish Walter Yetnikoff, who had no interest whatsoever in allowing any artist to dictate his own terms.

There were, apparently, several occasions upon which a deal seemed close, but every time, something screwed it up. Finally, Yetnikoff is said to have loudly declared that Simon no longer had any kind of deal with the label—news of which immediately alerted Warner Brothers then-chairman Mo Ostin. He was a longtime fan of Simon's and would have loved to add him to the WB stable.

Whether Yetnikoff was serious about dropping Simon or not, all the singer needed to do was deliver one last album to Columbia, and his contract would be fulfilled. It was the nature of that album which now infuriated the label head—one of the world's greatest, and most successful, songwriters announced his next LP would be a collection of favorite covers.

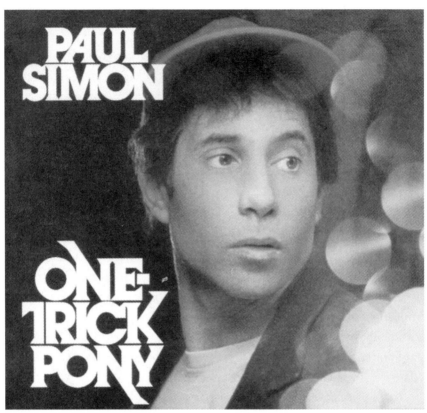

The movie did not set the world afire, but its soundtrack album remains a fan favorite.
Author's collection

It wasn't that outlandish a notion. Columbia labelmate Bob Dylan had come close to such a thing with his 1970 album *Self Portrait*—just seven of the double album's twenty-four tracks were Dylan originals, and Paul Simon's "The Boxer" was one of the songs that Dylan chose to cover. And three years later, with Dylan now recording his next album for another label, Columbia released *Dylan*, an album comprising nothing but covers.

That same year, David Bowie responded to a dispute with his publishing company by effectively going on strike and threatening his own album's worth of covers. They didn't believe him, so he went ahead with it, and *Pin Ups*, his tribute to the music he'd loved in London a decade earlier, remains one of Bowie's most unexpectedly delightful records.

So Simon's threat had precedent, but Yetnikoff was not in the mood for a history lesson. Instead he threatened to sue; Simon countersued; and even with the proffered Warner Brothers deal now a reality, the affair could have dragged on interminably.

Ultimately, however, the two sides settled—Simon abandoned the threatened LP and instead bought himself out of what remained of his contract for a reported $1.5 million. He then promptly wrote Yetnikoff into the script of *One-Trick Pony*. He is Walter Fox—the chosen surname being a direct translation of the executive's Yiddish nickname, Velvel.

There was another advantage to escaping Columbia and moving to Warner Brothers. The label was steeped in movie history. With their weight behind the project and one of their own staff producers, Anthea Sylbert, onboard the project, *One-Trick Pony* was off to the races already.

The search began for a director. Mike Nichols was Simon's first choice, but his calendar was full. Another choice, Alan Parker (*Midnight Express* and *Bugsy Malone*) was interested but wondered whether Simon would allow him the creative freedom he would require—ironically, Parker's next major project would be *The Wall*, the brainchild of one of rock's other notorious control freaks, Roger Waters.

Simon eventually selected Robert Young, better known as a documentary maker but a smart choice regardless. "His ego didn't get in the way," Simon told *People's* Jim Jerome when the film was released.

Simon's early choices for lead actor—Dustin Hoffman and Richard Dreyfuss, among others—also disappointed him, although their reasoning had less to do with script or freedom than with their inability see themselves lip-synching through the dozen songs that Simon had written and recorded for the movie and that would need to be seen to be performed. Both actors told him much the same thing—"Why don't you play the role yourself?"

Buoyed by the positive reviews that he'd garnered for Tony Lacey but aware that he could not expect to carry the entire movie based on so little experience, Simon hired method acting coach Mira Rostova, and he also set about a fitness regime, losing weight, building muscle.

It's perhaps a little much to say, as one of Simon's biographers would, that he was making himself "more physically attractive"; more likely, he

Paul and Shelley Duval attending the party thrown to mark Simon's first
TV special, 1977.   *Photofest*

was simply preparing himself for the long hours, bad food, and associated
other rigors of filming—and if he had not experienced them for himself,
his current girlfriend, actress Shelley Duval (they met on the set of *Annie
Hall*), could certainly fill him in on them.

Blair Brown was recruited as Jonah's wife, Marion; Rip Torn to play
Walter Fox; Simon's latest band—Eric Gale, Tony Levin, Steve Gadd, and
Richard Tee—would play Jonah's backing group; and New York legend
Lou Reed took a break from his own recording career to portray a record
producer.

The Lou Reed Connection

Some three and a half decades after he and Lou Reed came together for *One-Trick Pony*, Simon was among the guests at Reed's memorial concert in New York, alongside Patti Smith, Debbie Harry, Philip Glass, and many more.

Theirs was not necessarily a friendship that fans of either could have predicted. Indeed, there are few musical careers that could be described as more diametrically opposed than theirs.

At the same time as Simon and Garfunkel were singing "America" and slyly describing the "real estate" in their bag, Reed and his Velvet Underground were openly singing of "Heroin." While Simon's Mrs. Robinson was putting things in the pantry with her cupcakes, the Velvets' "Sister Ray" was enjoying seventeen-minute feedback parties with gay sailors and their ding-dongs.

But they shared a similar musical background. Like Simon, Reed's earliest work was as a contract songwriter and musician on the sub-Brill Building circuit; and, like Simon, Reed would enter the seventies and beyond ranked among New York City—and America's—most sainted contemporary songwriters

Furthermore, *One-Trick Pony* was only the first occasion upon which they would share the spotlight. In 1987, at the Homeless Children's Medical Benefit Concert at Madison Square Garden, Reed joined Simon, Bruce Springsteen, James Taylor, and Billy Joel as backup for vocalists for fellow guest Dion, as he resurrected his old hit "Teenager in Love." And Dion hit the nail on the head when he remarked, "These guys couldn't wait to do it. They all grew up in the fifties wanting to be the Belmonts."

Two years later, when Reed inducted Dion into the Rock and Roll Hall of Fame, Simon was there to duet with Dion on "The Wanderer." And when Reed was hospitalized toward the end of his life, Simon had the perfect gift for him: "We were only born a few months apart, so we listened to the same music, we grew up with the same music and when he was in the hospital I thought he must be so bored, so I sent him these albums of R&B from 1954, 1955, 1956."

For the memorial concert, Simon reached back to the Velvet Underground for his choice of song, a melancholy but perfectly realized "Pale Blue Eyes," saying: "I love this song; I'd sing it and think how beautiful the guitar and just the way he sings, even though he says he hated Long Island, I have his lyric *here because I sang this first and I thought, 'Yeah, what the fuck does that mean?' And I thought, 'Well, I just missed a lot of stories somewhere.'*

In the winter of 1979, the entire production decamped to Cleveland to begin filming. It was a generally light-hearted and problem-free shoot—perhaps the closest it came to disaster was when Simon announced a free concert at the local Agora Club, intending to film the audience for the movie's live scenes, only for the venue to be two-thirds empty on the day.

The accompanying soundtrack album was drawn, at least in part, from this show—two songs, "Ace in the Hole" and "One-Trick Pony" appear as genuine live recordings on the record. The remainder was taped at A&R Studios in New York City, and the initial portents were good, as the first single from the album, "Late in the Evening," made it to number six on the *Billboard* chart.

It's a strange album though. As if he was anxious, now, to draw attention away from the similarities between himself and Jonah Levin, Simon top-loaded the record with what felt (and still feels) like laid-back jazz-pop—yacht rock before its time.

His lyrics, too, seem more focused upon what was happening in the movie than their status as songs in their own right, leaving the listener with two primary thoughts—first, that the music made a lot more sense when accompanied by the movie, and secondly, if all of Jonah's music sounded like this, little wonder that he was the eternal one-hit wonder.

The movie opened on October 3, 1980, and again, early hopes were high. The initial reviews were particularly effusive: the *LA Times* claimed that "one of our most celebrated singer-composers has become an impressive actor and screenwriter"; Roger Ebert, in the *Chicago Sun-Times*, rated it "a wonderful movie"; and even the otherwise skeptical Janet Maslin, in the *New York Times,* professed herself impressed by the music industry scenes.

Which, in itself, was an achievement—most films that try to lift the lid off one aspect of the biz or another usually fall face-first when dealing with that side of things.

But those were the headline reviewers. The remainder weren't so generous, and some were downright hostile, with *Newsweek* speaking for many when it wrote *One-Trick Pony* off as a "vanity production." Which, in many ways, it was, but that in itself is not a problem. Where *One-Trick Pony* most obviously failed was in its audience's inability to distinguish one of the most famous faces in the world, Paul Simon, from one of the most least-known, and *that* was the downside to Hoffman and Geare's advice.

There is a reason why Mick Jagger's most beloved movie role is that of the reclusive degenerate rockstar Turner in Nic Roeg's *Performance*, and David Bowie's was the alien Thomas Jerome Newton in (Roeg again!) *The Man Who Fell to Earth*. Effectively, they are playing themselves, or at least that aspect of "themselves" that their audience most wants to identify with.

A great actor can play a multitude of roles, and that's fine. They are expected to do so. But a great rock star—even a so-called chameleon like Bowie—is not playing "a role." He or she is exemplifying a lifestyle, and stepping outside of that is a lot harder.

Purely on the strength of his scriptwriting and vision, Paul Simon could probably have made a successful movie out of almost any scenario he chose. Almost. Unfortunately, he selected the one that was least likely to be believed: failure. And that, in turn, ensured that the endeavor would become one.

The soundtrack album became Simon's first LP since *Sound of Silence* not to make the Top 10, and the accompanying tour proved less than a sterling draw. But the movie foundered even more desperately, its $8 million budget positively dwarfing the mere $850,000 or so that it grossed.

September 1980: "Late in the Evening"/"How the Heart Approaches What It Yearns" (Warner Brothers WBS 49511)

September 1980: *One-Trick Pony* (Warner Brothers XHS 3472)

"Late in the Evening"	"Oh, Marion"
"That's Why God Made the Movies"	"Ace in the Hole"
"One-Trick Pony"	"Nobody"
"How the Heart Approaches What It Yearns"	"Jonah"
	"God Bless the Absentee"

"Long, Long Day"
Album produced by Paul Simon and Phil Ramone
Recorded in New York City, except tracks 3 and 6, recorded live at the Agora
    Club, Cleveland, Ohio, September 1979

Musicians

Eric Gale—guitar
Hugh McCracken—acoustic guitar
Steve Gadd (drums); Tony
    Levin—bass
Ralph McDonald—percussion
Dave Grusin—horn arrangements
Richard Tee—piano
Hiram Bullock—guitar
Don Grolnick—synthesizer
Ralph McDonald—percussion

Anthony Jackson—bass
Jeff Mironov—guitar
Jon Faddis—flugelhorn
John Tropea—acoustic guitar
Patti Austin—vocals
Joe Beck—guitar
Lani Grove—vocals
Bob Friedman—horn/string
    arrangements

October 1980: "One-Trick Pony"/"Long, Long Day" (Warner Brothers
WBS49601)

February 1981: "Oh, Marion"/"God Bless the Absentee" (Warner Brothers
WBS49675)

"You Can Call Me Al" and Other Pictures

The sad fate of *One-Trick Pony* irrevocably flavored Simon's activities through the first half of the 1980s and convinced him, even on the eve of the career-revitalizing *Graceland*'s release, that his days in the spotlight might be numbered, as he said, "It could be that I've reached the point in my career where I can't be a viable commercial force in popular music."

Of course he did not retreat altogether; or, if he did, it was back into the past via that initially rapturous but ultimately self-destructing reunion with Art Garfunkel.

But *Hearts and Bones* in 1983 did nothing to relieve the agonies of *One-Trick Pony*; it even convinced him, in fact, to eschew the one

Paul's 1983 solo album started life as a Simon and Garfunkel reunion LP.   *Author's collection*

promotional medium that he might actually have excelled at, had he only regained the confidence to do so.

More than three decades on, it is difficult to imagine a time when music videos were not a part of the musical furniture—as hard as it is to truly quantify just how seismic an impact they had when they did arrive, in the form of MTV.

Artists had been recording what many described as "clips" for years. Both the Beatles and the Rolling Stones were old hands at the practice, but if you asked them why, it was generally because they were a labor-saving device. With a new single on the shelves, every television music show in the world would be demanding a moment of their time. A short promotional film, somehow themed around the song, would allow them to say "yes" to every one.

Of course that wasn't the only reason they did it. A good clip was also the chance to make a statement—political, cultural, artistic, whatever. David Bowie, at the height of his *Ziggy Stardust* glam rock phase was responsible for several massively popular (if, at the time, rarely seen) clips, all aimed toward heightening the efficacy of his image; and the film made to accompany Queen's "Bohemian Rhapsody" was a rock opera in its own right, as awe-inspiring as the record itself. Indeed, when, six years later, MTV flickered into life, more than one commentator was convinced that "Bohemian Rhapsody" was the first true rock video. And they may have been correct.

By 1983, the video was firmly entrenched in the artistic arsenal, a must-have for anybody even remotely considering competing in the musical marketplace.

Paul Simon, on the other hand, ignored it. Two singles were released from *Hearts and Bones*, "Allergies" and "Think Too Much," with a third, "René and Georgette Magritte with Their Dog After the War," somewhat courageously treated as a promotion for the entire album.

But there would be no official video for the first two, while the latter was celebrated with a succession of admittedly fascinating clips and images that might have been as obscure to many would-be listeners as the song itself.

With Simon credited as executive producer (Alan Kleinberg was producer), the video was the work of Joan Logue, of New York's Electronic Arts Intermix collective. The organization's website offers up the following description of the piece: "A witty tribute to Magritte's work and a haunting visual interpretation of Simon's music and lyrics. A photograph of the Magrittes serves as the point of departure for both the song and images, as Logue employs video effects to technologically echo and transform the eerie resonances of the surreal imagery of Magritte's paintings."

Now imagine the average early eighties video DJ trying to follow Duran Duran with *that*.

If his first step into the waters of music video was willfully obscure, Simon's second was almost doomed to failure. Almost.

Working with director Catherine Hardwicke, he shot the video for *Graceland*'s first single, "You Can Call Me Al," at the same time as he

Videos were huge in 1983, but the only one to fall from *Hearts and Bones* boasted one of the most uncatchy titles of the year—"Rene and Georgette Magritte with Their Dog After the War."   *Author's collection*

filmed his landmark *Saturday Night Live* performance, on the show's own Rockefeller Center stage.

He was never happy with the final result, though, and Lorne Michaels was one of the first people he apprised of the fact. Michaels, in turn, mentioned it to Chevy Chase and suggested that maybe he offer to help Simon come up with a better one.

The result, directed by Gary Weis, remains one of the most distinctive videos of the age, with Chase and Simon initially seated side by side until Chase takes the initiative in singing the song. Simon's disgruntled facial expressions alone are priceless, while Chase is utterly convincing as a lead singer, as personable and charming as the song itself.

That same sense of purpose carried over to Jim Bashfield's video for "The Boy in the Bubble," albeit via a super-stylized, animation-plus production that spoke loudest for the extent to which Peter Gabriel's "Sledgehammer" video had influenced the genre.

Chevy Chase reappeared briefly, alongside Steve Martin, in the 1990 video for "Proof," the first single from *Rhythm of the Saints*—fears that the pair might simply restate "You Can Call Me Al," however, were undone when the action switched instead to a street parade, with Simon and band performing from the back of a truck and his comedic guests' contributions restricted to a handful of scene-stealing vignettes.

From the same album, the video for "The Obvious Child" offered another carnivalesque location shoot, vibrant and colorful—like *Graceland* before it, the nature of *Rhythm of the Saints* all but dictated the content of its videos, and the finished things did not disappoint.

Unlike "Thelma," an (understandable) outtake from the sessions, which was granted a belated release in 1993 aboard the *1964/1993* box set. Shot with no apparent input from Simon, the video is little more than scenes of dancers and skydivers, and it probably looked a lot better on the storyboard than it did on television.

Wayne Isham, famed for his eighties and nineties work with Rod Stewart, the Rolling Stones, and a host of metal bands—more recently engaged by Sheryl Crow, Ricky Martin, and Britney Spears—handled 2002's "Father and Daughter," a solo guitar and vocal performance (visually, not musically) that was intercut with scenes from the animated movie *The Wild Thornberries*; *Surprise*'s solitary single "Outrageous" was overseen by P. R. Brown.

But videos had again receded in importance; the slow death of even the most rudimentary television outlet for such productions, coinciding of course with the rise of YouTube and Vivo, effectively marooned video production in a cultural Wild West dominated not by the established directors of the past but by any creator with the necessary software and a less than respectful ear for copyright restrictions.

Calling up any of Paul Simon's "official" videos online today reveals half a dozen, sometimes more, "unofficial" ones for every song, some drawn from live or broadcast performances, others relying upon the poster's own choice of visuals.

Video is still a lucrative promotional device, just as it was when it all began in the sixties. But as a window into the artist's own vision, technology has rendered it less important than it ever was in the past—a development for which Paul Simon, who has never seemed to be video's most vociferous champion, is probably rather grateful.

14

Enter the Capeman

The Capeman Murders were the sensation of the day. On August 29, 1959, one of New York City's most notorious gangs, the largely Hispanic Vampires, set out to avenge a recent attack on some of their members by the Irish-American Norsemen.

Traveling into Manhattan and making their way to the then-seething quarter known as Hell's Kitchen, the heart of the Norsemen's territory, the Vampires set about the first teenagers they could find, convinced that they had found their foe.

Tragically, they hadn't. The kids they attacked were unaffiliated with any gang. In the ensuing melee, however, Puerto Rico-born Vampire Sal Agrón stabbed and killed two of them, Anthony Krzesinski and Robert Young Jr., and then fled.

The youth had been in and out of trouble most of his life, and when his father sent him to Brooklyn to live with his mother, he quickly found a new life in the gangs. He ran with the Mau Maus for a time but switched his allegiance to the Vampires after meeting the president of the gang, Tony Hernández. It was his distinctive choice of weapon, a specially sharpened umbrella, and Agrón's equally recognizable mode of dress, a black cape with a red lining, that allowed witnesses to identify them, and the cape in particular gave the New York newspapers a name for the killer. He became the Capeman.

Swiftly captured and tried, Agrón fascinated the media, if only because of his utterly unrepentant stance. No matter that there were serious questions surrounding his guilt—the absolute absence of blood from his knife and clothing, for example—the youth appeared to relish his notoriety, and with the death sentence certainly hanging over him, the watching journalists could not get enough of his response: "I don't care if I burn, my mother could watch me."

Agrón was indeed sentenced to death—at sixteen, he became the youngest Death Row inmate New York City had ever housed. Now a fresh furor arose, as both the general public and popular personalities divided over whether the penalty should be carried out.

In the end, it wasn't; in 1962, Governor Nelson Rockefeller commuted the sentence to life imprisonment, and Agrón, who became a born-again Christian soon after his arrest, would remain in jail for the next fifteen years.

There, he learned to read and write; he gained his high school equivalency diploma and subsequently a Bachelor of Arts degree in sociology and philosophy from the State University of New York in New Paltz, New York. He became a published poet, and in December 1976, Governor Hugh Carey agreed to reduce Agrón's sentence. He would be released in late 1977; in the meantime, he was transferred to the Fishkill Correctional Facility and given day release to attended State University.

Just months before his release date, Agrón escaped. He was recaptured in Phoenix two weeks later, but in the ensuing trial he was found not guilty of the charge of absconding, due to a newly diagnosed mental illness. He left prison for the final time at the beginning of November 1979. He died seven years later, on April 22, 1986, from pneumonia and internal bleeding.

It was a short but sordid life of crime, but it captured the imagination, both at the time and following Agrón's release. Then as now, the gangs were a major cause for concern in America, even if Hollywood and Broadway had apparently done their utmost to glorify their existence— indeed, when Agrón first arrived in New York City, *West Side Story* was the toast of Broadway.

Paul Simon was certainly fascinated. Much the same age as Agrón, although their backgrounds were thoroughly opposed, he nevertheless felt a certain kinship with the killer—or, at least, with all that the killer seemed to represent. A rebel, an outsider, an out*cast*. Just for once, the young Simon daydreamed, wouldn't it be cool if the Parsons Boys, the gang that haunted his own neighborhood, instead of shaking him down for cash, asked him to join their ranks? "There were gangs in Queens [and] I felt the typical middle-class aspiration to be a part [of that]."

That yearning, of course, had long since passed. But, as he contemplated the imminence of his sixtieth birthday five years and counting... and indulged, as one does, in increasing nostalgia for his long-ago youth, so he recalled the feral thrill of early rock 'n' roll and the culture that had erupted around it on the streets of New York.

He contemplated, too, the Latin dance music that once permeated the ballrooms and the bars of late-fifties Queens, and the so-cool kids who danced to it, and slowly a culture that was as long gone as his youth began to consume his thoughts.

Simon remembered the Capeman killings—how he had been as enthralled by the ensuing newspaper coverage as any other New Yorker. He remembered hearing of Agrón's redemption, too, and looked out the poems that he'd written in his prison cell, published in sundry newspapers, streetwise ruminations with titles like "The Political Identity of Salvador Agrón; Travel Log of Thirty-Four Years," "Uhuru Sasa! (A Freedom Call)," and "Justice, Law and Order."

Even the killer's nickname felt "right." As a child, Simon had consumed pulp comics as avidly as any kid his age, through that late-1940s to mid-1950s era before Stan Lee's Marvel Comics came along to fill their pages with superheroes, and a title like The Capeman could conceal anything from a crime-fighting vigilante to a vampiric horror. Of course, Agrón's cape was affected solely out of allegiance to his gang's name, but that, too, was intriguing. Forgotten by modern culture, but once an intrinsic part of life, it was the stagecraft of the streets.

Unbidden and unexpected, a new project drifted into view.

His options, Simon knew, were limited—not by his talents or even the nature of the music industry (which, in the mid-1990s, was still healthy enough that the arrival of the internet felt light years removed from its own concerns) but by the medium in which he worked.

Broadway or Bust

A "concept album" was the obvious route to take, but it was also one that was studded by pitfalls. Since their heyday in the late 1960s and early to mid-1970s, the entire notion had become something of an albatross,

rightly or wrongly viewed as an artist seriously overreaching his importance at the same time as utterly overstating his audience's willingness to
sit through a protracted song cycle.

Far more concept albums have perished in a sea of much-deserved
mirth than have ever been acclaimed works of genius, and even the vast-
est ego on Earth ("well, *mine* will be different") could not overlook that.

A movie? Simon had already had his fingers burned in that respect.

A novel? He wrote songs, not prose, no matter how literate his work
might be.

A play?

That was interesting.

Other artists had flirted with such productions in the past. In fact,
Simon himself had glanced in that direction when he agreed to com-
pose a score for Murray Schisgal's tale of an aspiring, fictional Greenwich
Village folkie named Jimmy Shine in 1967.

He quickly pulled out again, though, when he realized that, just as he
had with *The Graduate*, there were only so many hours in the day. John
Sebastian of the Lovin' Spoonful replaced him on *Johnny Shine*; Dustin
Hoffman took the lead role, and the entire production had been and gone
by early 1968.

David Bowie mooted several possible stage shows during his most
adventurous 1970s pomp—adaptations of George Orwell's *1984* and
his own *Ziggy Stardust*—but they had come to naught. Ray Davies of
the Kinks engineered a string of records that same decade that would,
in an ideal world, have made the transition to the stage but ultimately
succeeded only in delivering a single British television play (1974's
Starmaker).

But that was a different age, a time when the audiences for, and expectations of, rock and Broadway were very different. How telling, at least in
the United States, that the only truly successful hybrids of the two—the
likes of *Hair, Godspell, Grease,* and the output of Tim Rice and Andrew
Lloyd Webber—were the work of writers who were *not* rock 'n' rollers at
heart, who utilized the body but not the soul of the music as they put
together their singalong, toe-tappable tunes.

Indeed, Simon had himself been fairly outspoken on the subject,
back in 1973, with the sixties idealism of *Hair* still flashing peace signs

on Broadway. "The best writers of popular songs never wrote for the stage. Consequently you get people who did poor imitations getting the big hits."

That had now changed. By the mid-1990s, the kids who had come of age with rock 'n' roll, the first wave of post-war baby boomers, *were* now the denizens of Broadway. The more Simon thought about it, and the more he discussed his still formulating notions with people, the more he thought he could do it.

There would be mountains to climb, of course, including his own feelings on the nature of the traditional musical; the suspension of reality that is necessary before you can accept that the people you are watching on stage really are predisposed to burst into song every few minutes.

However, he had also devised a way around that, musing on the theme of musicals back in 1970—a giant radio set, prominent above the stage. Every time a song was required, a performer would climb a few steps and switch it on.

So Simon had thought about Broadway in the past. Nevertheless, he spent much of the early 1970s ducking suggestions that he was actively considering a move into theater, conceding only that it might be something to think about one day. Now that day had come.

Or, more accurately, it was coming.

Tommy

Simon first began contemplating the Capeman story before he started work on *The Rhythm of the Saints*, and it would take a necessary back seat for a couple of years more. By the time he returned to it, however, the Broadway landscape had changed even further—in 1993, the theatrical version of Pete Townshend's *Tommy* song cycle made its Broadway debut and went on to become one of the hits of the age, running to 899 performances at the St. James Theatre before closing in June 1995. It then moved on to similarly successful runs in Canada and the United Kingdom.

Of course *Tommy* had a reputation behind it. In previous lives, it had been both a concept album *and* a rock movie. But it was also one of those rare contributions to both genres that had not been mercilessly skewered by the critics, if only by virtue of being—if not the first (that dubious honor is generally ascribed to the Pretty Things' *SF Sorrow*)—one of the very earliest of its ilk ever released.

But it was also utterly fantastical, the tale of a deaf, dumb, and blind boy who excels at pinball and, as a consequence, is proclaimed a new messiah. Could there have been a starker corollary than the story of Salvador Agrón?

Simon returned to the notes he had made a couple of years earlier; the plot outlines and even the handful of songs he had sketched out; the interviews he had conducted with, among others, Agrón's mother, Esmeralda, and his sister, Anna.

He revisited his notes on Sing Sing, the prison where Agrón served out his sentence, and the observations he made when he travelled to Mayagüez, the Puerto Rico town where the boy was born.

He hunted out photographs of the Asilo de Pobres, the poorhouse where the Agrón family lived and where his mother worked, and reacquainted himself with the Brooklyn to which the fifteen-year-old was transplanted. And, as he noted in the liners to the eventual soundtrack album, he relived his own teenaged years as well, and "the summer between high school and college, [when] the story was all over the papers and on TV." He continued: "I remember thinking here was a kid my age—a kid who had the look. Salvador Agrón looked like a rock 'n' roll hoodlum. He looked like the 1950s."

The story told itself. Too often in the realms of real life dramatization, the drama took precedence over the reality—subtle, and sometimes not-so-subtle, shifts would be applied to even the most important points in order to heighten the excitement or simplify a relationship.

Indeed, Agrón's story had only just dodged that particular bullet itself, when a television movie of his life was proposed around the time he was released from prison. Perhaps mercifully, it never materialized.

Simon had no intention of traveling down that route, however. He resolved that the only inventions in his script would be the dialogue and, of course, the songs. And, perhaps, the imposition of his own interpretation of the culture of the age.

There were hurdles he would have to surmount, of course. For a start, he had only the vaguest notion of how one would go about writing a musical stage show. It was not, after all, simply a matter of putting words and tunes onto paper. Stage directions needed to be issued. Choreography needed to be arranged. Sets needed to be designed, and while other people—the director, the choreographer, the designer—would each have their own input into those things, still the writer was required to give them the outline of what was required.

Simon mused on the possibility of drawing in a collaborator and hoped for a time to interest novelist E. L. Doctorow, whose 1975 novel *Ragtime* was in the process of being adapted for theater. (The play would open in 1998.)

He, however, was not interested, and he was not especially impressed with Simon's intention of adhering to the facts. There was a story to be told, Doctorow explained, but it would require far more emotional depth and moral analysis than a straightforward retelling of events could manage. Perhaps, he suggested, Simon could redraft it as fiction?

Unabashed, Simon next approached his friend Derek Walcott, the Saint Lucian poet whose writing had so inspired the singer that "The Coast," one of the highlights of *The Rhythm of the Saints*, had been dedicated to him.

He *was* interested. Both men knew it would not be an easy process— for a start, neither was especially well-versed in what a written collaboration actually necessitated, while Simon had shown his disdain for other people's opinions during the doomed gestation of *Think Too Much*.

But while Walcott worked on the dialogue, Simon got to work on the music, so intent upon recapturing the precise vibe of the era that he insisted that Walcott's contributions to the lyrics be matched to the tunes that Simon was creating, as opposed to Walcott's insistence on the opposite approach. Simon's insistence might not be precisely the way one should treat a Nobel Prize-winning poet, but Walcott agreed.

"Writing songs in a '50s style was very appealing to me," Simon's soundtrack liner notes continue. "And so was writing songs in a Latin style, which was a significant and sort of exotic New York subculture to me when I was growing up. Since I was working at the time with Brazilian drums and West African guitars, it wasn't too much of a leap to begin thinking about music from Puerto Rico."

Still there were problems. The songs were great, the writing was excellent. But the main character that the pair insisted was their focus, Agrón himself, remained utterly unlikeable. Friends, including Simon's longtime advisor Mike Tannen, may not have *begged* Simon to try and redress the balance, but they did strongly advise him to do so. Creating an antihero was one thing—the arts are littered with characters whose sole purpose was to be loathed by the audience, and didn't the audience love loathing them?

The Agrón that Simon and Walcott placed on paper did not have that quality. No matter what other virtues *The Capeman* might have had, and everyone agreed there were many, its leading character was its fatal flaw.

They were prophetic words. And Simon ignored them.

Upending the System

Simon eschewed other conventions, too. There would be no drawn-out hunt for traditional Broadway investors, no courting of big-name directors. Whatever hoops other playwrights leaped through in their quest to mount a production, Simon chose to reject. He would do things his way.

Cast auditions opened in May 1995, with Simon announcing a talent contest for young doo wop singers—a tall order in the age of grunge, techno, and bland boy bands. But they came anyway, lured as much by the promise of the $10,000 prize money as any hope of actually snagging a role in the play.

He determined that his cast would be largely Latino—the first major Broadway production (for that is how he saw it, already) to do so. Singer Marc Anthony, a New Yorker born of Puerto Rican parents, was to play the young Agrón; Panamanian Rubén Blades the older one. Priscilla Lopez would play his mother.

He courted a variety of directors whose work he admired, regardless of their status or experience, and settled on Susana Tubert, fresh from directing Jim Luigs's *Rock 'N' Roles from William Shakespeare* at the Actors Theatre of Louisville in Louisville, Kentucky.

Set designer Bob Crowley and choreographer Mark Morris completed the team, at least for now. Creative disputes, however, would see the production tumble into turmoil from the outset. Tubert departed; she was replaced by Eric Simonson—whose virtues included an almost familial link to Simon through the play *Jacob Zulu*, featuring the music and dance of Ladysmith Black Mambazo.

Soon, however, the portents were looking even less hopeful. Simonson's reign saw *The Capeman* undergo a workshop performance at the Westbeth Theatre Center in December 1996, performing to friends and investors, and all agreed it was a success. All except Simon, who could see only the mistakes and the flaws. Simonson was fired, and Mark Morris—who Simon had wanted for the job all along—became the show's director.

The *New York Times* pricked up its ears. Just as Simon was not the first (nor would he be the last) personality to walk into an alien environment with the insistence that he'd be doing things *his way*, neither was he the first (nor again the last) to discover that the job was not quite as simple as it appeared from without.

Broadway worked to its own rules, and inconceivably hidebound though they might strike an outsider, they were in place for a reason. Because they worked, and had many, many years of past successes to prove that. They could not be changed overnight, and even if they could be, there was a vast internal mechanism in place to ensure that they wouldn't be.

Tales of strife within the *Capeman* camp were already rife, with singers, actors, and dancers being shown the door, or finding it themselves. A budget that was out of control ($11 million and rising), and investors who were growing increasingly nervous. Three directors within a year. An out-of-town preview was enthusiastically mooted, but was then precipitously cancelled.

A fall 1997 opening night was announced and then delayed. The *New York Daily News* tabloid, so often delighting in the downfall of the rich and famous, published a story that reiterated the life of the "real" Capeman and asked whether such a person was really deserving of being immortalized on Broadway. *Newsday* followed up with a piece that described Simon as a neophyte and the show as being reliant upon "untested talent."

Tickets went on sale in September, and the *New York Daily News* pounced again: "Teen Slay Caper Nearing Stage" bellowed the headline, and again the question, this time framed by one of the murdered boys' uncles, "Why would anyone want to write a show about a guy who killed two boys? Is he going to sing and dance?"

Now things started to become surreal. That same month, off-off-Broadway at the Castillo Cultural Center in SoHo, Salvador Agrón's post-prison psychiatrist, Fred Newman, debuted his own play about his patient, *Salvador (Fictional Conversations)*, and even wrote a veteran pop star/would-be stage writer named Paul Simon into the story. Writer Dan Friedman, editing a collection of Newman's plays in 1998, went on to describe *Salvador (Fictional Conversations)* as "Newman's greatest love story to date." Paul Simon, on the other hand, remained stoically silent on the subject.

Songs from the Capeman

He did, however, release a new album, *Songs from the Capeman*, a thirteen-song-strong collection that combined his own performances with a handful of cast recordings. Excerpts from a 1959 interview Agrón gave with NBC's Gabe Pressman were strewn between several of the songs, and it is ironic that the CD—had it been released in its own right, without any of the attendant distractions—would itself have made a more than worthy addition to the slim canon of concept albums that actually worked.

The lyrics told the story without ever resorting to dragging it along with unnecessary exposition or detail; the music recaptured the era and the shifting moods with ease. The liners, brief though they were, gave the uninitiated an idea of what they were listening to; and the commentary that Simon had wanted to deliver—the prejudice and racism that was rife in that world, the lack of opportunity that awaited migrant families, the violence that leeched out of every shadow—was illustrated with some of the most concise, and incisive, writing of his life.

Capeman onstage at the Marquee Theater, 1998 run.   *Photofest*

1997: *Songs from the Capeman* (Warner Brothers 9 46814-2)

"Adios Hermanos"

"Born in Puerto Rico"

"Satin Summer Nights" (with Marc Anthony)

"Bernadette"

"The Vampires"

"Quality"

"Can I Forgive Him"

"Sunday Afternoon" (with Ednita Nazario)

"Killer Wants to Go to College"

"Time Is an Ocean" (with Marc Anthony and Ruben Blades)

"Virgil"

"Killer Wants to Go to College II"

"Trailways Bus"

Produced by: Paul Simon

Associate producers: Roy Halee and Oscar Hernandez

Recorded at The Hit Factory, New York

Musicians

Angel Ramirez—vocals
Angelo Aponte—vocals
Arlen Roth—guitar
Bakithi Cumalo—bass
Barry Danielian—flugel
Bernie Misoso—bass
Bill Holloman—saxophone, trumpet
Bobby Allende—percussion
Bobby Bright—vocals
Bobby Franceschini—saxophone
Briz—vocals
Chris Eminez—vocals
Crusher Bennett—shaker
Danny Rivera—vocals
David Davila—vocals
David Mann—saxophone
David Rodriguez—trumpet
Derrick James—vocals
DeWayne Snype—vocals
Diomendes Matos—guitar
Ed Vasquez—vocals
Edgar Stewart—vocals
Edgardo Miranda—cuatro
Edwin Montalvo—congas
Frank Negron—vocals
Hans Giraldo—vocals
Harper Simon—guitar, harmonica
Hechter Ubarry—vocals
Horace Ott—piano
Janet Hafner—violin
Jay Leonheart—bass
Jimmy Sabater—conga, cowbell
John Beal—bass
John Walsh—trumpet
Johnny Andrews—timbales

Juliet Hafner—viola
Karen Bernod—vocals
Kevin Harrison—vocals
Kia Jeffries—vocals
Krista Feeney—violin
Laura Bontrager—cello
Luis Lopez—trombone
Luis Marrero—vocals
Marc Quinones—timbales, congas, cua
Marcia Butler—oboe
Mike Ramos—accordion
Milton Cardona—vocals, percussion
Mitch Frohman—saxophone
Myrna Gomila—vocals
Nelson Gonzalez—tres, plenaro
Nestor Sanchez—vocals
Oriente Lopez—flute, organ
Oscar Hernandez—keyboards
Ozzie Melendez—trombone
Pablo Calogero—saxophone, clarinet
Pablo Nunez—bongos, cowbell
Paul Griffin—piano
Paul Livant—guitar
Paul Peabody—violin
Ray De La Paz—vocals
Ray Vega—trumpet
Renee Connell-Adams—vocals
Richard Crooks—drums; Robby Ameen—drums
Robby Turner—pedal steel
Robert Vargas—vocals
Ruben Rodriguez—bass
Sara Ramirez—vocal
Saturninho Laboy—guitar

Sean Pully—vocals

Shannon Ford—drums; Steve
    Cropper—guitar

Stewart Rose—French horn

Teana Rodriguez—vocals

Tony Garnier—bass

Donte Sutton—vocals

Trent Sutton—vocals; Vincent
    Nguini—guitar

When a mother sings out, during "Can I Forgive Him," "this city makes a cartoon of crime, capes and umbrellas the glorification of slime," Simon was tapping into the same line of reasoning that conjured "The Sound of Silence"; while "Quality"'s dialogue between a teen idol and a chorus of girls is effectively every high school love song ever written, rewired around the kind of questions that may lie behind their own lyric.

Jerry Landis would have been proud, and so was Simon. In fact, when the *New York Times Magazine*'s Stephen J. Dubner confronted Simon on the manifold dramas and difficulties into which *The Capeman* had strayed, the controversies over its subject matter, and the glee with which the media appeared to be predicting its downfall ("Dis-graceland" was another of the *Daily News*' choice headlines), Simon effectively shrugged them all away, saying: "This is about an incredible love of sound. This is all about music. This is about how I fell in love with music and who I was when that love happened."

He was more forthcoming when *Vogue* asked similar questions: "I couldn't care less what the theater community, or whatever it is that they call themselves, think about [The Capeman]. I didn't write it for Broadway. I wrote it for me."

The storm clouds continued to gather. *The Capeman*'s opening date of January 3, 1998, was pushed back a full month after Jerry Zaks became its fourth director. Unease about the (still largely unseen) play's portrayal of a teenaged killer prompted demonstrations in the streets outside the theater. And, when the first night's reviews finally came in at the end of the month, they stunk.

The Capeman, for all of its production problems, was a beautifully realized play. Crowley's exquisite sets not only captured the New York of the age, they brought to vibrant life the city scenes that were projected, as photos or film clips, onto the video screens around the stage. The

The *Songs from Capeman* soundtrack album.   *Author's collection*

music . . . well, we already knew how good the music was. The dancing was spectacular.

Even the long-echoed fears that Simon had written an antihero without a single heroic quality were stilled by the assured performances with which he was portrayed. One still felt no sympathy or empathy, but like the gratuitous true crime dramas with which modern (twenty-first century) television seems to be littered, it was difficult to tear one's eyes away.

Whether Simon would accept, let alone be complimented by, the assertion that he played midwife to what would soon become the epitome of trash television is another matter entirely. But if his scrapbook should contain any of the reviews he received, it's a dishonor he has probably learned to live with.

The premiere was attended, of course, by a star-studded audience—TV and Hollywood A-listers; Agrón's sister and her family; the investors, of course—and all gave the play a rousing reception. But the news corps were out in force as well, and their thoughts were somewhat less generous. *The Capeman* was "a sad, benumbed spectacle" (the *New York Times*); a listless smorgasbord of "damp, sputtering logs of received non-wisdom" (*The New Yorker*); "a dud" (*USA Today*).

Variety praised the songs, but again, Simon could have received that accolade if he'd merely released a new album—and even that joy was snatched away as the album peaked humiliatingly outside the Top 40.

Advance ticket sales, scarcely healthy once past the opening few days of availability, plunged another 30 percent, and while the show's publicity office continued to shout the odds, predicting that *The Capeman* would still be in town for the Tony Awards, few people agreed.

The show closed just a few weeks later on March 29. Simon was in tears as he said his goodbyes to the cast and crew, but still he had some defiance left within.

As the curtain came down for the last time and a sympathetic audience gave *The Capeman* one of the most boisterous ovations of its short life, Simon—taking his bows with the rest of the cast—called out, "If this is a failure, what's success?"

15

Bobby, Paul, and Brian

There is little that has occurred in the history of rock, at least in the years since its initial flames were quenched by the rise of high school pop, that cannot be said to have been influenced by Bob Dylan.

The first songwriter to be anointed a poet, the first folkie to rock, the first rocker to paint true pictures with his words, Dylan has sparked riots and incensed his admirers, has been covered by almost every artist out there and has covered a multitude in return, and had at least a finger in every stylistic musical pie of the sixties and seventies, which have baked since then.

It was Dylan who, when he first picked up an electric guitar in anger, dragged the New York folk scene into the international spotlight in the early 1960s (and who sent it spiraling back into obscurity in 1965). His vision inspired the Beatles to *Revolver* and the Beach Boys to *Smile*; his lyrics predicted war and prayed for peace.

One song, "Blowing in the Wind," is so firmly established as the ultimate protest anthem that it seems hard to believe it was even written by one man—it should have been handed down through the ages, every fresh crisis precipitating another verse; and it's not alone. If the twentieth century could ever be said to have produced its own version of the Child Ballads, it's the Bob Dylan songbook.

Paul Simon has never hidden his admiration for Dylan, not even at a time when the two could be considered rivals, not even when it sounded as though he was putting him down.

Interviewed by the *New Musical Express* in 1965, Simon was adamant that much of Dylan's success was attributable to what less polite voices would have described as "hype" rather than his natural talent. Joan Baez, he said, "is probably the only folk singer to have happened naturally," establishing herself, "without the fantastic barrage of publicity that built up Dylan." Simon recalled seeing Dylan play a guest spot at a Baez concert in Forest Hills, early on in his career. "He sang two numbers at the end of the concert and got booed off stage."

But he never tired of recounting the phone call he received from Dylan, either, one day early in Simon and Garfunkel's career.

Initially, he thought it was somebody playing a prank on him. "This guy rang me in Greenwich Village and said he was Dylan." The following conversation then ensued:

> Dylan: "I hear you went to Tahiti, and bought a gold earring?"
>
> Simon: "No, it was Jamaica and I bought a gold ring to put through my nose so I could follow the Village hippies!"
>
> Dylan: "What's the weather like in the Village?"
>
> Simon: "Stuffy—it's always stuffy in the Village."
>
> Dylan: "Yeah, well goodbye."

He would never deny Dylan's influence, either. Simon told *Mojo* in 2000: "I tried very hard not to be influenced by him, and that was hard. 'The Sound of Silence' I never would have wrote it were it not for Bob Dylan." At the same time, however, Simon never felt the need to try and imitate what Dylan was doing. "Not because I didn't admire it but because I didn't see any way out of being in his shadow if I was going to be anything like that."

At the same time, Simon was never averse to putting Dylan down when the opportunity arose. During his time in London, he shared an apartment for a while with singer-songwriter Al Stewart. One day he walked in to find Stewart listening to "Desolation Row," the epic closing cut on Dylan's newly released *Highway 61 Revisited* LP.

Simon was not impressed. Dismissing the song as nothing more than "half-baked Ferlinghetti lines," he truly lost his temper when Stewart responded by telling Simon that he'd never write a song that good, not if he lived to be one thousand years old.

According to Stewart, Simon walked out of the apartment and did not return for two days.

Bob Dylan onstage at his 30th Anniversary Concert in 1993. *Photofest*

It was producer Tom Wilson (whom the duo shared with Dylan) who suggested Simon and Garfunkel cover the master's "The Times They Are A-Changin'" on their debut album, and you can hear their misgivings as an inaudible subtext throughout their performance.

At the same time, as Simon acknowledged, without Dylan's example, there would never have been the original "The Sound of Silence"; and without him, there might not have been the electric version, either. Without Dylan, the London-based Simon would never have performed

"Don't Think Twice, It's Alright" or "Man of Constant Sorrow." (Some nights, he even liked to imitate Dylan's vocal.)

And, without Dylan, Simon and Garfunkel would never have undergone the torture of a gig at Gerde's Folk Club, just as they were completing that album, while Dylan sat at the bar with *New York Times* critic Robert Shelton, laughing loudly throughout their performance. Small wonder that Simon composed "A Simple Desultory Philippic" soon after, perhaps the most accurate Dylan takeoff until National Lampoon nailed him with their "Those Fabulous Sixties."

"A Simple Desultory Philippic"

Two versions of this strange song have been recorded and released: the first in 1965 aboard Paul Simon's *Songbook* LP, the second the following year on the album *Parsley, Sage, Rosemary and Thyme*.

Subtitled for the then-US Secretary of Defence, "A Simple Desultory Philippic" was an excellent Dylan parody whether Simon intended it to be one or not. The song is also renowned for the long list of names that appear within the lyric—a list, incidentally, that was changed between the original version and its rerecording.

The 1965 recording features the following:

Larry Adler	James Joyce
The Beatles	Jack Kerouac
John Birch	Barry Kornfeld (guitarist on Simon
Walter Brennan (actor)	and Garfunkel's first LP)
Lenny Bruce	John Lennon
Cassius Clay	Krishna Menon (Indian politician)
Diz Disley	Ayn Rand
Walt Disney	The Rolling Stones
Art Garfunkel	Dylan Thomas
Mick Jagger	Andy Warhol
Lyndon B. Johnson	Tom Wilson (producer)

The following year, the song immortalized:

Lou Adler	Lenny Bruce
The Beatles	Art Garfunkel

Roy Halee (producer)

Mick Jagger

Norman Mailer

Robert McNamara

John O'Hara

Ayn Rand

The Rolling Stones

Barry Sadler ("The Ballad of the
Green Berets" hit maker)

Phil Spector

Maxwell Taylor

Dylan Thomas

Andy Warhol

"I'm always being compared to Bob Dylan," Simon complained to the *New Musical Express* while in London. "[But] our philosophies are different. He is always dumping [on] people more than I do. It's really easy to put somebody down. The biggest thing Dylan has going for him is his mystique."

By the mid-1970s, the playing field had leveled. Dylan's recording of "The Boxer" on 1970's *Self Portrait* may not have been as generous a gift as it would have been a year or two earlier—the album was widely regarded as the worst of Dylan's career so far, a gloomy roost it continued to inhabit until 2013 brought the *Bootleg Series, Volume 10: Another Self Portrait (1969–1971)* reappraisal and convinced people it wasn't as awful as they thought after all.

Nevertheless, "The Boxer" was a reach—Clinton Heylin, in his peerless anatomy of Dylan's studio career, *The Recording Sessions*, recalls those critics ("they shall remain nameless") who "have sought to suggest that Dylan sees the boxer in the song as his old self, parrying every blow and accepting each come-on," justifying this interpretation by the presence of two wildly opposing lead vocals on the track: one the familiar nasal honk, the other "sweeter [and] somehow younger."

"All very convincing," Heylin concludes, but "the finished article still sounds pretty damn unlistenable."

But simply acknowledging Simon as a writer worth covering (Gordon Lightfoot was the only other contemporary songwriter to feature on the set) was a lofty compliment from a man who was not exactly renowned for distributing such things; and, as revered as Dylan's 1974 opus *Blood on the Tracks* might have been, Simon's *Still Crazy After All These Years* matched it the following year.

A dramatic poster celebrating the union of two true rock legends.   *Author's collection*

Indeed, beyond those two records, plus Neil Young's *On the Beach*, it would be impossible to visualize a more lucid document of the mid-decade, post-Vietnam American apocalypse blues, as reviewer Bob Woffinden enthused in the *New Musical Express*.

> *Blood on the Tracks* apart, *Still Crazy* is the best album you're likely to hear all year. Two warnings: If you like your albums to be raw, unsophisticated, and sound as though they were made up at the last minute, maybe you should turn the page; if you consider on the other hand that the making of a record should be as meticulously planned as an Apollo moonshot or an Everest ascent, then

stay tuned. A second warning is that if you're of an emotional or nervous disposition, maybe you should experiment with something a little less heartrending.

Twenty-five years later, with the twentieth century about to pass into history, only Dylan's seemingly (and, at the time of writing, still ongoing) insatiable appetite for live work and prolific vinyl output truly separated him from Simon in terms of legendary status. Well, that and the way they continued to deliver their songs.

"One of my deficiencies is my voice sounds sincere," Simon mused to the UK magazine *Uncut*. "I've tried to sound ironic. I don't. I can't. Dylan, everything he sings has two meanings. He's telling you the truth and making fun of you at the same time. I sound sincere every time."

Perhaps Simon, with the failure of *The Capeman* still hard in the rear view mirror, was feeling more bruised by recent events. Dylan's most recent album, 1997's *Time Out of Mind*, on the other hand, had attracted some of his most adulatory reviews in years, if not decades. Nevertheless, Dylan was effusive when he was asked a similar question—how did he rate Paul Simon? "I consider [Simon] one of the pre-eminent songwriters of the times. Every song he does has got a vitality you don't find everywhere."

Two Bards on the Road

Simon resolved to retire following the collapse of *The Capeman*. His domestic life, married now to singer Edie Brickell, was settled and blissful; their third child, Gabriel, was born in 1998, a brother to six-year-old Adrian and three-year-old Lulu). His son from his first marriage, Harper, was grown now and enjoying his own career in music; he even guested on the *Songs from the Capeman* album.

Simon did not need the constant struggle for further recognition, further fame, to cast shadows across his happiness. It was not the first time he'd threatened to give it all up, of course, but even before the stageshow's demise, he'd acknowledged, "I'm thinking of *The Capeman* as a very big ending."

No more tours, no more records, no more movies, no more stage shows. And, for the next year or so, he seemed determined to make it stick. And then he was offered a co-headlining tour with Bob Dylan, and he bounced back onto the horse without so much as a backward glance.

The tour was announced in early April, just two months before the opening show; a joint statement—which, in truth, really doesn't sound like either of them—explained "We have been great fans of each other for years and are really looking forward to touring together."

They had already started planning the layout of the shows. Early meetings between the two stars saw them discussing the handful of duets that would highlight the show—Dylan was apparently keen to handle "The

A bootleg CD from Paul's 1991 Japanese tour.   *Author's collection*

Boy in the Bubble" and "The Only Living Boy in New York"; Simon, for his part, chose "To Ramona" and "Forever Young."

Ultimately they settled for regular performances of "The Sound of Silence" and "Knocking on Heaven's Door," and sundry oldies medleys ("I Walk the Line/Blue Moon of Kentucky"; "That'll Be the Day/ The Wanderer"), with the occasional deviation toward "The Boxer" and "Forever Young" for variety.

As author Andrew Muir remarked in his study of Dylan's "neverending tour," *Razor's Edge*: "[The] duets were 'fairly nice' in a very bald way; amusing, too, for their very awkwardness, but not too obnoxious. Or at least not until the reggae-lite 'Knockin' on Heaven's Door' was jarred by the monstrous perversion of incorporating some absurd lines from a Simon song into the Dylan original." (This didn't happen too often—the pair were just as likely to drop "I Hear You Knocking" into the song.)

Neil Strauss, in the *New York Times*, too, was unimpressed. "Though singing harmony is second nature to Mr. Simon, trying to harmonize with Mr. Dylan is like trying to catch a fly with chopsticks. As a result, 'The Sound of Silence' turned from a haunting ballad to a cacophonous prophecy punctuated with a harmonica solo."

The shows were arranged so that each artist would "headline" on alternate nights, and that too showed up the disparity between the two. Dylan's set was roughshod and spontaneous; Simon's well rehearsed and largely unchanging. If anybody ever needed a single object lesson in the most profound difference between the two, and their approach to performance, these evenings were it.

In terms of spectacle, nevertheless, it was a big-ticket item, and the tickets themselves were priced accordingly. Dylan was no stranger to the superstar double headers—tours in the eighties with the Grateful Dead and Tom Petty and the Heartbreakers, and a more recent outing with Van Morrison, had all been successful, and in terms of ticket sales, this summer spectacular was no different. But fans paid heavily for the privilege of seeing the two together, as the *Philadelphia Inquirer* complained: "Nationwide, prices for premium seats are going through the amphitheater roof, particularly for superstar acts favored by baby boomers."

Prices for Simon and Dylan's local performance, at the Waterfront Entertainment Centre, raced towards the $100 mark, while "industry buzz has it that [the pair] will split $525,000 a night."

Those prices, continued the *Union Tribune*, were why ticket sales were slow. "For those fans who can afford it, hearing them together might be worthwhile at any price. But for many more, this tour may be remembered more for its prohibitive cost to attend than for its music."

On the Road—The Dylan Simon Tour, 1999

June 5—Denver, Colorado
June 6—Colorado Springs, Colorado
June 7—Denver, Colorado
June 9—Salt Lake City, Utah
June 11—Vancouver, Canada
June 12—Portland, Oregon
June 13—The Gorge Amphitheater, Washington
June 14—Eugene, Oregon
June 16—Sacramento, California
June 18—Concord, California
June 19—Mountain View, California
June 20—Anaheim, California
June 22—Los Angeles, California
June 25—Chula Vista, California
June 26—Paradise, Nevada
June 27—Phoenix, Arizona
June 30—New York City, New York
July 2—Minneapolis, Minnesota
July 3—Duluth, Minnesota
July 4—Milwaukee, Wisconsin
July 6—Detroit, Michigan
July 7—Clarkston, Michigan
July 9—Tinley Park, Illinois
September 18—Dallas, Texas

July 10—Maryland Heights, Missouri
July 11—Cincinnati, Ohio
July 13—Virginia Beach, Virgina
July 14—Raleigh, North Carolina
July 16—Bristow, Virginia
July 17—Camden, New Jersey
July 18—Burgettstown, Pennsylvania
July 20—Albany, New York
July 22—Mansfield, Massachusetts
July 24—Hartford, Connecticut
July 27—New York City, New York
July 28—Holmdel, New York
July 30—Wantagh, New York
September 2—West Palm Beach, Florida
September 4—Atlanta, Georgia
September 5—Charlotte, North Carolina
September 8—Antioch, Tennessee
September 9—Noblesville, Indiana
September 11—Memphis, Tennessee
September 12—Lafayette, Louisiana
September 15—Austin, Texas
September 17—The Woodlands, Texas

Simon's set did not vary much through the tour. "Bridge Over Troubled Water" was the perhaps surprising set opener, "The Boxer" the most frequent final encore, and in between times, a smart run through solo career highlights would focus on past hit singles, with only one further reference to the distant past ("Mrs. Robinson") thrown into the pot.

Some terrific performances emerged; even in the occasionally low-fidelity hell of audience recordings, it's hard to tire of the graceful "Slip Slidin' Away," which opened into the evening's closing salvo—"Diamonds on the Soles of Her Shoes" and "You Can Call Me Al."

"Trailways Bus," from *The Capeman*, was another sometimes surprising highlight—of course, Simon had surely said all there was to say about cross-country bus travel in "America," but this was another occasion upon which a little repetition was not a bad thing, all the more so as the song opened up to look at the lives of the people the bus was passing, as opposed to those it carried.

As an allegory for the tour itself, too, the song was effective; posters for the outing depicted the headliners as speeding locomotives racing down parallel tracks, but it had been a long, long time since either Dylan's or Simon's career could have been compared to that.

No, they were indeed akin to a couple of buses, meandering thoughtfully down America's highways and byways, halting where they chose, watching the scenery as it flashed by, contemplating the lives of the people they passed, noting the changes that had been wrought since the last time they'd taken that route, and predicting, perhaps, those that were still to come.

Reviews of the tour were generally supportive, with the *New York Times* report on the Madison Square Garden show speaking for most of them with its opening caveat: "They were no Simon and Garfunkel, no Bob Dylan and the Band. They weren't even as good a match-up as Bob Dylan and Elvis Costello singing 'I Shall Be Released' during the encore of an impromptu Dylan show the night before at Tramps. But Bob Dylan and Paul Simon weren't exactly the odd couple either."

The success of the tour did not guarantee a lifetime's friendship and cooperation, of course. A decade later, working on the title track for his new album *So Beautiful or So What*, Simon invited Dylan to join him.

He told *Uncut* what happened (or didn't happen) next: "I thought Bob could sing, put a nice voice on the verse that begins: 'Ain't it strange the way we're ignorant/ how we seek out bad advice.' I thought it would be nice if he sang that, since his voice has become so weathered I thought he would sound like a sage. I sent it to him, but I didn't hear back. I don't know why."

That was still to occur, however. In the meantime, the tour thoroughly reinvigorated Simon's musical urges. Even at the height of his resolved retirement, he had continued noting down song ideas; off the road following the Dylan tour, however, he wrote as though he were possessed. Barely one year after he and Dylan played their final show in Dallas, Texas, Simon had written, recorded, and released a new album, *You're the One*—the first step in what *The New Yorker* would later describe as "one of rock music's greatest late-career comebacks."

Beginning with that record, "Simon has turned out a series of clever, quietly audacious albums, containing some songs that are as good as any he has made."

And now he was hungry to promote it.

2000: *You're the One* (Warner Brothers 9362 47844-4)

"That's Where I Belong"   "Señorita with a Necklace of Tears"
"Darling Lorraine"   "Love"
"Old"   "Pigs, Sheep and Wolves"
"You're the One"   "Hurricane Eye"
"The Teacher"   "Quiet"
"Look at It"

Produced by: Paul Simon

Recorded at The Hit Factory, New York

Musicians

Abraham Laboriel—bass   Evan Ziporyn—bass clarinet
Alain Mallet—keyboards   Howard Levy—harmonica
Bakithi Kumalo—bass   Jay Elfenbein—vielle, vihuela
Clifford Carter—cello   Jimmy Haddad—percussion
Dan Duggan—hammer dulcimer   Larry Campbell—pedal steel

Mark Stewart—cello, guitar
Peter Herbert—upright bass
Skip LaPlante—96-tone harp
Steve Gadd—drums

Steve Gorn—bamboo flute
Steve Shehan—percussion
Vincent Nguini—guitar

"The thing about getting older is I really know what I like," Simon told *New York* magazine. "And when I find it, I'm in heaven. And that's what I try to do: Make a record that is so pleasurable for people who like what I like that they can just swim in it. I really tried to do that."

He was rewarded, among other things, with—deep breath!—a Gold disc and a Grammy nomination for Album of the Year for *You're The One*, a primetime PBS TV special, his induction as a solo artist into the Rock and Roll Hall of Fame, and being named the Musicares 2001 Person of the Year.

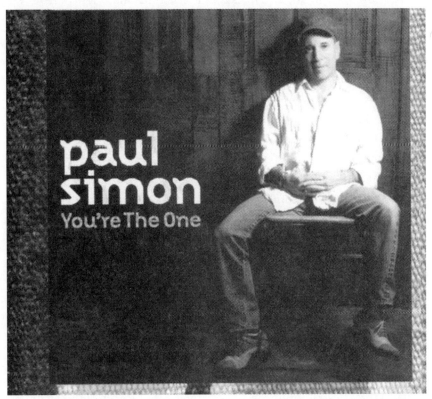

Simon's *You're the One* was released less than a year after he came off the road with Dylan.

Author's collection

He even added to his collection of Beatles performances, first when Paul McCartney (always his favorite member of the band) joined him onstage at the Greek Theater on June 13, 2001, and then, the following evening, when he guested with McCartney at his Landmine Benefit Gala. (Simon also played a short set at the show.) At both, they performed McCartney's own "I've Just Seen a Face," a track from the Beatles 1965 *Help!* album and a song whose own harmonies could have easily slipped into Simon and Garfunkel's period repertoire.

Simon was also among the wealth of guests turning out to pay tribute to the music of Beach Boy Brian Wilson at Radio City Music Hall on March 29. On a bill that also featured Ricky Martin, Vince Gill, Billy Joel, and Elton John, Simon turned in a spectacular "Surfer Girl," alone with his acoustic guitar, and it was at these latter pair of events that Simon decided to invite Wilson to join him on his upcoming tour.

The pair were mere acquaintances at the time, although Wilson was certainly aware of Simon and had long since fallen under his influence—back in 1966, Simon loaned his copy of *Music of Bulgaria* ("recorded in 1955 in Paris by a chorus of Bulgarian farmers," he explained) to Al Kooper, who played it for Wilson, who, in turn, became one of its greatest proselytes.

"He got blown out by that," Kooper later remarked, and it isn't too difficult to see the LP's impact on the sessions Wilson was then overseeing for the Beach Boys' legendary *Smile* album.

Twenty-eight cities around the country would play host to the outing, which—perhaps disappointingly on this occasion—would not feature any duets. Both musicians, however, were conscious of both their legacy and their future. Unlike Dylan, who could never be relied upon to even play his biggest hits on any given night, Wilson and his band pieced together a full ninety minutes of pop radio memories. Simon had no choice but to respond in kind—with, of course, a few surprises thrown in.

The *Chicago Tribune* caught the show: "Backed by a stellar international band, Simon zipped through nearly two hours of material, mixing a hefty chunk of his strong new album, *You're the One*, with virtually all the hits the audience could want."

His largesse was not unconditional, however. "Me and Julio Down by the Schoolyard" surrendered its reggae beat to a straightforward rock

Brian Wilson (center) and the Beach Boys, the quintessential sound of the American 1960s. *Photofest*

arrangement, flamenco guitar haunted "The Sound of Silence," and "50 Ways to Leave Your Lover" went electro. "Simon and company consistently delivered the musical goods with energy and style."

The tour was a success and the spirit of collaboration was unquestionably abroad. For barely was Simon off the road with Wilson when he began scheming his next partnership. One that might be described as an utterly unexpected, or an absolutely predictable, reunion. Or both at the same time.

Edie Brickell was not even born when Simon and Garfunkel scored their first hit singles. She was just four years old when the duo broke up and had yet to graduate high school when they reunited for the first time. Almost from the moment she and Simon met, however, at *Saturday Night Live* on November 5, 1988, she has been alongside him every step of his career, and just a few nights into his 2018 farewell tour, the couple celebrated their twenty-sixth wedding anniversary.

Born in Dallas, Texas, Brickell's musical career began in 1985 when a group of friends from Southern Methodist University invited her to try out for their folk rock band, the New Bohemians.

It was not something that she ever expected to happen. In fact, her one attempt to join a band, a few years ago, frittered out after just one phone call. Answering the band's "singer wanted" ad, she was asked where her musical tastes lie. She answered honestly: Al Green, Aretha Franklin, Willie Nelson, "everything." The voice on the other end of the phone said "Okay, thanks," and that was the end of that.

Finally a mutual friend introduced her to the New Bohemians, and just in time, as she said, "I was waiting tables and going to art school and, frankly, I just didn't want to be bored anymore."

A single tryout gig blossomed into a career. Within a year, the group had self-released its first album, a cassette of songs titled *It's Like This*.

Featuring several of the songs that the band would rerecord for their major-label debut two years later ("What I Am," "She," "Air of December"), the tape was produced in a limited edition of just 500 copies, but everybody who heard it, it seemed, was entranced—both the songwriting and performance demanded far more attention than the cassette could ever offer them and, within eighteen months, the group was signing to mogul David Geffen's eponymous label.

Shooting Rubberbands at the Stars duly appeared in 1988, and was itself immediately shot skyward. Sales of 2.5 million saw the record turn double Platinum; tours with Bob Dylan and Don Henley saw the band playing auditoriums before many people had even seen them in clubs and theaters.

All placed the band firmly at the forefront of the now-burgeoning Americana music scene, as that threatened to become the defining flavor of nineties American rock.

San Francisco's *Sunday Chronicle* captured the group's appeal—or, rather, that of its so-effervescent vocalist. "Brickell is a different breed of rock star, one who instinctively resists the trappings of fame. Her appearance—long, wavy brown hair, old jeans, loose-fitting tops and not much makeup—doesn't

Edie Brickell, at the outset of her recording career in 1988.   *Photofest*

vary from street to stage. In concert, she appears awkward, crossing her legs and leaning shyly into the microphone like a grade-school kid giving her first class presentation."

Or, as the *Los Angeles Times* put it: "She has a guileless persona of the sort that a lot of older bohemians love to hate—charmingly introverted and innocent, apparently unaffected and given to writing sweet, sketchy, sensitive verse about life and rocky relationships outside the big city. 'I don't think it's uncool to write about squirrels!' she protested."

In the event, the success of Nirvana and the birth of grunge would firmly derail all such predictions, but the New Bohemians had already passed from view by that time. Though it was arguably musically superior, their second album, 1990's *Ghost of a Dog*, was scarcely as successful as its predecessor, a wide-ranging foray through the band's full, eclectic mindset; and by the time Brickell and Simon married, on May 30, 1992, the band seemed to be over.

Her first solo album, *Picture Perfect Morning*, appeared in 1994, with Paul Simon in the production chair. It was, she said at the time, for the sake of expedience as much as anything else—why spend time auditioning outside producers, when she already had the perfect choice sitting across the breakfast table from her? He shared her musical tastes, applauded her musical instincts, and he knew how to get the sounds she wanted. Only when it came to the actual songwriting did she hold him at arm's length.

Brickell told writer Larry Katz: "I wouldn't show him the songs until I was comfortable with them. He's sensitive to that. I would never listen to his ideas as far as writing goes. It wouldn't feel right. It wouldn't be natural."

As writers, too, she was aware of the differences between them. "He's a great songwriter. But there's something missing in his songs for me personally. I use words that he doesn't use. There are things that I want to talk about and sing about that he hasn't sung about. There are emotions I want to express I feel are lost on me as a listener when I listen to his songs. There are some hopes I feel that he doesn't express and I have to."

An excellent album, *Picture Perfect Morning* was nevertheless not the beginning of a new career—just a single episode within a series of occasional new releases and reappearances. A New Bohemians reunion, for example, would deliver *Stranger Things* in 2006, and then nothing until a US tour in fall 2018. She would not follow up her solo debut until 2003's *Volcano*, and that would not be offered a successor until 2011.

But she reassured *Vanity Fair*: "I haven't ever stopped thinking about music or writing music or playing music." Indeed, alongside the *Edie Brickell* album, she had also completed a similarly eponymous offering with the Gaddabouts, a band formed with Welsh singer-songwriter Andy Fairweather Lowe, and Steve Gadd, from Simon's regular band. And, on this occasion, questions regarding her husband's possible influence on any of this music were deftly swatted aside.

"Paul has not heard either of these records," Brickell said. "I'm very private about showing him anything because, to me, songwriting is a very spiritual

kind of practice. It's that evolving into your own, and that's extremely important to me, to have that and to try to get into that sense of self-discovery. So
he can't be a part of that process."

They've been married for over a quarter of a century. But musically, they
keep their distance.

16

Hello Artie, My Old Friend

On February 23, 2003, at Madison Square Garden, the National Academy of Recording Arts and Sciences presented Simon and Garfunkel with a Career Achievement Grammy.

Throughout the run-up to the event, speculation was rife as to whether one or the other would even attend, let alone acknowledge one another's presence if they did so. Instead, the pair placed a decade of distance behind them and reunited as performers to deliver a sincerely moving "The Sound of Silence."

Mere months later, they announced a new tour. But they would not be doing it alone. Their childhood idols the Everly Brothers would be joining them.

Ticket prices, incidentally, would top out around $250 apiece.

Accepting Simon and Garfunkel's inauguration into the Rock and Roll Hall of Fame, Paul Simon suggested that the institution consider adding a special wing for feuding partners—Simon and Garfunkel, Ray and Dave Davies, Ike and Tina Turner, and so forth. A few years earlier, he could easily have added Don and Phil Everly to the roll call.

When the brothers parted company in 1973, they brought to an end a career that stretched back to the dawn of rock 'n' roll.

Behind them, there stretched a run of thirty-seven American hits and thirty British smashes that only begin to tell the story. By 1973, however, such glories were far behind them, and the brothers were constantly at one another's throats. Their live performances were restricted to the supper club circuit, a dispiriting series of concerts that ended onstage at the John Wayne Theatre in Knotts Berry Farm, California, on July 14.

There, a drunken Don spent much of the show insulting his brother until, finally, Phil smashed his Gibson guitar and simply walked off, pledging never to "get on a stage with that man again."

Don completed the show on his own, reassuring the audience that they really shouldn't be concerned over what they'd witnessed. "The Everly Brothers died ten years ago," he told them. Over the next decade, the only occasion upon which Don and Phil would meet one another was at their father's funeral.

The two immediately launched solo careers. Phil cut a string of well-received albums and appeared in the hit movie *Every Which Way but Loose*; Don linked with British country-blues rockers Heads Hands and Feet, featuring ace guitarist Albert Lee, and cut his own solo album, the superlative *Sunset Towers*. He gigged constantly, but like Phil, he was never able to shake the "ex-Everly Brothers" cachet from his name.

Into the early 1980s, the two brothers remained adamantly solo. Around them, however, interest in their old career was growing—particularly in the United Kingdom. Nick Lowe and Dave Edmunds formed their own Everlys tribute act, the Beverley Brothers, performing both the Everlys' own old songs and their own soundalikes.

A TV-advertised compilation of the Everlys' greatest oldies, *Love Hurts*, spent more than five months on the British chart in early 1983, while Don scored his first ever solo hit single when he combined with local hero Cliff Richard and Dire Straits guitarist Mark Knopfler for the Top 10 smash "She Means Nothing to Me."

Behind the scenes, too, much was happening. Finally willing to talk with one another again, the brothers quickly discovered that the differences that once sundered them had long ago been forgotten. In June 1983, therefore, they announced that they were getting back together, beginning with a reunion concert at the most venerable venue the United Kingdom had to offer, London's Royal Albert Hall, on September 23. In the words of their own 1960 hit single "Like Strangers," the brothers had vowed, "Let's forget that we were angry and swear not to be like strangers anymore."

Tickets for the event sold out within hours, while the audience was rapidly revealed as a star-studded gathering of rock 'n' roll heroes who themselves

One of the highlights of the entire reunion tour, at London's legendary Royal Albert Hall.   *Author's collection*

had grown up listening to the Everlys. For anybody too slow off the mark and unable to attend, the show would be filmed for TV and home video release, and recorded for a double live album.

Of course there was no doubt that the emphasis would be on their greatest hits—what few of the assembled observers expected was just how fresh and dynamic those hits would sound.

With the duo kicking off the show with "The Price of Love," the R&B rocker that had given the Everly Brothers a number two UK hit in 1965, the decades rolled back as those heavenly harmonies rang out through the august venue. It was a dramatic start and it only got better as the performance ranged across the duo's career and as every new song brought back an old memory—the storming "Walk Right Back," Roy Orbison's wonderful "Claudette," the heartbreaking "Crying in the Rain."

Another late-in-the-day British hit, 1965's call-and-response chorused "Love Is Strange" followed—the group hadn't scored a significant American hit since 1962, when they were sprung from a short-lived stint in the US Marines, but Britain had remained fiercely loyal and was rewarded with some of the Everlys' strongest music yet. 1966's *Two Yanks in England* album, recorded with the likes of Jimmy Page, John Paul Jones, and Graham Nash, was the duo's way of saying thank you at the time—tonight at the Royal Albert Hall they proved that they remembered that age-old devotion.

The folky ballad "Take a Message to Mary" opened a heart-stopping medley of lesser-known favorites—the 1957 B-side "Maybe Tomorrow" and, from as late as 1969, the country themed "I Wonder If I Care as Much." Then it was back into the monster hits: "When Will I Be Loved," a song that had earned further immortality via versions by both Linda Ronstadt and Dave Edmunds; 1960's "So Sad (To Watch Good Love Go Bad)"; and 1958's rockabilly "Bird Dog."

That led into a dramatic take on Gene Vincent's classic "Be Bop A Lula," a song the Brothers recorded on their first-ever LP back in 1958; then came two songs from their second album, the aptly titled *Songs Our Daddy Taught Us*: "Lightning Express" and "Put My Little Shoes Away"—the song that Simon and Garfunkel performed at their very last show together in 1970.

By now, the Brothers were effortlessly mixing the worldwide hits with the specialist surprises but were well aware that the audience knew every single one of them. "Step It Up and Go" was followed by "Bye Bye Love," the hit that started it all for them; that was succeeded by "Gone Gone Gone," the title track from a beloved 1964 LP.

"All I Have to Do Is Dream," their first British number one, slid smoothly into "Wake Up Little Susie," their first American chart topper; the summertime ballad "Devoted to You" reawakened long-forgotten memories of schoolyard loves that were shattered by the holidays; and "Ebony Eyes" proved it was still one of the most haunted, haunting death ballads ever written, a plane crash epic that will always bring a chill.

Now we were into the home stretch. "Love Hurts," a song that Gram Parsons and Emmylou Harris had seemingly made their own back in the early 1970s, was effortlessly recaptured. Don's "Cathy's Clown" was next, the first song ever released on the Warner Brothers label in 1960, after the label paid an unprecedented $1 million for the duo's services; this led into 1959's effervescent "('Til) I Kissed You"; they moved on to their trademark break-neck assault on Bing Crosby's "Temptation" and, finally, the riotously rocking finale—"Lucille," "Let It Be Me," and the all-purpose manic meltdown, "Good Golly Miss Molly." The lights came up, the curtain came down, and the crowd was still on its feet, calling for more.

It was not to be—not that night, anyway. The following year, however, brought a new studio album from the Everly Brothers, their first in eleven years and their best in twenty. Produced by Dave Edmunds, *EB84* gave the Everlys another massive hit single when a song Paul McCartney wrote especially for them, "Wings of a Nightingale," reached number four in Britain.

Paul Simon took advantage of their reunion to deploy their still-stunning harmonies on *Graceland*. In 1986, the Everly Brothers were inducted into the Rock and Roll Hall of Fame; two years after that, a granite statue of the pair was unveiled in Central City, in their home state, Kentucky.

Paul (and Art's) childhood heroes, the Everly Brothers, at the peak of their 1950s powers.   *Photofest*

The honors continued and so did the music. Tours and records are more sporadic than they once were, but the magic remained just as powerful. A lot of people, possibly suffering from a surfeit of "American Pie," talk about the day when the music died. Well, now it was reborn.

Simon and Garfunkel's set list was impeccable. Opening with "Old Friends" and its gentle drift into "Bookends," the duo offered up a solid primer in all that made their sixties so sensational—"A Hazy Shade of Winter," "I Am a Rock," "America," "At the Zoo"—and that was just the opening salvo.

Behind them, the band was more muscular than any they had previously worked with, a rocking septet fronted by Simon's musical director

The probably inevitable live CD souvenir of the reunion tour.   *Author's collection*

Mark Stewart and conspiring to push the duo to unprecedented heights whenever they felt the need.

"Baby Driver" made even its so-energetic album equivalent feel somehow undernourished, all the more so as it led into what Garfunkel, nightly, described as "a song I had to have in the show, because I think it's Paul's most beautiful love song."

"Kathy's Song" was rendered with all the sensitivity it ever demanded, even if Garfunkel's voice no longer possessed the angelic purity it had once achieved so effortlessly. He was already feeling the first symptoms of the vocal problems that would eventually take him away from the stage for three years, but right now, he was feeling fine. "It's pretty easy to sing when the songs are this good."

It was at this point in the show, twenty-five or so minutes in, that the duo fell to reflection. Art started it:

> Paul and I go back to the sixth grade, which is when we met each other. We were both growing up outside Manhattan and they cast us both in the elementary school play; we were in *Alice in Wonderland* together. From those early days to today, with just a few interruptions, this is now a fifty year friendship that we cherish.

Paul picked up the thread:

> We were eleven years old when we met. I was the White Rabbit, a leading role; he was the Cheshire Cat, a supporting role. We started to sing together when we were thirteen years old, started to argue when we were fourteen years old, so that makes this the forty-seventh anniversary of our arguing. But we don't argue any more—we're exhausted. Now we say, 'That's your opinion and I respect that.'

Back to Art:

> There's really only one big thing we argue about, and it goes back to the very earliest days of our group. I wanted to call us Garfunkel and Simon. But he very cleverly convinced me that it really should be alphabetical.

"You don't have to be that clever," interjected Simon.

But Garfunkel continued, "When we were sixteen we made our first record, 'Hey Schoolgirl in the Second Row,' and it went like this."

The song would be over within a minute or so, just a glimpse really.

"But the sound of our voices, the sound that we aspired to, that came from the Everly Brothers. The Everlys were our heroes, so it's a tremendous pleasure for me to be able to introduce . . ."

And on they strode, older obviously, but still looking, and sounding, fabulous. "Wake Up Little Susie," "All I Have to Do Is Dream," "Let it Be Me," "Bye Bye Love"—whether they performed as a duo in their own right, or with Simon and Garfunkel throwing their voices into the mix alongside them, time itself evaporated.

Even the backing musicians, warming to the occasion, were suddenly transformed from a twenty-first-century band to a note-perfect fifties rockabilly combo, which in turn transformed the dreariest concrete aircraft hanger into the kind of high school sock hop where Simon and Garfunkel themselves first fell in love with the brothers' sound. And created their own.

The show went on: "Scarborough Fair," "Homeward Bound," "The Sound of Silence," "Mrs. Robinson"; Paul slid "Slip Slidin' Away" into the running order, and a few songs later, "American Tune."

But around them frolicked "El Condor Pasa (If I Could)," "Keep the Customer Satisfied," "The Only Living Boy in New York," "My Little Town," "Bridge Over Troubled Water," "Cecilia," "The Boxer," "The Leaves That Are Green," "The 59th Street Bridge Song (Feelin' Groovy)."

Two hours of tunes that, more than any of their previous reunions, felt not like a reunion but a rebirth, as though Simon and Garfunkel were finally ready to pick up where they first left off.

For almost a year, the old friends toured together, closing triumphantly with a free concert in front of the Colosseum in Rome, before a staggering 600,000 people. And, almost as soon as that was over, they immediately began preparing for their next outing.

The following year, 2005, they performed at the Hurricane Katrina benefit concert at Madison Square Garden, with Aaron Neville joining them for the closing "Bridge Over Troubled Water"; they were together again for a similarly short set when Simon played the Beacon Theater in

2007; and they undertook a money-spinning tour of Asia and Australia in 2009.

And then it was over. Onstage headlining day two of the 2010 New Orleans Jazz and Heritage Festival, Garfunkel's voice effectively disappeared.

Simon did his best to carry him; the audience, knowing something was wrong, did its utmost to keep him going. When his voice failed, they would still applaud; when he made it through a song without too much difficulty, they would celebrate.

But by the time they reached "My Little Town," it was clear that Garfunkel couldn't continue, not now and not in the near future, either. He was diagnosed with an enlarged vocal chord, a condition which saw him withdraw altogether. Not until 2013 was he ready to sing again, going out on the road in his own right and, in 2015, selling out Carnegie Hall at the climax of his latest US tour.

Today, too, he still keeps his music at arm's length, still seems happier undertaking long, private tours on his own (between 1998 and 2014, he completed his goal of walking from Ireland to Turkey—albeit a little bit at a time) than planning similar excursions with a band and an audience.

He even wrote his autobiography, *What Is It All But Luminous—Notes from an Underground Man*, a playful but disjointed amalgam of lists, letters, poems, prayers, dreams, ruminations on circumcision, and guides to his favorite books.

Memories, too, but not so many, and not too illuminating, either. There are moments when you feel you have a direct line to Garfunkel's soul and others when you know that is the very last thing he wants you to have.

And a reunion seems further away than ever.

In May 2015, four decades after their parting, Art Garfunkel talked about his feelings toward his former musical partner ahead of a solo tour; how, he told the British *Daily Telegraph*, Simon's decision to break up the duo was "very strange," and then, with that off his chest, he said: "I want to open up about this. I don't want to say any anti-Paul Simon things, but it seems very perverse to not enjoy the glory. Crazy. What I would have done is take a rest from Paul, because he was getting on my nerves. The jokes had run dry. How can you walk away from this lucky place on top of the world, Paul? What's going on with you, you idiot? How could you let that go, jerk?"

When the *Telegraph* interviewer suggested that Simon might have a "Napoleon complex," Garfunkel agreed, adding that, at school, he felt sorry for his friend because of his height, so he in turn offered him friendship as a compensation. "And that compensation gesture has created a monster," he says. "End of interview."

For his own part, Simon told NPR in 2016:

The fact is, is, like, we did do two big reunions, and we're done. There's nothing really much to say. You know, the music essentially stopped in 1970. And, you know, I mean, quite honestly, we don't get along. So it's not like it's fun.

If it was fun, I'd say, "OK, sometimes we'll go out and sing old songs in harmony. That's cool." But when it's not fun, you know, and you're going to be in a tense situation, well, then I have a lot of musical areas that I like to play in. So that'll never happen again. That's that.

But there's always room for maneuver. Always the hope of rapprochement. In 2017, on a promotional tour for his book, it was inevitable that the old wounds would be reopened, by interrogators if not by interrogatee.

But Garfunkel had no hesitation in shutting down one telephone interview after being asked, once again, to comment upon certain of his more coruscating pronouncements.

"I'm sorry I couldn't give you more time, and hear more quotes of things I've said in the past," he said softly. Then he hung up the phone. And the following year, reliving his own career on his farewell tour, Paul Simon avoided making any mention of his former partner whatsoever.

17

Twenty-First-Century Philanthropist

Paul Simon has always worn his heart on his sleeve, at least when it comes to what could be termed "political" causes but which others might prefer to describe as humanitarian concern.

His politics themselves are a matter of record. A lifelong Democrat, he has performed for candidates ranging from George McGovern to Hillary Clinton (he sang a shaky "Bridge Over Troubled Water" at the DNC in 2016), and he gleefully endorsed Bernie Sanders's co-opting of "America" for his run at the presidency that same year.

Indeed, according to the *New York Times*, when the entire campaign was done and dusted, the minute-long commercial that the Sanders campaign set to that tune was elected the most popular ad of all that were thrown at the electorate throughout that season. It made people feel happy.

Simon's leanings were confirmed, too, throughout the sixties—the journey from "He Was My Brother" to the ill-fated PBS documentary *Songs of America* was pocked with commentary, while *Graceland*, too, was the work of a man moved by injustice and determined to act against it, even if it meant flying in the face of popular opinion and wisdom.

His work in the field of musical education for the young, meanwhile, was exemplified by the songwriters workshop that he held in early 1970 (see chapter 6). But his appearance the following year on *Sesame Street* also spoke for his commitment to that same cause, as did the 1976 benefit he staged at Madison Square Garden, to raise a total of $30,000 for the New York Public Library.

A cofounder of the Children's Health Project in 1987 (see below), Simon sits, too, on the board of directors of the Little Kids Rock nonprofit organization, which aims to provide free lessons and musical instruments to the public school system.

A list of the other charities with which he has reportedly become involved includes: the American Foundation for AIDS Research, Autism Speaks, the Entertainment Industry Foundation, Every Mother Counts, the Fund for Imprisoned Children in South Africa, the Joe Torre Safe at Home Foundation, Life College, Love Hope Strength Foundation, MusiCares, Project ALS, the Rainforest Foundation Fund, Rosie's Theater Kids, the Starkey Hearing Foundation, the Doe Fund, the Nature Conservancy, Tibet House US, and Ubuntu Education Fund.

In 2014, Simon was awarded the Service to America Leadership Award by the NAB Education Foundation (NABEF) for his longtime commitment to providing healthcare to children.

Much of his charitable work and giving goes unreported, at least by Simon—the million bucks that he and Edie gave to the Hurricane Harvey relief fund in 2017 was a very rare example of them speaking out about their donations.

Less easy to obscure, however, has been the alacrity with which Simon agrees to perform at, or organize, benefit concerts—not just for the causes with which he is directly involved but a multitude of others, too.

Onstage during his farewell tour, he assured audiences that he intended to continue performing live to raise funds for causes he believed in—"occasional performance[s] in a (hopefully) acoustically pristine hall"—while, at the other end of his solo career, his first ever live appearance following the breakup of Simon and Garfunkel was at an anti-war benefit in 1970.

The Summer Concert for Peace (1970)

Organized by the New Mobilization Committee to End the War in Vietnam, the Summer Concert for Peace was the sensibly titled successor to the Winter Concert for Peace, staged at the Fillmore East earlier in the year.

The summer event was to be held at Shea Stadium on the twenty-fifth anniversary of the atomic bombing of Hiroshima, with a lineup that included Creedence Clearwater Revival, Johnny Winter, Poco, the Paul Butterfield Blues Band, Steppenwolf, the James Gang, the cast of *Hair*,

Miles Davis, and a one-off reunion of Janis Joplin and Big Brother and the Holding Company. Simon and Garfunkel were then approached to headline the whole event, but while Simon was enthusiastic, Garfunkel was not.

Their split had yet to be made public; they themselves were only dimly aware that it had occurred. Simon's decision to go solo for the show, then, was a portent that few comprehended.

From the outset, it was clear that this show was to be very different from its predecessor. Ticket sales barely half-filled the massive stadium, and when the audience did take their seats, it was to find that the stage was way out on second base while they were confined to the bleachers.

The makeup of the crowd, too, was different. At the winter event, the show attracted an audience that was wholly committed to the cause. The summer concert, on the other hand, primarily drew people who wanted a day out in the sunshine, listening to music and getting drunk or stoned. They didn't think much of Paul Simon, either. On a day packed with loud, hard-driving rock and blues, his short acoustic set (he did not, of course, headline) was scarcely audible.

Three songs in, midway through "Scarborough Fair/Canticle," the cat calls began, and Simon did not even try to quell the audience's discontent. He left the stage, never to return.

The Concert for George McGovern (1972)

Simon's next benefit concert, and his next live appearance too, was a benefit for Democratic candidate George McGovern on June 14, 1972. Organized by actor and activist Warren Beatty, Together for McGovern took place at Madison Square Garden and is best remembered for the Simon and Garfunkel reunion that highlighted the event.

In fact, neither were particularly devout McGovern supporters; they were more interested simply in stopping President Richard Nixon from winning a second term. Earlier in the campaign, Simon favored Shirley Chisholm, the first black candidate, and the first woman, too, ever to seek the Democratic nomination. He was disappointed when she lost out to

Governor George McGovern. Paul played a benefit for his election campaign in 1972.   *Photofest*

McGovern in the primaries and even more so when McGovern lost to Nixon in the general election.

"When Nixon was elected, I cried. I actually cried. I remember puttin' on the TV set in the morning, and I saw he was coming down to make his acceptance speech. Tears started rolling down my eyes."

The Library Benefit Concert (1976)

Jimmy Cliff, Phoebe Snow, and the Brecker Brothers joined Simon at Madison Square Garden on May 3, 1976, for a benefit aimed at raising $30,000 for the New York Public Library system.

With Jessy Dixon and Phoebe Snow reprising their familiar roles, Simon's fourteen-song set largely echoed his recent live repertoire, comprising: "Still Crazy After All These Years," "You're Kind," "Have a Good Time," "I Do It for Your Love," "50 Ways to Leave Your Lover," "My Little Town," "The Boxer," "Loves Me Like a Rock," "Some Folks Lives Roll Easy," "Gone at Last," "American Tune," "Bridge Over Troubled Water," and "Me and Julio Down by the Schoolyard."

The Concert in Central Park (1981)

Art Garfunkel was back at Simon's side for his next major benefit appearance, in Central Park in 1981 (see chapter 9).

Hopes that they would regroup once more for Live Aid, four years later, were dashed however, although Simon did appear on the "We Are the World" USA for Africa single.

The Homeless Children's Medical Benefit Concert (1987)

Basking in the massive success of *Graceland*, Simon threw himself into a benefit for the newly launched New York Children's Health Project.

The goal was to raise the money to purchase a fully equipped hospital van, with a staff of five, to tour the city's homeless shelters. It was estimated that the mobile medical unit would cater to around a quarter of New York's estimated twelve thousand homeless children.

It was a cause which Simon had already aided financially. In 1986, the former medical director of USA for Africa, pediatrician Dr. Irwin Redlener, took Simon to one of New York's most notorious welfare hotels, the Martinique in Herald Square. Simon later recalled: "You would look into a room, and a young mother with a couple of young kids would be in there, with dishes in the bathtub and a little hot plate she tried to cook on which wasn't allowed. The children would be on long lines to get one hot meal a day, and when they ran out of food, the kids at the end wouldn't get any."

Before the end of the year, Simon had donated $80,000 from his personal fortune, and he would also hand over a similar amount from the proceeds of the Graceland tour.

Now, his organization of the concert was drawing together a remarkable bill: Ladysmith Black Mambazo, Lou Reed, Billy Joel, James Taylor, Laurie Anderson, Grandmaster Flash, Chaka Khan, Nile Rodgers, Debbie Harry, and Grace Jones (who provided the distinctive backing vocals for Reed's "Walk on the Wild Side"), with unannounced guest appearances from comedians Chevy Chase, Whoopi Goldberg, and Bill Cosby; baseball stars Ron Darling and Don Mattingly; and, introduced to the stage by the latter, Bruce Springsteen.

Highlights of the performance were manifold, with Simon on and off the stage all evening, performing a few songs here, a few songs there— "The Boy in the Bubble," "Crazy Love Volume 2," and "I Know What I Know" at the start of the show; "Still Crazy After All These Years," "Late

Paul alongside (clockwise from left) Lionel Richie, Daryl Hall, Quincy Jones, and Stevie Wonder at the *We Are the World* recording session.   *Photofest*

in the Evening," and "Diamonds on the Soles of Her Shoes" at the end; "Homeless," "Graceland," and "You Can Call Me Al" in the middle; and a clutch of surprises, too.

"Glory Days," with Simon joining Springsteen and Joel onstage, was one standout, of course, prefaced by Springsteen joking, "Rhymin' Simon is going to be rockin' Simon." But "Teenager in Love"—with Simon, Springsteen, Taylor, Joel, and Ruben Blades in full voice behind Dion—is the one that most commentators recall.

Before the concert, Simon cautioned, "It's not about being pretentious enough to think that we can solve the homeless problem in this country; all we're trying to do is to look at one particular aspect of this horror and provide medical care to homeless children." But the event more than met its aims—not only was the medical unit purchased, but a fleet of mini buses was, too.

There would be no film released of the concert and no official live album, either. "This was for New York," Simon remarked once it was over.

Bluff Aid (1990)

It sounded trivial, but to residents of the New York community of Montauk, out in the Hamptons, to conservationists, and to lovers of America's natural beauty, it was a serious affair.

For centuries, the surf had been gnawing away at the monumental bluffs that overlooked the Atlantic Ocean from the edge of Long Island, constantly eroding them.

The Montauk Point Lighthouse, the fourth-oldest continually functioning lighthouse in America (it was erected in 1796), had long fought a battle against the waves, while homes that included Paul Simon's $10.5 million mansion and Andy Warhol's $50 million compound were also watching their property fall into the ocean.

A cottage on Simon's land, built by artists Balcomb Greene and Gertrude Glass, was so close to the edge that Simon would eventually be forced to have it physically moved away from danger.

The lighthouse was the gravest concern, however, and on August 30, 1990, at Montauk's Indian Field Ranch, Simon staged Bluff Aid to help raise the $500,000 needed for its protection with landscaping and seawalls.

He was the headliner, of course, turning in an eighteen-song set that covered all the bases, and Billy Joel took the stage amidships for a three-song set that concluded with a wild rock 'n' roll medley.

The American Tribute to Vaclav Havel and a Celebration of Democracy in Czechoslovakia (1991)

The collapse of the Iron Curtain and the dismantling of the Soviet Union stand among the most significant historical events of the late twentieth century, and its heroes were proclaimed across the western world.

Vaclav Havel was a Czech writer and statesman who, throughout his homeland's Communist era, was regarded as a dissident—a status that he encouraged through his patronage of the Western arts in general, and rock 'n' roll in particular. It was no coincidence that, following his death, the tribute concert staged in his memory in Prague was headlined by a Velvet Underground tribute act—Lou Reed's old outfit was far and away Havel's favorite band.

The Velvets were absent from the Cathedral of St. John the Divine on the night of February 22, 1990, when the arts came together to celebrate his election to the presidency of his newly liberated homeland. But still producer Joseph Papp arranged an event fitting for both man and venue, with Placido Domingo, James Taylor, Roberta Flack, and Paul Simon.

The Simple Truth (1991)

It was the refugee crisis of the age—millions of Kurds fleeing their homes following the outbreak of the first Gulf War, and the Iraqi crackdown on some of its longest-established domestic opponents.

Both repeating an old story and rehearsing for future injustices, the warring nations—the Iraqis and the coalition of allies pieced together by the United States and its president, George H. W. Bush—had little time to aid them.

Lou Reed (left) and Jimmy Cliff (right), together in the late 1970s.   *Photofest*

It was left, as it so often is, to public sympathy and outrage, and on May 12, 1991, performers scattered across three continents were linked by five satellites to a massive festival at London's Wembley Stadium to raise funds for the International Committee of the Red Cross. Simon was among those who appeared at the Wembley event.

The five-hour broadcast was watched in thirty-six countries and raised $15 million.

Tibet House (1994)

The Tibet House US Cultural Center of H. H. the Dalai Lama was founded in 1987 by, among others, composer Philip Glass, actor Richard Gere, and Columbia University professor Robert Thurman, at the behest of the Dalai Lama, Tenzin Gyatso.

Dedicating to preserving the arts, music, spirituality, and culture of Tibet in the face of the Chinese occupation of the nation, Tibet House staged its first annual benefit concert in 1989, and rapidly the event established itself among the highlights of the New York concert calendar.

Simon was a longtime friend of Glass, both socially and musically—in the liners to 2011's *So Beautiful or So What*, Simon describes him as someone who "seems to know how to untangle the harmonic knots that I occasionally miscreate in my songs."

Their collaborations now date back over thirty-five years; Glass was among the contributors to *Hearts and Bones*, while Simon was one of the singers invited to partake in Philip Glass's 1986 album *Songs from Liquid Days*—Suzanne Vega, Laurie Anderson, Linda Ronstadt, Bernard Fowler, and David Byrne were also involved.

Glass had already "fashioned a set of six songs which, together, form a cycle of themes ranging from reflections on nature to classic romantic settings"; the "long and difficult process of casting" of featured vocalists was then undertaken with producer Kurt Munkacsi and conductor Michael Riesman. Simon's contribution, the ten-minute "Changing Opinion," was the album's opener.

The 1994 Tibet House event was very much a family affair for Simon; aside from Glass, his wife Edie Brickell and the Roche sisters, students at that long-ago songwriters class at NYU, were also on the bill alongside Allen Ginsberg, Spalding Gray, Richie Havens, Nawang Khechog, and Natalie Merchant.

The performance, too, would be highlighted by some remarkable collaborations, not least of all Simon and Glass combining for a performance of "The Late Great Johnny Ace." Simon was then joined by Canadian fiddler Ashley MacIsaacs for a thrilling "Duncan" before Brickell took the stage and the trio introduced the title track from her newly released album, *Picture Perfect Morning*.

America: A Tribute to Heroes (2001)

For many observers, Paul Simon's impossibly moving *Saturday Night Live* performance in the immediate aftermath of 9/11 remains among the most emotional performances of his entire career (see chapter 10). But it was matched, a week previous, by his solo performance of "Bridge Over Troubled Water" at the Tribute to Heroes event.

Arranged jointly by the television networks ABC, CBS, NBC, and Fox, and produced by Joel Gallon, the entire concert took place on a candlelit stages in three cities—Los Angeles, London, and New York—with the performances linked by telethon-style messages and appeals.

It was broadcast live across all four American networks and many cable channels too. The event raised over $200 million for the United Way's September 11 Telethon Fund.

Paul at the Tribute to Heroes concert in 2001.   *Photofest*

Bruce Springsteen, Tom Petty, Steve Wonder, Willie Nelson, and Wyclef Jean were among the performers who joined Simon on that night, with "Bridge Over Troubled Water" ending the main set. Celine Dion's "God Bless America" and an ensemble "America the Beautiful," from the Los Angeles stage, closed the show.

A month later, further celebrities staged the Concert for New York City at Madison Square Garden, an event which opened with David Bowie's poignant, radical, but nevertheless beautiful rearrangement of "America."

It was a message that spoke as loudly to the United States at large as it did to New York City itself, as Bowie acknowledged: "I was looking for [a song] which really evoked feelings of bewilderment and uncertainty because, for me, that's how that particular period felt. And I really thought that ['America'], in this new context, really captured that."

From the Big Apple to the Big Easy—The Concert for New Orleans (2005)

On September 20, 2005, little more than three weeks after Hurricane Katrina wreaked unparalleled havoc and destruction across the Gulf Coast and New Orleans, two simultaneous concerts were organized at Madison Square Garden and Radio City Music Hall.

Featuring performances from Jimmy Buffett, Ed Bradley, John Fogerty, Irma Thomas, Bette Midler, Elvis Costello, and Elton John, the event generated proceeds that approached $9 million for the Bush Clinton Katrina Fund, Habitat for Humanity, MusiCares, and the Children's Health Fund.

"It was kind of a rare moment where the whole country was a community," Simon reflected on the aftermath of the storm. "Everybody focused on how to help. If we could bottle that, it's a more efficient way of problem-solving,"

Simon and Garfunkel, midway through their latest reunion (see chapter 16), performed "Mrs. Robinson" and "Homeward Bound" before being joined onstage by Louisiana legend Aaron Neville for the closing "Bridge Over Troubled Water."

Turkana Basin Institute Benefit (2012)

Headed up by paleontologist Dr. Richard Leakey, the Turkana Basin Institute is a nonprofit organization dedicated to the assembly of a full fossil record of mankind's origins in sub-Saharan Africa. And Leakey himself admitted that Paul Simon's support was unlikely—"I really don't like music and he really doesn't like old bones."

They met around 2008 when Simon paid a visit to the institute; now he was proposing a benefit concert to be held at the beginning of May 2012 at the Highline Stages in Manhattan's old meatpacking district.

It was a cosy affair, a dinner more than a concert, with two hundred guests, including the likes of David Rockefeller Jr., real estate developer Leonard Stern, financier James H. Simons, and Richard Gelfond, the CEO of IMAX. There was also an auction with the items up for grabs, including a painting by the Kenyan-born artist Wangechi Mutu (which fetched $42,000) and a nine-day Kenyan safari ($46,000).

Simon, for his part, performed a short, Simon and Garfunkel-era-heavy set with guitarist Mark Stewart—opening with "The Boxer," closing with "The Sound of Silence"

The audience listened attentively—at least for the most part. According to *Huffington Post* writer Mike Hogan, however, "Charity audiences are notorious for yammering through concerts, but this audience was reverentially silent—so much so that a fist fight nearly broke out following the performance when two guests accused a third of talking over the music."

The benefit raised over $2 million.

The Children's Health Fund 25th Anniversary Benefit Concert (2012)

A quarter of a century on from its tentative beginnings, the Children's Health Fund was now a powerful force not only on New York's health scene but across the nation. A fleet of fifty mobile medical, dental, and mental health clinics is in operation, working on a daily basis with hospitals and community health centers around the country but also available for disaster response, too. Children's Health Fund was involved in the aftermath of Hurricanes Andrew, Katrina, and Sandy.

Fundraising remained its most important source of income, however, which led to Simon and cofounder Dr. Irwin Redlener organizing the silver jubilee benefit at Radio City Music Hall on October 4. Guest performers included Sting and his wife, Trudie Styler; comedian Steve Martin; James Taylor and Caroline Taylor; Tina Fey and Jeff Richmond; and more.

There was also an appearance from father-and-daughter Stevie Wonder and Aisha Morris, the inspiration behind the hit song "Isn't She Lovely," while Simon was joined by Edie Brickell.

Standing out among the highlights of the evening was the ensemble finale of "Loves Me Like a Rock" and "America the Beautiful."

A Night for Freedom—FTS (Free the Slaves) Benefit (2012)

Performing two songs, Paul Simon was a surprise guest at the November 27 event at New York's City Winery. Hosted by jazz performer Esperanza Spalding, the event was designed to raise funds and awareness of the international lobby group Free the Slave's campaign against modern slavery.

Bobby McFerrin and Gretchen Parlato were among the other performers, although the after-show talk seemed dominated by the star item at the accompanying silent auction. Asking Prince for a donation, Esperanza said she would accept anything, even an old sock. Prince promptly mailed her one. A few days later, however, he also sent a guitar, and that was what was eventually sold.

Robin Hood Benefit Concert (2013)

Both Sting and Paul Simon were booked to appear, separately, at the May 14, 2013, Madison Square Garden event—old friends and former neighbors, however, they decided to take the stage together, initiating the partnership that would soon see the pair touring together (see chapter 18).

Staying Put Benefit (2013)

On September 29, 2013, four of the highest-profile residents of New Canaan, Connecticut—Paul Simon, NBC anchor Brian Williams, his actress daughter Allison Williams, and singer Harry Connick Jr.—joined forces for a tribute to the town's first responders. Proceeds were donated to Staying Put, a nonprofit that allows senior citizens to continue to live in their own homes.

With the Williamses as cohosts, the event took place at the New Canaan High School. Brian Williams enthused: "This may be the largest single collection of star power in the town's history. Concertgoers around the world have lined up to see Paul Simon and Harry Connick Jr., but never at the same time, under one roof."

Seventh Annual Performance Series of Legends Benefit Concert for the Duke Ellington School of the Arts (2014)

Stevie Wonder, the scheduled bill-topper, was forced to cancel, so Sting headlined the benefit—staged at the Music Center at Strathmore in North Bethesda, Maryland, on March 12, 2014—and brought along his own special guest, Paul Simon.

While the school's cofounder, Peggy Cooper Cafritz, celebrated "the most successful benefit we've had since 1994," Rep. Jim Moran (D-VA) was simply mortified to hear the predominantly youthful audience sing along with the headliners. "Nooo, you're too young."

Simon's guest slot was brief—a duet of "The Boxer" and a Simon solo through Sting's "Fragile." Sting alone then performed "America." Later, Simon returned to the stage in the company of the school's pupils (who also performed during the evening) for "Bridge Over Troubled Water" (see chapter 18).

A Tribute to Phil Everly (2014)

Phil Everly passed away in 2014 from complications caused by chronic obstructive pulmonary disease (COPD). On October 29 that same year, the COPD Foundation staged a fundraiser at the mansion home of Sylvia Roberts, 1358 Page Rd., Nashville, Tennessee. Tickets for the event started at $500.

On a tiny stage erected in the grand hallway, Simon and guitarist Mark Stewart performed both Simon's own material and a clutch of Everlys classics—"When Will I Be Loved" and "All I Have to Do Is Dream"—with a passing Brenda Lee joining in on harmonies. All she'd done, she told the audience, was drop by the dressing room "to say hello, and [Paul] said, 'You're gonna sing, aren't you?'"

"I am grateful for the support of Paul Simon in helping to raise awareness about this devastating disease and to be a part of this special evening with proceeds going towards the COPD Foundation," Everly's widow, Patti, said later.

Rainforest Fund Benefit Concert (2014)

Simon was back in action with Sting at the Rainforest Fund benefit, on April 17, 2014, at Carnegie Hall, on a bill that also featured James Taylor (who wore a lampshade on his head for the occasion), Dionne Warwick, Stephen Stills, Chris Botti, Dionne Warwick, and more. Sting's daughter and son, Eliot and Joe, ran respectively through "Born to Be Wild" and "Smells Like Teen Spirit," and Rolling Stones backing vocalist Lisa Fischer stepped out of her customary shadows to deliver rousing versions of "Start Me Up" and "Jumpin' Jack Flash."

Simon's headlining appearance included "Graceland" and the first of his expected duets with Sting, "The Boxer," together with a handful of what were, from all accounts, appalling jokes. When Sting shook his head in (presumably) feigned despair, Simon responded that only native Amazonians, with their dry sense of humor, would understand them.

Sting got his own back swiftly, saying: "You know, when Artie would sing, he'd send Paul off the stage. Well, tonight, Paul, I'm not going to send you off the stage. I want you to stand right there while I sing your song."

He then swam into "Bridge Over Troubled Water," but for once, a different song ended the evening, a *tout ensemble* rendition of Stephen Stills's "Love the One You're With."

The Nearness of You Benefit (2015)

Staged at Frederick P. Rose Hall, Jazz at Lincoln Center on January 20, 2015, the benefit was a tribute to late saxophonist (and longtime Simon sessioneer) Michael Brecker.

With James Taylor and Bobby McFerrin sharing the bill, proceeds were donated to cancer research at Columbia University Medical Center (CUMC) and the work of Siddhartha Mukherjee, MD, PhD and Azra Raza, MD, a specialist in Myelodisplastic Syndromes, the disease that killed Brecker in 2007.

Fistula Foundation Benefit (2015)

On October 1, 2015, this benefit was held both to raise funds for The Life You Can Save charity and to mark Princeton professor Peter Singer's seventieth birthday and life's work.

A longtime friend of Simon's, Singer was a founder of the The Life You Can Save, which is dedicated to reducing the unnecessary suffering and premature death of those living in extreme poverty. It was when the two men were named among *Time* magazine's 100 People Who Shaped the World that Simon suggested celebrating with a benefit concert and asked Singer to choose the beneficiary. The Fistula Foundation was his choice.

The home of Katja Goldman and Michael Sonnenfeldt was turned over for the evening, and Fistula Foundation CEO Kate Grant recalled: "The living room was filled with exceptionally generous people there to hear Paul Simon and help women in need. I think I had bruises from pinching myself. To be recommended by Peter Singer, whose work deeply inspires me, and hear music from a man whose brilliance has brightened my life over decades, as he has millions around the world, was simply priceless."

The concert raised over $150,000 to fund fistula surgery for women in need.

(Five days later, on October 6, Simon was among the performers at New York's PlayStation Theater, for the Country Music Hall of Fame Benefit.)

A Tribute to Allen Toussaint, Featuring Paul Simon and Friends (2015)

This December 8, 2015, event was originally scheduled as a benefit for New Orleans Artists Against Hunger and Homelessness, a charity formed by Allen Toussaint thirty years before as a means of allowing the local artistic community to battle poverty in the city. Toussaint himself would have headlined.

His death from a heart attack less than a month before the event, on November 10, saw the nature of the show radically altered. It would remain a benefit, but Toussaint and his miraculous musical legacy was now the focus of the performance at the 370-person-capacity Le Petit Theater.

"If it's true that he can see and hear us," Simon told the audience, "I'm sure he'd approve. It's the cause that he wanted to support. And I'm happy to help."

Toussaint-heavy sets by a succession of Crescent City luminaries—Davell Crawford, John Boutte, Erica Falls, Cyril Neville, and Deacon John, all accompanied by Toussaint's own band—set the stage for Simon's arrival. He did not offer up any of the old master's material, but he did reveal that Toussaint (who had guested on *There Goes Rhymin' Simon* in 1973) had recorded a version of "American Tune"; and, as he prepared for the final number, a desolate "Homeward Bound," he said, softly, "For you, Allen."

"I love New Orleans," he remarked to the audience at one point.

A voice floated out of the audience. "We love you too."

Allen Toussaint was originally scheduled to headline a New Orleans charity benefit in November 2015. His death a month before transformed the event into a benefit concert, headlined by Simon.   *Photofest*

The Life You Can Save Benefit (2016)

Exactly twelve months on from his last The Life You Can Save-related benefit, Paul Simon was in Los Altos Hills, California, on October 1, 2016, to raise funds for the organization itself. The benefit took place at the home of Julie and Carlo Panaccione. "Performance, food and cocktails limited to 150 people," warned the advance reporting.

Materials for the Arts (MFTA) Benefit (2017)

In September 2016, Simon was introduced to artist Skip LaPlante, who had recently created no fewer than 130 wind chimes using materials he found at the MFTA facility.

Initially, the singer was intending only to discover whether the chimes would be appropriate for his upcoming *Stranger to Stranger* tour; once on campus, however, he became fascinated not only with the facility itself but also with the programs it runs for children.

Immediately he suggested a benefit concert, which took place on April 5, 2017. Simon was joined by Mark Stewart and, playing those wind chimes, LaPlante.

The Half-Earth Tour (2017)

Nobody who has read Edward O. Wilson's book *Half-Earth: Our Planet's Fight for Life* can fail to be, in turn, moved, infuriated, and, to an extent, left feeling utterly helpless by the conservationist's account of how easy it would be (at least theoretically) to save the world from the barrage of environmental disasters that mankind seems intent on foisting upon it. Simply set half the planet aside for conservation.

That is the goal of the Half-Earth Project, and as Paul Simon read the book—he was reviewing it for the *New York Times*—he formed an idea.

"The point of no return is fast approaching," Simon wrote. "Questions of human rights, racism, democracy versus tyranny and sexism are just that: human rights. But there will be no rights, or humans, if we do not preserve and conserve a habitable planet. Still, Wilson is an optimist and believes we can preserve our jewel-like planet if we do the job we must do. 'Half-Earth' is compulsory reading if we care about the lives of our children, our children's children and all of the species alive today. A paradise!"

He was planning to tour in 2017, a monthlong outing that began in St. Augustine, Florida, on June 1 and wound up in Denver, Colorado, on June 28. Now he was planning to give away the entire proceeds: "[I]f I do a tour, I can keep singing, I can keep my skills up. I can keep my band together.

The Montauk Point lighthouse.   *©Alex Potemkin/iStock/Getty Images*

And I can give all the profits to [the E. O. Wilson Biodiversity Foundation], and that will make me feel that I am making a greater contribution than putting more money in my pocket, which I don't need, or becoming more famous, which I really don't need."

Harvey Can't Mess with Texas (2017)

Simon joined Willie Nelson, James Taylor, and Bonnie Raitt to headline a benefit for victims of Hurricane Harvey on September 22 at the Frank Erwin Center in Austin.

In addition, he and wife Edie also handed $1 million to the relief fund. As Brickell put it, "I'm sad when it happens anywhere. When it's your home state I feel a greater responsibility to come in and do what I can."

They targeted their donation as widely as they could. "We're not giving to one big umbrella. We're giving a lot of little umbrellas all over."

Montauk Music Festival Rocks the Lighthouse (2018)

On August 27, shortly before launching the final leg of his farewell tour, Simon made an unannounced surprise appearance at Montauk Music Festival. Accompanied by a local band, the Montauk Project, he performed four songs: "Late in the Evening," "50 Ways to Leave Your Lover," "Me and Julio Down by the Schoolyard," and "You Can Call Me Al."

18

Still Questing After All These Years

Paul Simon's first "concert in the park" took place in New York in September 1981; the second, there again in August 1991. Perhaps there should have been a third in 2001, but the horrors of 9/11 would have wiped it from the memory.

Simon's third parkland performance, then, took place on July 15, 2012, when he headlined the second night of the Hard Rock Calling Festival at London's Hyde Park and brought twenty-plus years of music to bear on a sprawling outdoor audience—a "mere" (by past standards) sixty thousand people.

The shortfall was understandable, of course. It was not a free concert this time, just another in the ever-longer list of branded shindigs that proliferate today, and which heap up in the memory as anonymously as the corporate concrete blocks that now stand in for the familiar, locally-named stadia in which such affairs once were staged. If you've attended one Soft Drink Sponsored Festival in one Telecommunications Giant Arena, you've attended them all.

Simon did not appear to care. The show, after all, was not simply one more feather in his already richly beplumed hat. It was an opportunity, too, to stroll through his career once more and then pause to regard its most historic moment, with a complete performance of *Graceland*.

Age had taken its toll, of course, and time, too. The *Daily Telegraph* may have seemed a little indelicate when it remarked, "Some of the original members of Ladysmith were unavoidably unable to take part in this reunion concert due to being dead." But it at least tried to make amends by continuing, "But their high kicking replacements introduced a jaunty energy on stage." And recounting how, later in the set, "Tony Cedras's accordion opening [to "The Boy in the Bubble"] was greeted like a returning old friend."

Which, of course, it was.

The festival itself was beset by difficulties, most pronounced of them all being the curfew that curtailed Bruce Springsteen's headlining performance the evening before—he had barely had time to introduce special guest Paul McCartney, to blast through the Beatles' "I Saw Her Standing There," when the creatures of the officious deep arose to declare that the party was over.

There would be no such curtailment for Simon; in fact, he took the stage early to be sure of it, launching into a string of hits before he turned the stage over to reggae hero Jimmy Cliff (see chapter 7).

2017: The Concert in Hyde Park (Legacy 88985404822)

"Kodachrome"
"Gone at Last"
"Dazzling Blue"
"50 Ways to Leave Your Lover"
"The Harder They Come" (Jimmy Cliff)
"Many Rivers to Cross" (Jimmy Cliff)
"Vietnam" (with Jimmy Cliff)
"Mother and Child Reunion" (with Jimmy Cliff)/
"That Was Your Mother"
"Hearts and Bones"
"Mystery Train"
"Wheels"
"Me and Julio Down by the Schoolyard"
"Slip Slidin' Away"
"The Obvious Child"
"Homeless" (with Ladysmith Black Mambazo)
"Diamonds on the Soles of Her Shoes" (with Ladysmith Black Mambazo)
"I Know What I Know"
"The Boy in the Bubble"
"Crazy Love, Vol. II"
"Gumboots"
"Under African Skies" (with Thandiswa Mazwai)
"Graceland"
"You Can Call Me Al"
"The Sound of Silence"
"The Boxer" (with Jerry Douglas)
"Late in the Evening"
"Still Crazy After All These Years"

Executive Producer: Mike Kauffman

Producer: Paul King

Concert film directed by: Matthew Amos

Musicians

Andy Smitzer—saxophone, percussion, vibes, vocals

Bakithi Kumalo—bass

Barney Rachabane—saxophone, penny whistle (*Graceland* set only)

Isaac Mtshali—drums (*Graceland* set only)

Jamey Haddad—percussion

Jim Oblon—drums, guitar, vocals

John Selowane—guitar, vocals (*Graceland* set only)

Mark Stewart—guitar, harmonica, saxophone, vocals

Mick Rossi—keyboards, percussion

Ray Phiri—guitar (*Graceland* set only)

Tony Cedras—trumpet, keyboards, accordion, percussion, vocals

Vincent Nguini—guitar, vocals

Cliff's short set ended as Simon rejoined him for "Viet-Nam," which drifted in turn to the song it so profoundly influenced, "Mother and Child Reunion," and more hits too, as Simon made his way towards *Graceland*.

The set was exquisite—a handful of numbers may not have ranked among the most unabashed audience favorites, but it was impossible not to get caught up in either the moment or in the sheer sense of happiness that radiated from the stage.

The cameras caught it. Too many of Simon's peers, captured on DVD today, simply look bored, just doing their job for the cameras while a backing band filled with hired hands mug for the cellphones and play their scheduled notes. There's no joy, no sense of occasion, no tomfoolery, and no deviation from the rehearsal script.

Simon and co *weren't* simply making up the show as they went along. But they looked as though they could be, and that is half the battle won right there, particularly if you know the concert is being filmed and that audiences will be studying facial expressions and body language for years, and decades, to come.

Hugh Masekela appeared, echoing Cliff and Ladysmith Black Mambazo by performing two songs of his own ("Stimela" and the anthemic "Bring Him Back Home (Nelson Mandela)"); and *Graceland* wrapped up with "You Can Call Me Al."

Jimmy Cliff was one of the stars of Simon's Concert in Hyde Park.   *Photofest*

"It's all unfathomably tight," mused the critic from *The Independent*, "[and] the only criticism is that Simon's light tone just can't compete with the other singers. It would have been nice too to have heard *Graceland* in order, maybe. [But] he made up for it with a one-man encore of "The Sound of Silence" that reduced the crowd to a fitting hush."

Perhaps surprisingly, given the alacrity with which other artists pump such things out, the DVD of the concert was not released until 2017—five years after the fact. But Simon's workload had scarcely let up in recent years, even as he maintained the relaxed trickle of new albums that he'd fallen into thirty years before.

Surprise in 2006 was followed by the so-richly homespun *So Beautiful or What* in 2011, but only one song from either, the latter's "Dazzling Blue," appeared in the Hyde Park set list.

Their absence was noted, and mourned. *Surprise*, in particular.

A Beautiful Surprise

Surprise, Paul Simon's 2006 album was recorded with producer Brian Eno—and that, for longtime watchers of either man, was itself justification for the album's title.

The album was largely written in the wake of 9/11 and the years of conflict that followed it; somewhat presciently, "Wartime Prayers" was written *before* the invasions, yet it quickly became one of the key anthems of the anti-war protests that sprang up in their aftermath.

Given that both men's entire careers have been built around evading the expected, it was perhaps as inevitable as it was unlikely that Paul Simon and Brian Eno should wind up working together.

First sighted aboard Bryan Ferry's art/glam rock band Roxy Music in the early 1970s, the man who was born Brian Peter George St. Baptiste de la Salle Eno remained with the group for two albums, and two hit singles, before his insatiable curiosity with other forms of music led to his departure.

An album of drones, bleeps, and atmospheres, recorded with King Crimson's Robert Fripp and aptly titled *No Pussyfooting*, opened this phase of his career in 1973, and over the years that followed, a succession of solo records saw Eno's music shift from incisive, if fiercely left-field, pop songs toward what would now be titled "ambient" music—a term, incidentally, that Eno both coined and applied to his own work.

It remains the most commonly used description for his music, yet it only begins to scratch the surface of his canon. Though he seldom deviates from the realms of purely electronic expression, Eno's eye for experimentation has never wavered, whether he is conjuring what he has, at different times, titled *Music for Airports, Music for Films, Possible Musics*, or even, simply, *Atmospheres*. Yet his sense of adventure reaches far beyond his own prolusions.

Taking on the mantel of producer, he was an integral ingredient in Talking Heads' journey into what was not yet called world music, the *Remain in Light* album. He conspired with David Bowie across what is fondly termed the Berlin Trilogy—a sequence of albums that included the massive hit "'Heroes.'" And, just as the outside world had pegged him as the ultimate musical dilettante, without a commercial notion in his entire body, Eno struck up a relationship with U2 at a time when they were firmly on course to be anointed the biggest rock band in the world.

The Unforgettable Fire was their first LP together, in 1984; three years later, *The Joshua Tree* followed, and the union has remained largely intact ever since.

But he has also worked with Laurie Anderson, Peter Gabriel, Coldplay, Grace Jones, Sinead O'Connor, Soul Makossa, Anna Calvi, Dido, Hector Zazou, and Suede, sometimes as an outsider remixer, other times as an integral part of the recording process. And in every case, and despite the congeries of imitators and clones that his work has inspired, what he brings to the proceedings is forever utterly unique, absolutely timeless, and irrefutably Eno.

Simon and Eno originally met at a dinner party in London, with Eno admitting he was prepared to dislike his new acquaintance. His work with Talking Heads, after all, was widely acclaimed as one of the first successful rock albums to incorporate "world" rhythms as an integral part of its construction, and Eno was understandably proud of that fact.

"I realize now that what I was feeling was envy," he told the *Guardian* newspaper in 2006. A musical landscape that he had very much pioneered (he described it as a "wonderful private beach") had suddenly been invaded, no only by Simon but by "all these people." For a while, Eno admitted that he was "sort of annoyed." But then he heard a track from *Graceland*, and he said, "I found myself liking it."

He was also astonished to discover how easy Simon was to work with. In that same interview, Eno explained how Simon, ordinarily "so controlling and anxious to get everything right," was also always willing to listen to other people's suggestions. "If you say to him, 'Well look, I think you're wrong about that, why don't we try it this way?' he'll do it with complete commitment."

There was a secret to arriving at that state, however—send Simon out to the stores. Working on one particular piece of music, with Simon standing over him passing (generally negative) comments, Eno finally looked up and observed, "Isn't it Mother's Day next week?" Simon nodded. Yes, it was.

Well, replied Eno, "This is quite a good neighborhood for shopping." And off Simon went, leaving Eno to get on with the music.

"I worked like a pig to get something that was really substantial," Eno continued, and his efforts paid off. Simon returned from the stores, listened to what had been accomplished while he was away, and was blown away by it. "That's fantastic," he raved, before adding, "I think I've got an old song that would work with that." "He played it," Eno concluded, "and suddenly we had a whole new piece." Simon never again objected when Eno sent him shopping.

For his part, Simon claimed that the album took two years to record, although, he said: "The actual time I spent with Brian was twenty days, split into four periods. We found we could really work intensely for five days, and after that it was a bit of a burnout."

He surprised his audience, too, by admitting that he never took his finished songs for granted. In fact, he told *USA Today*:

> I'm much more judgmental these days. Finishing a song is more satisfying now because I'm grateful, whereas when I was twenty-eight, I expected it. Now if I find something to say, and I say it in a way that I think is artful and true, I'm relieved I wasn't frustrated or stymied.
>
> I'm trying to be as honest as I can editing out what might be considered obscure but not trying to oversimplify or be condescending. And then I have to let go, even if I don't immediately understand the words. What I meant eventually reveals itself. Sometimes, instead of manipulating the craft, you have to just be the vessel through which some sort of inspiration will flow.

2006: *Surprise* (Warner Brothers 49982-2)

"How Can You Live in the Northeast?"
"Everything About It Is a Love Song"
"Outrageous" (Paul Simon/Brian Eno)
"Sure Don't Feel Like Love"
"Wartime Prayers"
"Beautiful"
"I Don't Believe"

"Another Galaxy" (Paul Simon/Brian Eno)
"Once Upon a Time There Was an Ocean" (Paul Simon/Brian Eno)
"That's Me"
"Father and Daughter"

Produced by: Paul Simon

Recorded at The Hit Factory, New York; Clinton Studios, New York; Sony Studios, New York; Right Track Studios, New York; Mayfair Studios, London; Lansdowne Studios, London; Capitol Studios, Los Angeles; Ocean Way, Nashville

Musicians

Abraham Laboriel—bass
Adrian Simon—vocals
Alex Al—bass
Bill Frisell—guitar
Brian Eno—electronics
Gil Goldstein—harmonium
Herbie Hancock—piano

Jessy Dixon Singers—choir
Leo Abrahams—fretless bass
Pino Palladino—bass
Robin DiMaggio—drums
Steve Gadd—drums
Vincent Nguini—guitar

2011: *So Beautiful or So What* (Hear Music HRM 32814-02)

"Getting Ready for Christmas Day"
"The Afterlife"
"Dazzling Blue"
"Rewrite"
"Love and Hard Times"

"Love Is Eternal Sacred Light"
"Amulet"
"Questions for the Angels"
"Love and Blessings"
"So Beautiful or So What"

Produced by: Paul Simon and Phil Ramone

Musicians

Charles Pillow—clarinet
Chris Bear—electronics
David Finck—bass

Desiree Elsevier—viola
Diane Lesser—English horn
Doyle Lawson and Quicksilver—vocals

Dr. Michael White—clarinet
Edie Brickell—vocals
Elizabeth Mann—flutewijk—celeste
Gabe Witcher—fiddle
Gil Goldstein—arrangements
Golden Gate Jubilee Quartet—vocals
    (sample)
Jeanne LeBlanc—cello
Jim Oblon—drums
Joshua Swift—dobro
Karikiudi R Mani—Indian ensemble,
    vocals
Lois Martin—viola
Lulu Simon—vocals
Mary Abt—clarinet
Mick Rossi—piano
Nancy Zeltsman—marimba
Pamela Sklar—flute

Rev. J. M. Gates with congregation—
    sermon (sample)
Richard Locker—cello
Sara Cutler—flute, harp
Skip LaPlante—gongs, wind chimes,
    96-note harp
Sonny Terry—harmonica
Steve Gorn—bansuri flu
Etienne Stadte
Steve Shehan—bass, djembe, talk-
    ing drum, anglung, glass harp,
    brushes
V Suresh-Ghatan—clay pot
VB Madhusadanan—tabla
Vincent Lionti—viola
Vincent Nguini—guitar
Yacouba Sissoko—kora

2016: *Stranger to Stranger* (Concord CRE 39803-02)

"The Werewolf"
"Wristband"
"The Clock"
"Street Angel"
"Stranger to Stranger"
"In a Parade"

"Proof of Love"
"In the Garden of Edie"
"The Riverbank"
"Cool Papa Bell"
"Insomniac's Lullaby"

Produced by: Paul Simon and Roy Hallee

Musicians

Alan Ferber—trombone
Alex Sopp—flute
Andy Snitzer—saxophone
Bakithi Kumalo—bass
Bobby Allende—congas
Bobby McFerrin—vocals
Carlos Henriquez—bass, acoustic
    bass

C. J. Camerieri—horns, trumpet,
    French horn; Clap! Clap!—elec-
    tronic drums, synthesizer, loops
    – beats
Dave Eggar—cello
David Broome—Chromelodeon

Dean Drummond—percussion [bamboo], marimba, Zoomoozophone

Gil Goldstein—string arrangements

Golden Gate Jubilee Quartet—vocals (sample)

Jack DeJohnette—drums

Jamey Haddad—performer [Hadjira], percussion, handclaps, finger snaps

Jared Soldiviero—cloud-chamber bowls, marimba [Bowed], vocals

Jim Oblon—drums, percussion, electronic drums

Katie Kresek—viola

Keith Montie—vocals

Marcus Rojas—tuba

Mark Stewart —percussion, mbira

Mick Rossi—harmonium, keyboards

Nelson González—tres, maracas

Nico Muhly—celesta, bells

Nino De Los Reyes—percussion, handclaps, finger snaps

Oscar De Los Reyes—percussion, handclaps, finger snaps

Paul Halley—pipe organ

Sergio Martínez—percussion, handclaps, finger snaps

Steve Marion—slide guitar

Vincent Nguini—guitar

Wycliffe Gordon—trombone

Not all ears were receptive to the resulting record. The website Pitchfork dismissed *Surprise* as little more than a midlife crisis. "It appears Simon is still narcissistic after all these years. While that's not inherently bad, here it's ill-advised. *Surprise* drowns in signifiers of experimentalism—wobbly U2 electric guitars, drones, whizzes, and oh-em-gee programmed beats—that already sounded stale when 'electro-folk' was actually a fad. Meanwhile, when Simon isn't probing the mysteries of aging, he's singing about his own writer's block." Pitchfork then suggested that the narcissism "is just the metaphysical underpinning for a bunch of post-hippie New Age nonsense."

The *Guardian*, too, was dubious. "The problem with *Surprise* is the songs Simon has chosen to undergo the Eno treatment. As with its predecessor, *You're the One*, anyone scouting for a memorable tune may as well pull up a chair—you'll have to wait until track eight, 'Another Galaxy.' The lyrics are similarly opaque: the shadow of war and a divided America haunts the songs, but it's a bit difficult to work out what Simon thinks about either."

It was left, as it so often is with artists of Simon's stature, to *Rolling Stone* to give the album a more appreciative listen. "Eno outfits some of

Simon's most elegant songs yet with spacey accouterments, ranging from the shimmery atmospherics of 'That's Me' to the buzzy electro-folk groove of 'Another Galaxy.' Despite the album's shiny surface, Simon sounds like Simon," here dropping "self-conscious barbs with the same pained wiseass spirit that made him poet laureate of New York alienation in the early Seventies," there delivering "tender ruminations on time and tide, pledging eternal love to his little girl and working up a gospel-tinged elegy for conflict-ravaged families."

If there was no common consensus on the album itself, the tour that inevitably followed in the record's wake was somewhat better received. Twenty-seven dates over the course of five months offered Simon a leisurely outing; and of course he continued to find ways of surprising people.

He would do so again with *Surprise*'s 2011 successor, *So Beautiful or So What*—an album that Simon suggested could be rooted in a quest for the meaning of life. However, when he was interviewed by *Mojo* around the time of its release, he sounded far more excited to be talking about a wildebeest: "[The album] came from asking myself, 'What do I like about *Surprise*?' That led me to begin again from a harmonic perspective, not a rhythm as I have been doing for a long time. So I sat in a room on my own with my guitar, began writing and went into areas that I hadn't touched since 'Still Crazy After All These Years.'"

The poster for the Hang Out festival in 2011.

Author's collection

There was no bass guitar on the record—"I just decided I really don't like bass!" But there was a wildebeest. "In that song 'Rewrite,' the bass 'doom' at the end of the 'doodle-e-doom' part all the way through the track is a wildebeest we recorded on a family holiday. So in the studio it was all 'More wildebeest!' and 'Too much wildebeest!' The critics will say, 'Not the old wildebeest trick again.'"

"Rewrite" would be among the songs that Simon would take on the road with him as he performed his 2018 farewell tour, where he revealed another, less flippant, aspect of the song. The kid who got on the bus in the song "America," he said, is the same guy who now works at the car wash in "Rewrite." It's an admission that casts both songs in a wholly different light, just as *So Beautiful* in general allowed Simon, again, to reinvent his muse.

"Simon's first album in five years," mused *Rolling Stone*, "is full of heavy business: life's meaning, beauty, brutality and brevity. Simon is pushing 70; it's appropriate that he's got mortality on his mind. But the songs rarely feel heavy. Instead, they combine the freewheeling folk of 1972's *Paul Simon* with the brilliant studio sculpting of *Graceland*. It's his best album since 1990's *The Rhythm of the Saints*, and it also sums up much of what makes Simon great."

With co-producer Phil Ramone helping forge an overall atmosphere of intimacy and spontaneity that was absent from *Surprise*, *So Beautiful . . .* feels almost live, as though the musicians are seated in the studio just a few feet from the listener and playing for the sheer love of it.

Energy sparkles through every song, even when Eno-esque ambience is in the same room, and if *Surprise* was the sound of Simon toying with the textures of the twenty-first-century studio, now he was back with his old R&B records, wondering what made them sound so electrifyingly timeless.

Strangers

Yet again, it would be all change in the years that separated *So Beautiful or So What* with its successor, *Stranger to Stranger* (2016), as Simon now threw himself into a smorgasbord of wild experimentation.

It is a maddening potpourri. There are dance beats created by Italian electronica figurehead Clap! Clap!; there are contributions from composer-arranger Nico Muhly, Alex Sopp, and yMusic figurehead C. J. Camerieri; there is even custom-made instrumentation created in the spirit of music theorist Harry Parch—who is a proponent of the still contentious theory that an octave features forty-three tones, as opposed to the more commonly accepted twelve, and who designed his own instruments to enable him to prove the fact.

So, microtones and zoomoozophones, echoes and rhythms, gospel and gopichan. *Stranger to Stranger* is a creation, in its own way, as revolutionary as either *Graceland* or *The Rhythm of the Saints* yet as personal, too, as "America" or "Duncan." The album also featured one of his most curious ever looks at fame, in the form of "Wristband"—the possibly but not necessarily fictional tale of the day he stepped outside of the theater to have a smoke and check his e-mail and wasn't allowed back in. He didn't have the necessary wristband.

But then it twists until the wristband becomes emblematic of everything that holds people back in life, the riots that start with "the homeless and the lowly" but spread through the towns, to the cities, to everyone held back in life because they don't have the money, the breeding, or the smarts to "make it" in the modern world. To everyone who doesn't have the wristband.

Not all the notions deployed on the album were, Simon acknowledged, "new." He told the *Irish Times* magazine: "I almost never listen back to my old work, but the other day I was showing a song to a musician that I was thinking of working with, and I came to the song 'You're the One'—which is from the album of the same name—and it could have come from *Stranger to Stranger*. There was the same level of surprise and mystery."

Among those surprises was the manner in which he conjured such an energetic album from ideas that, Simon said, "didn't begin that way." He continued: "It began very slowly—they usually do—but then focus becomes apparent, and with that you get energized. Maybe we can't do the all-night sessions anymore, but the thinking is still crackling."

Nevertheless, *Stranger to Stranger* would have been a courageous release for any so-called "established artist," a shifting of boundaries and

2011's So Beautiful or So What LP.   *Author's collection*

foundations once again. But of course, Simon is not the average "established artist."

As *Billboard* put it in 2016, "[He is] the exception to the usual rules. Most boomer rock stars long ago settled into quasi-retirement, recycling their greatest hits on tour and recording albums that attempt to replicate those songs. Simon remains a seeker, continually pushing into new territory."

His audience pushes alongside him. *Stranger to Stranger* crashed into the *Billboard* Top 100 at number three, the highest chart entry of his entire career, while Simon teased Jon Pareles of the *New York Times* with the suggestion that it might be the last album he would ever make: "I often think, I don't have to do this. I'm doing the idea I had when I was thirteen. Sixty years later, it's a thirteen-year-old's idea. Do I still want to do it? That's a good question. I usually ask it when I start off on each album. Then I start. I grumble, I grumble, and then some idea comes along. And I always say this after every album: I really don't know if I want to do it again. But this time I really do mean it."

And then a shrug. "But I always mean it."

That was in May, 2016, when he was still reeling from the shock he received the night that he looked out at an audience and saw four great white mountains looming behind them. It was a vista that, most certainly, you would not expect to encounter from a Philadelphia stage. But it was only later, with his spectacles on, that he realized they were tents.

By October, however, he was reassuring the *Los Angeles Times* that he was "never going to retire," although he was considering "slow[ing] down and step[ping] away from the touring."

19

Come On, Take Me to the Next Frontier

Paul Simon is, and forever will be, best known for one single, special partnership. But, particularly in these later years, he has thrived upon initiating more, as if to say, "You think that was my best shot? Well, listen to this."

He toured with Sting, the former frontman with the Police who was, for a considerably longer period, as idiosyncratic of a performer as Simon himself. The pair were longtime friends, ever since they found themselves neighbors in an Upper West Side apartment building. They had been musical collaborators, however, only since they performed together at the 2013 Robin Hood Foundation in New York City (see chapter 17).

Two songs, "The Boxer" and the former schoolteacher's "Fields of Gold," were all it took for them to begin discussing a longer collaboration; and, through 2014–2015, they toured North America, Europe, and Australia.

It was, acknowledged the *Guardian*, a bizarre coupling: "At first glance, the Paul Simon and Sting on Stage Together tour is reminiscent of those bizarrely unlikely 1960s package tours where Jimi Hendrix would appear on the same bill as Engelbert Humperdinck. Paul Simon is a Greenwich Village folkie whose towering songbook stretches from Simon and Garfunkel to world-music experiments with *Graceland*; his Geordie counterpart a former Police-man who has careered from new wave to a lute. Together, the gangly, hipster-bearded Sting and shorter, hat-wearing New Jerseyan could audition for *The Odd Couple*."

But it worked. For all the distance between the dawns of their careers—Simon enjoyed his first hit record in 1958; Sting, with the Police, scored his in 1978—there are only twelve years between them in age, and their thirty-seven-song-strong live show saw the pair playing and singing

Sting performing at New York's Live Earth: The Concerts for a Climate in Crisis show in July 1997.   *Photofest*

on highlights from both men's careers—from "Homeward Bound" to "Every Breath You Take"; from "Mother and Child Reunion" to "Roxanne"—as if to remind us that both, at significant junctures in their career (Simon's first solo hit, Sting's first hit full stop), played reggae off against itself.

A sixteen-piece band dropped peculiar flourishes and a surprisingly successful tuba into the brew; they celebrated the legalization of cannabis in Colorado with a slightly reworded version of "Late in the Evening" ("stepped outside to smoke my legal 'J'"); and they wound up with an Everly Brothers finale. Their rousing "When Will I Be Loved" was as successful as any Simon ever pulled off in any other duet of his career.

There is no shortage of competition, though.

In 2015, and again in 2017, Simon guested onstage with Billy Joel, and it is a mark of just how removed he has become from what might once have been considered his traditional orbit that that felt far more of a shock to his fans than, say, his collaboration with hip-hop star Wyclef Jean a decade earlier.

"Fast Car," from Jean's *Carnival Vol. II: Memoirs of an Immigrant* album, indeed has more in common with Simon's twenty-first-century music than "Uptown Girl" and "We Didn't Start the Fire" ever could.

The Other Great (or, at Least, Memorable) Duets

2017: "You May Be Right" with Billy Joel and Miley Cyrus (Madison Square Garden)

2016: "Bridge Over Troubled Water" with Josh Groban (Grammys)

2016: "Wristband" with Chris Thile, Sarah Bird, Andrew Jarosz (*Prairie Home Companion*)

2015: "The 59th Street Bridge Song" with Stephen Colbert (*The Late Show with . . .*)

2015: "New York Is My Name" with Dion (LP *New York Is My Name*)

2015: "Mother and Child reunion" with U2 (Madison Square Garden)

2014: "Like to Get to Know You" with Edie Brickell (single)

2014: "Me and Julio Down by the Schoolyard" with Michael J. Fox (Michael J. Fox Foundation Benefit)

2012: "You're The Reason Our Kids Are Ugly" with Edie Brickell (Children's Benefit Concert, Radio City Music Hall)

2012: "Loves Me Like a Rock" with Sting, Stevie Wonder, Aisha Morris, Vince Gill, and James Taylor (Children's Benefit Concert, Radio City Music Hall)

2011: "Cecilia" with Jimmy Fallon (*Late Night with Jimmy Fallon*)

2001: "I've Just Seen a Face" with Paul McCartney (Landmine Benefit Concert)

1994 : "The Late Great Johnny Ace" with Philip Glass (Tibet House)

1992: "Graceland" with Willie Nelson (Farm Aid)

1983: "The Blues" with Randy Newman (LP *Trouble in Paradise*)

1975: "Gone at Last" with Phoebe Snow and Jessy Dixon (*Saturday Night Live*)

1975: "Gone at Last" with Bette Midler (demo)

1975: "Here Comes the Sun" with George Harrison (*Saturday Night Live*)

1972: "Mother and Child Reunion" with improvised lyrics by unnamed child (*Sesame Street*)

Plus, an honorary mention for:

1998: "Superstition" with Stevie Wonder and Don Henley (MTV Awards Paul on tambourine!)

Simon and Brickell joined comedian Steve Martin to perform a bluegrass number called "Pretty Little One"; Simon alone worked up a new version of "Questions for the Angels" with jazzman Bill Frissell, and he performed glorious sets for *Prairie Home Companion* and *Austin City Limits*, both of which sounded so fresh and alive that it was impossible to believe that their maker, and performer, was now halfway through his seventies *and still hadn't tired of toying with people's expectations.*

Or with his own.

Neither was he afraid to buck the modern convention of his career. He has rarely resorted to sampling, for example. If Simon wants a sound, as he has proved with every album since *Graceland*, he will hunt down its source, whether that demands flying to another country or having somebody build him a Chromelodeon.

One can count on one hand the number of times Simon has resorted to samples, and always they are exquisitely well chosen and well found too. He discovered the sermon that sounds out during "Getting Ready for Christmas Day," the opening cut on *So Beautiful and So What,* on a collection of vintage gospel and religious recordings gathered and boxed together as *Goodbye Babylon*—a six-CD collection packaged in its own handcrafted wooden box by the archive-scouring Dust to Digital label.

He held off the modern obsession with electronics until he found himself in the presence of the field's undisputed master, Brian Eno; and even the accepted twenty-first-century wisdom that the album, as a single artistic statement, is dead holds no water with him.

True, it is a gloomy prospectus that seemingly gets aired whenever artists, or fans, of a certain age gather to discuss the predominance of streaming music and custom-built playlists. But that does not make it a reality.

He told *Drowned in Sound*: "If your mind is such that you like it when it's on shuffle and you go from hearing Beyonce to Hank Williams to Django Rheinhardt to some Debussy piece to the Beatles—if you like it when things jump like that, then that way of creating interest will find

Portrait of Artist and Guitar.   *Photofest*

its way into the album form. Because really, when things are on shuffle, it's just like a big album. The individual artist can't possibly change from one person to another, but they can change enough to keep you interested and entertained."

That, he continued, was what *Stranger to Stranger* was all about. Think about the album's very name, after all. The title track reads straightforwardly enough—two lovers wondering what might happen were they to meet again for the first time.

But the title also sums up the musical journey that the album as a whole will be taking, from strange (the opening howl of "The Werewolf") to stranger still ("Wristband," the most recent—2015—composition on the album), and thence to stranger yet. *Stranger to Stranger* was *made* to be listened to on shuffle.

You might even say it was how he's conducted his entire career.

A career that he suddenly, or so it seemed from the outside, had decided to bring to an end.

No stranger to suggesting he might soon retire only to recant the next time he sat down for an interview, Simon announced that he had changed his mind again in January 2018. Only this time, he had the farewell tour already booked, and there would be no going back. He had often wondered how it would feel to curtail his performing career of his own volition. Now he had found out—a combination of relief, exhilaration, and, perhaps, trepidation. He still enjoyed making music, and he especially enjoyed working with the band that he had assembled around him. His voice, unlike so many of his peers, was largely unscarred by the years, and his health was good. But it was time.

Homeward Bound—The Farewell Tour, 2018

May 16—Vancouver, Canada	May 30—Denver, Colorado
May 18—Seattle, Washington	June 1—Dallas, Texas
May 19—Portland, Oregon	June 2—Houston, Texas
May 22–23—Los Angeles, California	June 4—Austin, Texas
May 25—Oakland, California	June 6—Chicago, Illinois
May 27—Las Vegas, Nevada	June 8—St. Paul, Minnesota
May 28—Los Angeles, California	June 10—Detroit, Minnesota

June 12—Toronto, Canada

June 13—Montreal, Canada

June 15—Boston, Massachusetts

June 16—Philadelphia, Pennsylvania

June 19—Greensboro, North Carolina

June 20—Nashville, Tennessee

June 30—Stockholm, Sweden

July 1—Oslo, Norway

July 3—Copenhagen, Denmark

July 5—Antwerp, Belgium

July 7–8—Amsterdam, Holland

July 10—Manchester, England

July 11—Glasgow, Scotland

July 13—Dublin, Ireland

July 15—London, England

September 5—New Orleans,
    Louisiana

September 7—Tampa, Florida

September 8—Ft. Lauderdale, Florida

September 11—Orlando, Florida

September 12—Atlanta, Georgia

September 14—Washington, DC

September 15—Newark, New Jersey

September 17—Pittsburgh,
    Pennsylvania

September 20–21—New York City,
    New York

September 22—Flushing Meadows,
    New York

20

Homeward Bound

In 1990, as he prepared for his benefit for the Montauk Point Lighthouse, Simon was chatting about the future with Elda Gentile, who was once numbered among the most energetic presences on the New York art and music scene of the seventies but who more recently was content to pursue more leisurely occupations.

In fact, it was she who now coordinated many of the events that took place around Montauk, and her friendship with Simon allowed her to circumvent many of the barriers that an artist of his stature is traditionally surrounded by. (This included convincing him to undertake a promotional interview with Johnny Carson for inclusion in the event's own literature.)

It was during a break in the midst of these events that their conversation touched upon the subject of retirement. Gentile had long ago put her years as a performer on hold, but Simon doubted he could ever make a similar step.

"What would I do with my time?" he asked plaintively.

Close to three decades on, he was about to find out.

It was as he put the final touches to what became his 2016 *Stranger to Stranger* album that he first sensed a change in the wind. "A funny thing happened when I finished," he told NPR two years later. "I literally felt like a switch clicked and I said, 'I'm finished.'"

He could not bring himself, immediately, to acknowledge that fact, and even when he did speak the words, he still vacillated. But, as the months slipped by, one particular reality was inescapable. He had not written a new song since that album's "Wristband."

Or, at least, anything that he considered to be a song, although he had "been fooling around with a little guitar piece," he confessed to NPR in September 2018.

It wasn't writer's block that was keeping him from writing new songs. He was certain of that. He'd experienced it before, and experienced, too, the crushing sense of frustration that accompanies it. This was not the same sensation.

He hadn't run out of things to say. If anything, for an artist of Simon's political and cultural convictions, the events that would unfurl over next couple of years promised (or should that be "threatened"?) to give him more to speak out about than ever before.

Indeed, when he was onstage throughout the entire span of his 2018 farewell tour, his rage and frustration—and, perhaps, also his despair—at the present state of the world were almost palpable as he closed each evening with "The Sound of Silence."

Never, it seems, had those lyrics appeared more apt.

But perhaps the time for lyrics was through.

At last, he had also solved a riddle that had exercised his mind for some time now—maybe since that long-ago conversation with Elda Gentile. If he was not writing songs, where would his creative impulses lead instead? Because they would certainly have to find an outlet somewhere.

What he was interested in, he said, were his dreams. Going back to the age of four, he had suffered from "violence dreams"—he hesitated to describe them as nightmares, but plainly, they shook him at the time, and they were not something he grew out of, either. In fact, talking in 2018, he declared, "those dreams, they got so intense a few years ago that I took a trip down to Brazil to see this healer, John of God."

He didn't know, he confessed, whether he would find what he was looking for—he simply acted upon the recommendation of some friends, at the same time as admitting, "I really don't need much arm-twisting to go to Brazil. So I said 'okay'."

In the event, John of God did not have any kind of answers, or cure, for the dreams. But maybe Simon did.

"I've been thinking about it more and more," he said, "and in the last year or so, my dreams are getting longer and—explosions of anger sometimes come out, but sometimes I feel I can almost control the dreams and

I have an insight into what it is, and I feel like this is a long story and I'm beginning to understand things about my life and who I am."

Music, he determined, was simply the vehicle that brought him to this place in life, one whose purpose ("aside from giving me intense enjoyment") was to allow him to begin to understand "what [his] life was about and what it meant."

That is one of the ways in which he visualizes occupying his future. Rather than devoting his time to wondering how he can continue to work in music, or in any other creative form, he intends to throw himself deeper into his ecological and humanitarian interests and pursuits and what he calls the "spiritual" battle lines that appear to be forming in twenty-first-century culture.

He will, he has said, spend his money supporting such causes and buying land so that it can be preserved, and he will continue to raise his voice against the political decisions that oppose those beliefs. He hesitates to describe those decisions as "evil," preferring to call them "mistaken" instead. But his goals are clear regardless—to protect the planet. The planet he wants to leave to his children.

This time, however, there would be no new lyrics, no fresh songs, with which he would document what he saw, what he thought, what he felt. And that despite the release, during that same brief span, of no fewer than two new albums bearing Simon's name.

Into the Light

The first of these was the *Graceland—The Remixes* album, which simply handed off the entire original LP to a variety of esteemed dance remixers (see chapter 11); the second, released just weeks before his farewell tour was due to conclude, was *In the Blue Light*, a collection of past favorite Simon compositions that offered a brand new musical perspective by Simon himself.

Describing *In the Blue Light*, he said: "[It comprises] songs that I thought were almost right, or were odd enough to be overlooked the first time around. Redoing arrangements, harmonic structures, and lyrics that didn't make their meaning clear, gave me time to clarify in my own head what I wanted to say, or realize what I was thinking and make it more easily understood."

Not, then, the kind of *greatest hits redux* collection that so many other artists feel justified in releasing as their careers draw toward their close; more a reminder that the greatest hits are but the tip of Simon's song-writing iceberg and that, for every "Kodachrome" or "You Can Call Me Al," there is a "One Man's Ceiling Is Another Man's Floor" or "René and Georgette Magritte with Their Dog After the War" ("the longest song title I've ever written," he would joke from the stage in the album's aftermath).

Ten songs were drawn from seven albums—*There Goes Rhymin' Simon* (1973), *Still Crazy After All These Years* (1975), *One-Trick Pony* (1980), *Hearts and Bones* (1983), *The Rhythm of the Saints* (1990), *You're the One* (2000), and *So Beautiful or So What* (2011), with Simon and the inevitable Roy Halee accompanied by a stellar cast of musicians (see sidebar).

As Simon wrote in the album's liner notes: "It's an unusual occurrence for an artist to have the opportunity to revisit earlier works and re-think them; to modify, even completely change parts of the originals.

"Happily, this opportunity also gave me the gift of playing with an extraordinary group of musicians, most of whom I hadn't recorded with before. I hope the listener will find these new versions of old songs refreshed, like a new coat of paint on the walls of an old family home."

It was a challenge, of course. Though the songs themselves may not have been the first on any mainstream list of Paul Simon favorites, every one of them had earned its place in his canon; every one is somebody's favorite. He was not simply reading upon his own past; he was readdressing other people's, too.

September 2018: In the Blue Light (Legacy 19075841442)
All words and music by Paul Simon

"One Man's Ceiling Is Another Man's Floor"

Paul Simon—vocal, percussion   John Patitucci—bass
Joel Wenhardt—piano   Edie Brickell—finger snaps
Nate Smith—drums   C. J. Camerieri—trumpet
Jim Oblon—guitar   Andy Snitzer—saxophone

"Love"

Paul Simon—vocal, acoustic guitar, percussion, harmonium

Bill Frisell—electric guitar

Steve Gadd—drums

Renaud Garcia-Fons—bass

"Can't Run But"

Paul Simon—vocal

C. J. Camerieri—trumpet, piccolo trumpet

Alex Sopp—flute, alto flute

Hideaki Aomori—clarinet, bass clarinet

Rob Moose—violin

Nadia Sirota—viola

Gabriel Cabezas—cello

Arrangement by Bryce Dessner based on the original arrangement from Rhythm of the Saints by Marco Antônio Guimarães

"How the Heart Approaches What It Yearns"

Paul Simon—vocal

Sullivan Fortner—piano

Nate Smith—drums

John Patitucci—bass

Wynton Marsalis—trumpet

"Pigs, Sheep and Wolves"

Paul Simon—vocal, percussion

Wynton Marsalis—trumpet

Marcus Printup—trumpet

Dan Block—clarinet

Walter Blanding—saxophone

Arrangement by Wynton Marsalis

Wycliffe Gordon—tuba

Chris Crenshaw—trombone

Marion Felder—drums

Herlin Riley—tambourine

"René and Georgette Magritte with Their Dog After the War"

Paul Simon: vocal, electric guitar

C. J. Camerieri: trumpet, piccolo trumpet

Alex Sopp: flute, alto flute

Arrangement by Robert Sirota

Hideaki Aomori: clarinet, bass clarinet

Rob Moose: violin

Nadia Sirota: viola

Gabriel Cabezas: cello

"The Teacher"

Paul Simon: vocal, percussion

Odair Assad: guitar

Sérgio Assad: guitar

Renaud Garcia-Fons: bass,
   percussion

Walter Blanding: saxophone
Jamey Haddad: percussion

"Darling Lorraine"

Paul Simon: vocal, percussion
Bill Frisell: electric guitar
Vincent Nguini: electric guitar
Mark Stewart: acoustic guitar
Steve Gadd: drums
John Patitucci: bass
C. J. Camerieri: trumpet, piccolo
   trumpet
Arrangement by Rob Moose

Alex Sopp: flute, alto flute

Hideaki Aomori: clarinet, bass
   clarinet

Rob Moose: violin

Nadia Sirota: viola

Gabriel Cabezas: cello

"Some Folks' Lives Roll Easy"

Paul Simon: vocal
Sullivan Fortner: piano, celeste
Jack DeJohnette: drums

John Patitucci: bass

Joe Lovano: saxophone

"Questions for the Angels"

Paul Simon: vocal, acoustic guitar,
   bass harmonica, percussion
Bill Frisell: electric guitar
Skip LaPlante: percussion

Sullivan Fortner: harmonium,
   Chromelodeon
John Patitucci: bass

Generally he succeeded, a triumph that he was quick to assign to the accompanying musicians: "It was really easy because the musicianship is extraordinary. When they play it's so good."

It was not, he knew, a project that he could have undertaken in the past, when his career was that of an active, creative, musician. Both *In the Blue Light* and the accompanying farewell tour would, under those terms, have been little more than an exercise in procrastination, disguising the fact that he had nothing new to say (or, perhaps, trying to distract from it) by making as much noise as possible around the things he'd said before. Only as part of a last farewell could he have justified (at least to himself) such a self-indulgent exercise.

At the same time, however, *In the Blue Light* did represent a significant piece of work. Songs were rethought and elements were rewritten, while his choice of backing musicians ensured that, even without such revisions, entire new landscapes would have been draped over the songs he chose.

Among Simon's own personal favorites, "Darling Lorraine" stood proud because, he said: "I thought [it] was one of the best songs I ever wrote." At the same time, however, he felt the original backing track was "so interesting and eclectic that I thought you couldn't follow the storyline because you were distracted by the sounds. So this time, I came and was very careful to try and allow for the storyline to go right through because if you don't follow the storyline then the ending doesn't have its power."

This new performance was given further resonance, Simon later acknowledged, as it marked the final occasion on which he worked with guitarist Vincent Nguini, his guitarist since the days of *Rhythm of the Saints*.

In fact, it was the last recording that Nguini would ever make, and perhaps that, too, fed into Simon's thinking as he contemplated his future. A few more weeks would elapse before he would announce his decision to retire to the world. He still had the time to change his mind.

But the loss of "the most creative musician [Simon] ever worked with" certainly weighed heavily on his thinking, as he acknowledged in his notes for the farewell tour souvenir program: "Nguini's passing was "not the only reason I've decided to stop touring, but [it was certainly] a contributing factor." Nguini, he continued, was "an extraordinarily melodic rhythm guitarist. By that I mean his rhythm parts were usually repetitive lines—very West African—rather than strumming chords. His style was unique and can't be fully understood except by the most sophisticated players."

Nguini's guitar work on "Darling Lorraine" is as vibrant and brilliant as any he has ever played before. Indeed, throughout the song cycle, Simon's choice of accompanying players was as breathtaking as the abilities he intended to tap, his usual posse of players joined by Bill Frissell, Wynton Marsalis, and, perhaps most revolutionary of them all, New York City neoclassicists yMusic.

yMusic and More

yMusic were recruited for three cuts: "Darling Lorraine," a glorious reworking of "René and Georgette Magritte with Their Dog After the War," and, most impressively of all, "Can't Run But."

Simon's relationship with the sextet stretched back to 2013, when trumpeter C. J. Camerieri was added to the band—he is one of the stand-out players on *Stranger to Stranger*.

Described by Simon as "an exceptional group of young neoclassical musicians" and by *Performance Today* as "one of the groups that has really helped to shape the future of classical music," yMusic's lineup of string trio, flute, clarinet, and trumpet has also attracted the attention of Ben Folds, Son Lux, and John Legend.

The Simon engagement, however, was certainly their highest profile in the rock mainstream, not least of all when the group joined him onstage at the Eaux Claires Festival in Wisconsin in 2017. Now their contributions to *In the Blue Light* confirmed their impact upon his repertoire, all the more so after they were not only invited to join the farewell tour but also to contribute their own thoughts to the arrangements.

"Often when we collaborate with a band, the arrangements are already set in stone," violinist Rob Moose told *Billboard*. "With Paul, we're not left out of that process of a song evolving over the course of a tour. Every day, he's trying to be a little more correct."

"Can't Run But" (originally recorded on *Rhythm of the Saints*) is noteworthy, too, for the involvement of Bryce Dessner in creating the arrangement that yMusic would play. Although he purposefully modeled his work on Marco Antônio Guimarães's original arrangement, there is much, too, that is different—in keeping with Dessner's own "day job" as a member of the National, a band that it is not difficult to imagine Simon being especially fond of listening to. They share, after all, a similar sense of musical adventure, and literary lyricism as well.

Key to the album, too, was surely the inclusion of "Love," one of four songs from *You're the One*, if only because its lyric, heard anew in the wake of his decision to say farewell, offers another reminder of the time-less universality of Simon's best lyrics.

Or, as the *Guardian*'s review put it, "Simon doesn't sound at peace with the post-crash, Trump-era world at all, and the exquisite new arrangement of 'Love' emphasizes lines such as: 'When evil walks the planet, love is crushed like clay.'"

In the Blue Light was generally well received by the media. A few critics would question Simon's jazzier inclusions, and perhaps with good reason—there are certainly moments on the album where the musicianship seems wholly at odds with the song. But Simon's own instincts, and his willingness to step outside of both his or his audience's comfort zone, can only be applauded.

The Last Days on Tour

There were less shocks on the tour. Even guest appearances were kept to a minimum. The appearance of Edie Brickell for "Me and Julio Down by the Schoolyard" at the final two shows, at Madison Square Garden and Flushing Meadows, marked the only occasion all tour that Simon had invited another performer onstage to join him. And even she was only called upon to whistle.

Video footage accompanying some of the songs did offer some additional perspective on the career that the show was intended to celebrate—and, perhaps, a little perspective upon how Simon himself regarded it.

There was next to no mention of Art Garfunkel in the montage, and though Simon would occasionally introduce "Bridge Over Troubled Water" as a song he gave away for "someone else" to sing, he steadfastly avoided naming that someone. Besides, he explained, now he was reclaiming it for himself. He knew he could have notched up a whole new level of audience ecstasy if he'd acknowledged his old singing partner (or even, as many hoped, brought him onstage for a final bow).

Instead, he omitted him altogether, and the music blog *BrooklynVegan* probably spoke for many when it mused, "If this is truly his final tour, it would've been nice to hear him break out more of his Simon & Garfunkel classics (only five of his 26 songs were S&G songs) and go a little lighter on the latter half of his career."

That was not Simon's way, however, and never has been. In terms of content, he adamantly refused to take the most obvious route through his career. Even the new album, *In the Blue Light*, received only a brief look-in ("René and Georgette Magritte with Their Dog After the War," "Can't Run But"—both featuring the accompaniment of yMusic—and "Questions for Angels"), but the 140-minute show continued to mine the less feted corners of his catalog nevertheless, with just the occasional hit thrown in for the casual attendee.

As he said at the Corona Park finale: "Most of these songs that I'm going to play tonight I think you'll be familiar with, maybe a few you'll be less so. But the rhythm tunes are all written with the idea you'll get up and dance."

Indeed, *Variety*'s review gloried in the realization that, "One of Simon's great talents as a band leader is being able to come up with fresh concert arrangements that drift far enough away from the studio versions to please listeners with curious ears, but stick just close enough to the familiar that less adventurous souls don't have cause to gripe."

Or, as the the *Guardian* put it, "If farewells imply the prospect of greatest hits karaoke, Simon is emphatically not that kind of guy, and Homeward Bound is not that kind of tour."

Nevertheless, it was not until the encores that the crowd was blatantly invited to rise to its feet and wave cellphones in the air, first for a blast of solo hits and then for a volley of Garfunkel-era oldies. And still, the sense of occasion, and the celebration that arose from it, was never less than luminous.

So was Simon's sense of humor.

"It was a cold winter night when Paul Simon began his farewell tour in Los Angeles," he declared onstage at the Hollywood Bowl. "So, the thing about a farewell is well, I've changed my mind. What it is is that it's not so much a final tour that I like as I like raising the ticket prices to the level . . ."

There was a multitude of highlights as the tour rolled on, and Simon was determined to enjoy them all.

On the opening night in Vancouver, said the *New York Times*, "he was far more a curious musician than a self-congratulatory, self-repeating pop star," fronting a sixteen-man band whose "numbers and flexibility give Mr. Simon an instrumental arsenal that can include, as needed, a button accordion, a piccolo, a clay drum, a French horn, a prepared piano (with assorted objects placed on and between its strings), or a penny whistle."

"There's a big video screen," the *New York Times* continued, "but the tour's real special effects are its arrangements and orchestrations." Just as he would on *In the Blue Light*, he was "still tweaking—or iterating—songs that he could easily have delivered as jukebox copies."

In Chicago, the local *Tribune* lionized a concert, claiming: "[It appeared] less a victory lap than a testimonial to a career defined by a restless musical search. [Simon] was still exploring his songbook for new meanings, treating it not as an immutable canon but a road map to who knows where."

Reviewing the Denver show, writer Adam Perry recalled the woman sitting to his left, who remarked that Simon looked "a lot older than when [she] saw him last year" but who, within moments, was marveling "that Simon was also having a lot more fun than the last few times she'd seen him on stage, 'talking a lot more between songs' and dancing around in his sleek black jacket with silver highlights. The jacket matched his black-and-silver acoustic guitar."

In terms of sheer resonance, however, his return for what was surely the final time to London's Hyde Park in mid-July was certainly paramount among the tour's highest spots.

Past Simon gigs at the venue had, after all, long since passed into legend and he seemed determined that his appearance at the British Summertime festival would as well. Sets by Bonnie Raitt and James Taylor paved the way for Simon's performance, about which the Upcoming, a British website, had no alternative but to wax rhapsodic.

"The flow of the powerful lyrics and the dancing beats were kept up for the length of 26 songs, covering just about all the favorites with multiple encores consisting of the greatest hits 'Diamonds on the Soles of Her Shoes,' 'You Can Call Me Al,' and 'Graceland.' One track followed another until finally Simon was left alone on the stage with an acoustic guitar for 'The Sound of Silence,' which beautifully closed the night."

The 2018 Farewell Tour—Songs Performed

"America"

"50 Ways to Leave Your Lover"

"The Boy in the Bubble"

"Dazzling Blue"

"That Was Your Mother"

"Rewrite"

"Mother and Child Reunion"

"Me and Julio Down by the Schoolyard"

"René and Georgette Magritte with
    Their Dog After the War"

Can't Run

But Bridge Over Troubled Water"

"Wristband"

"Spirit Voices"

"The Obvious Child"

"The Cool, Cool River"

"Questions for the Angels"

"Diamonds on the Soles of Her Shoes"

"You Can Call Me Al"

"Turn Up Your Night"

"Still Crazy After All These Years"

"Graceland"

"Late in the Evening"

"Homeward Bound"

"Kodachrome"

"The Boxer"

"American Tune"

"Mrs. Robinson"

"The Sound of Silence"

So Long, Paul Frederic Simon

"Thank you all for the ride," Simon said from the stage at his final show in Corona Park. "I had a great time." But, of course, there is no way of saying whether or not *In the Blue Light* will truly be Paul Simon's final album, or Homeward Bound will be his final tour.

Certainly he has given no concrete clue one way or the other; in fact, he even dodged the risk of being asked about his future plans by declining all but one of the interview requests he received in 2018. NPR was the sole exception.

But the "little guitar piece" he admitted to "fooling around with" in that interview suggests that he has not wholly abandoned his muse, while the obvious enjoyment he derived from reworking the songs on *In the Blue Light* proves that his lyrical light continues to burn strong, too.

The man in black.   *Photofest*

Onstage at Madison Square Garden, too, he admitted "I know I'm gonna continue to write music, that seems to just come." He has, after all, spent over sixty years writing songs. If nothing else, it will be a very difficult habit to break. And he would scarcely be the first musician to officially retire and then change his mind later.

However, he also declared, "I'd like to just stop and think a little bit, and maybe take a look around the planet—we're only here for a short time—and try and see the whole big picture of this beautiful gem of a world."

It all seems so irrevocably final today. But will it seems that same way in a few years time?

The voice is still there, and the energy, too, and there are moments (you'll find them on YouTube) when you could be watching a performer in his youthful prime, with years more of music-making overflowing the tank. Or, as the Cleveland *Plain Dealer* put it, following his performance there, "[Simon] at seventy-five has more stamina, panache and flat-out style than a rocker a third his age, rolling through twenty-five songs over more than two hours of non-stop music."

And the songs "all sounded so pure, so sweet, so real that it was as if the last fifty years hadn't happened yet."

Then there's Simon's confession to the Hollywood Bowl audience, at the outset of the excursion: "The way I see it is like, aside from the word 'final,' which evokes words like 'Oh, it's final, so you didn't study for your finals,' I don't know really what to make of the decision. I just find it somehow exciting to put some kind of casing around this entire career, and to look at it that way. So, I don't intend to stop writing music, or playing it."

At the time of writing, then, the most frequently asked question about Paul Simon is, "Have we really seen the last of him?"

And the smartest answer would appear to be, "Probably not."

Selected Bibliography

Books

Bayer Sager, Carole. *They're Playing Our Song*. Simon & Schuster, 2016.

Carlin, Peter Ames. *Homeward Bound: The Life of Paul Simon*. Henry Holt, 2016.

Daviau, Mo. *Every Anxious Wave*. St Martins Griffin, 2016.

Eliot, Marc. *Paul Simon: A Life*. Wiley, 2010.

Friedman, Dan. *Still on the Corner, and Other Postmodern Political Plays by Fred Newman*. Castillo Cultural Center, 1998.

Garfunkel, Art. *What Is It All but Luminous: Notes from an Underground Man*. Knopf, 2017.

Hilburn, Robert. *Paul Simon: The Life*. Simon & Schuster, 2018.

Humphries, Patrick. *Bookends: The Simon and Garfunkel Story*. Cherry Lane Music, 1983.

Jacoby, Richard, and Hubert Selby Jr. *Conversations with the Capeman: The Untold Story of Salvador Agron*. University of Wisconsin Press, 2004.

Kingston, Victoria. *Simon & Garfunkel: The Definitive Biography*. Sidgwick & Jackson, 1996.

Leigh, Spencer. *Simon & Garfunkel: Together Alone*. McNidder & Grace, 2016.

Morella, Joe, and Patricia Barey. *Simon and Garfunkel: Old Friends. A Dual Biography*. Birch Lane Press, 1991.

Simon, Paul. *The Songs of Paul Simon*. Alfred A. Knopf, 1972.

Swenson, John. *Simon & Garfunkel: A Musical Biography*. WH Allen, 1984.

Articles

Alterman, Lorraine. "Paul Simon." *Rolling Stone,* May 28, 1970.

Altham, Keith. Paul Simon interview. *New Musical Express,* April 22, 1966.

————. "Two Views on Baez by Paul Simon and Dana Gillespie." *New Musical Express,* July 30, 1965.

Barton, Laura. "Linda Ronstadt: I Don't Like Any of My Albums." *The Guardian*, September 28, 2017.

Charlesworth, Chris. "Art for Art's Sake." *Melody Maker*, October 11, 1975.

Clarke, Jude. "I Didn't Think 'Bridge Over Troubled Water' Was a Hit." *Drowned in Sound*, May 4, 2016.

Cooper, Mark. Concert in the Park review. *Q,* January 1992.

DeCurtis, Anthony. "Sounds of Simon." *New York Magazine,* October 9, 2000.

Delehant, Jim. "Inside the Mind of Paul Simon." *Hit Parader*, Aug–Sept 1967.

————. "My Favorite Records." *Hit Parader*, October 1967.

DeMain, Bill. "Surprise Surprise." *Performing Songwriter,* September 2006.

Dwyer, Jim. "Could This Be the End of Paul Simon's Rhymin'?" *New York Times*, June 28, 2016.

Fanelli, Damien. "George Harrison and Paul Simon Play 'Here Comes the Sun.'" *Guitar World*, October 13, 2017.

Farndale, Nigel. "Art Garfunkel on Paul Simon: 'I Created a Monster.'" *Daily Telegraph*, May 24, 2015.

Fricke, David. "Paul Simon: African Odyssey." *Rolling Stone*, October 23, 1986.

Gilbert, Jerry. "Artie Gets His Feet Wet." *Sounds,* March 30, 1974.

————. Paul Simon interview. *Sounds,* May 19, 1973.

Goldman, Vivian. "God Sent Paul Simon to Do This." *Q,* June 1987.

Greene, Andy. "Art Garfunkel Is Ecstatic: 'My Voice Is 96 Percent Back.'" *Rolling Stone*, February 19, 2014.

Griffiths, David. "I Thought I Was a Has-Been at 19." *Record Mirror*, April 30, 1966.

Grow, Kory. "Hear Dion, Paul Simon Duet on Heartfelt 'New York Is My Home.'" *Rolling Stone,* November 12, 2015.

Hinckley, David. "Homeward Bound in 'The Capeman': Paul Simon Returns to the New York of His Youth." *New York Daily News*, November 16, 1997.

Ingham, Chris. "Still Crazy?/Life After 'The Capeman.'" *Mojo,* November 2000.

Kreps, Daniel. "Paul Simon's 'Graceland' to Receive Dance Remix Album." *Rolling Stone,* April 7, 2018.

Jerome, Jim. "Still Creative After All These Years." *People*, November 30, 1980.

Landau, Jon. Paul Simon interview. *Rolling Stone,* July 20, 1972.

Marsh, Dave. "What Do You Do When You're Not a Kid Anymore, and You Still Want to Rock and Roll?" *Rolling Stone,* October 30, 1980.

Martin, Gavin. "Across the Tracks." *Vox,* December 1990.

McNair, James. Art Garfunkel interview. *Mojo,* September 2015.

Mokoena, Tshepo. "An Interview with Paul Simon, One of the Last Burning Stars in the Pre-Internet Galaxy." *Vice*, May 5, 2016.

Pareles, Jon. "Paul Simon's Ambition, and Inspiration, Never Gets Old." *New York Times*, May 18, 2016.

Pollock, Bruce. Paul Simon interview. *Playboy,* 1980.

Reel, Penny. *Graceland* review. *New Musical Express,* September 13, 1986.

Reynolds, Simon. "Simon Reports Back to Base." *Observer,* May 5, 1991.

Robins, Wayne. "It's Paul but Is It Art?" *Rolling Stone*, December 18, 1975.

Rosen, Jody. Paul Simon interview. *Billboard,* June 23, 2016.

Runtagh, Jordan. "Paul Simon's 'Graceland': 10 Things You Didn't Know." *Rolling Stone*, April 25, 2016.

Schwartz, Tony. Paul Simon interview. *Playboy,* February 1984.

Silverman, Rena. "Paul Simon Looks Back on the Anniversary of the Amazing 'Graceland.'" *National Geographic*, October 11, 2012.

Smith, R. J. "Still Mbaqanga After All These Years." *Spin*, January 1987.

Staunton, Terry. "The Boy in the Boycott." *New Musical Express,* April 4, 1987.

Sutcliffe, Phil. Paul Simon interview. *Mojo,* February 2011.

Thomas, Tracy. "New to the Charts: Enter the Intellectual S&G." *New Musical Express,* April 8, 1966.

Thomson, Graeme. "He Is a Foreign Man. He Is Surrounded by the Sound." *Uncut,* October 2010.

Turner, Steve. "Dixon Spreading the Gospel with Paul Simon." *Melody Maker,* August 19, 1978.

Valentine, Penny. Paul Simon live review. *Street Life,* January 10, 1976.

White, Timothy. Paul Simon interview. *Crawdaddy,* February 1976.

Williams, Richard. "Brian Eno: Working with Someone Is Like Dating." *Guardian*, May 19, 2006.

Woffinden, Bob. Paul Simon live review. *New Musical Express,* December 20, 1975.

Zollo, Paul. "Breakfast with Art Garfunkel." *Song Talk*, 1993.

———. "Paul Simon: Spirit Voices Vols 1 and II." *SongTalk,* 1990.

Index